Stone Murder

A Rock ‘n’ Roll Mystery

Howard A. DeWitt

STONE MURDER: A ROCK 'N' ROLL NOVEL

BY HOWARD A. DEWITT

HORIZON BOOKS
P. O. BOX 4342
SCOTTSDALE, AZ. 85261-4342

Horizon Books
P. O. Box 4342
Scottsdale, Az. 85261-4342
(925)-202-6005
E Mail: Howard217@aol.com

First Published 2012

ISBN: 0-6156-1301-2
ISBN-13: 9780615613017

Stone Murder

A Rock 'n' Roll Mystery

Howard A. DeWitt

ROCK N ROLL BOOKS
BY HOWARD A. DEWITT

Van Morrison: Them and the Bang Era, 1945-1968 (2005)

Stranger In Town: The Musical Life of Del Shannon (with D. DeWitt (2001)

Sun Elvis: Presley In The 1950s (1993)

Paul McCartney: From Liverpool To Let It Be (1992)

Beatle Poems (1987)

The Beatles: Untold Tales (1985, 2nd edition 2001)

Chuck Berry: Rock 'N' Roll Music (1981, 2nd edition1985)

Van Morrison: The Mystic's Music (1983)

Jailhouse Rock: The Bootleg Records of Elvis Presley (with Lee Cotten) (1983)

HISTORY AND POLITICS

Obama's Detractors: In The Right Wing Nut House (2012)

The Road to Baghdad (2003)

A Blow To America's Heart: September 11, 2001, The View From England (2002) (with Darin DeWitt)

Jose Rizal: Philippine Nationalist As Political Scientist (1997)

The Fragmented Dream: Multicultural California (1996)

The California Dream (1996)

Readings In California Civilization (1981, 4th edition revised 2004)

Violence In The Fields: California Filipino Farm Labor Unionization (1980)

California Civilization: An Interpretation (1979)

Anti Filipino Movements in California: A History, Bibliography and Study Guide (1976)

Images of Ethnic and Radical Violence in California Politics, 1917-1930: A Survey (1975)

Prologue

The Chef awoke from a deep sleep. He looked out at his neighborhood. He rubbed his eyes and squinted out at the cold gray morning. He lived in the Castro. There was no longer a dominant gay presence. His neighborhood was going straight. They called it gentrification. The Chef called it cheap housing. He walked down to Alonzo's market and poured a large coffee. It was a vanilla bean.

"Hey skinny," Alonzo remarked.

"Today is my day," the Chef continued, "I am off to collect my rightful royalties."

"You can move out of your dump then," Alonzo chuckled.

The Chef blanched at this remark. " I'm gonna be in the big money soon."

"Fat chance." Alonzo left the counter and began stacking beer cases near the cooler.

"The money is coming," the Chef remarked exiting the store.

His hatred grew as he thought of his plight. He was bent on destroying a rock music band that had never recognized his talents. They recorded his songs. They never appreciated his writing skills. He had a contract for 20% of the profits. The money was invested in mutual funds, and he was a wealthy man. No one knew that. That was in his past life thirty years ago.

With his royalties, he attended the California Culinary Academy. The sixty-week program blended classical and modern culinary techniques. Then to everyone's surprise the Chef went to work cooking for rock bands. He continued to write furtively, but never achieved the success of his early years. He wrote three classic rock songs that everyone recorded.

In the 1970s, he was a ghostwriter for Elvis Costello, Elton John, Billy Joel, Blondie and Tony Orlando and Dawn. The spot on Orlando's television show almost ended his writing career. There were only so many corny songs about tying yellow ribbons. He wan an illusive and mysterious character.

No one knew that he was a Michigan kid. It was another secret. Now he was well past fifty and still hoped to write some new rock and roll hits. He also wanted to write a book. But grunge, punk rock, techno, house, rap and hip-hop ended his career. No one wanted hits by a has been. It was futile. No one would listen to his demos. The chart topping rock and roll groups ignored him. Others in the industry returned his songs with a form letter. He was reduced to writing songs for cover bands that played the Holiday Inn circuit. Not only was this the last refuge of any rock band but that of the songwriter as well. He sold the rights and someone else took the glory and the money. He had substantial investments. He had a serious profession.

He hated the people who debased his lyrical gifts. He would have the ultimate revenge. He would destroy the band that ridiculed his talent. There was a new group, the Start Me Up Band, who played his non-copyrighted songs. They had copyrighted his tunes during a drunken, drug fueled night. They would pay for their blasphemy.

Looking at himself in the mirror, he smiled. He was a man of many talents. He was a songwriter, he was a master Chef, and he was a superb athlete. He was also a businessman. Few people knew about these skills. He would kill off those who failed to respond to his gifts. He had the perfect cover; a successful life with all the banalities of living an average life.

He was a large man, but a gentle one. Standing in the Castro he didn't really stand out. He looked boring. No one noticed him. His size was obscured by his deferential, gracious manner. He wore a t-shirt with the inscription "Punk Rules."

"Hey, asshole," a guy selling homeless papers hollered, "it's long past punk pal." The homeless guy chuckled. The down and outers always thought they were funny.

Few people remembered the Chef's infatuation with the Sex Pistols. He was a rock and roll junkie. One who had a feverish desire to be famous? It hadn't happened and it wouldn't happen. So death would come to those who ignored his talents. He would take a Rolling Stone cover band, known ubiquitously as the Start Me Up band, and make sure that they suffered not only death but humiliation. For a killer, he was mild mannered. It was the perfect cover.

The Chef entered his apartment. The phone rang: "Ya," he snapped.

"Ah, my favorite cook, do we have the batch ready."

Smiling the Chef sat down. "Oh, yes, it is a beauty. My finest potion. Call me later, I need some sleep." The Chef abruptly hung up.

It was late afternoon. He had partied into the night. He always loved the night. It gave him emotional security. He felt better when he could slip into a rock concert, poison a musician and leave without anyone realizing it. He had already ended the life of one drummer for the Start Me Up band. The police, a private investigator, and the security forces within the music industry were gearing up to catch him. They wouldn't have a prayer. He was not only too smart for them, he knew the rock and roll world inside out. It was predictable. They had no chance. But now it was the afternoon, he had to get ready to vanish into the night.

He moved quickly to clean up his small and tidy apartment. No one had any idea about his other life. The women's underpants on his bed brought him a nice reminder of last night. He smelled them. There was a hint of Agent Provocateur. His favorite perfume. He had performed at a karaoke night in a San Francisco transvestite bar, Auntie Charlie's. He won second place. A Diana Ross clone won the contest. She obviously had plastic surgery. The women's underpants had such fond memories. He put them on. They felt good. He rubbed them. He put on the red tube top and the tight Capri pants. The blonde wig added the final touch. He looked at himself in the mirror. He began chanting: "You are beautiful. You are beautiful." He lifted some weights. His upper body was still taut. He needed to remain muscular. He loved to look at himself in the mirror. He was balding but a special wig enhanced his looks.

He loved to dress in women's clothes. It made him feel feminine and powerful. But it was time for some serious work. He loved the feeling he got when the drummer's eyes registered instant fear and dropped dead in the dressing room. All three Start Me Up drummers died of food poisoning. It didn't matter. The unfeeling management simply rolled in another drummer. Everyone thought it was the rock and roll lifestyle that killed them.

No one had a clue. The Chef had a systematic way of killing. He used Tylenol and a drug that he invented Plenthenol. By crushing twenty tables in the food, the Chef induced a death in weeks. The beauty of Plenthenol is that it was manufactured from a special hair shampoo.

Planthenol 3 was an ingredient in shampoo that quickly turned into a poison. The Chef's college training in chemistry came in handy.

The Chef's food platters were rich and filled with different types of fish. He prepared them backstage before a concert. In combination with the drugs, death was delayed for ten hours to two weeks. Now the police were looking for him. There were rumors of a private eye hired to hunt him down. The San Francisco Police Department put their best man on it. Their best man was a woman. He was smarter than his hunters. He smiled like a fly on the wall that no one could see. He also had a foolproof method. Poisoning or electrical malfunction were his twin killers. He liked to vary death so as not to be predictable.

The Chef was a sophisticated killer. A fatal poison was the best method. His other means of death was a shock to the stomach or one to the body that brought a smile to the Chef's face. It didn't matter. A small explosive device strategically placed or, a short-circuited microphone also did the job. But food was the key. Poison was a slow and agonizing way to die. It gave the Chef pleasure. He spent hours putting together recipes in which the poison could not be detected.

He had been a star student in weekend classes at the California Culinary Academy. Around the city by the bay, he was known for his discriminating palate. For a time, he worked as the Phantom Restaurant Critic for the San Francisco Chronicle. He quit because of his increased notoriety. He was outed as a critic.

In San Francisco anonymity was one of the Chefs strongest traits. He was respected. He worked in a field that was considered prestigious, and he was a renowned Chef. He was also a chameleon who fit into the crowd. Despite his size, he was six feet five inches tall, he had an easy and ingratiating manner. People never saw him as a threat. He was the last person anyone would suspect of being a killer. He could fit anywhere and tonight it was Bill Graham's Fillmore Auditorium. The citadel of rock music was his place to commit homicide. He smiled. It felt good to think of those who would fall.

The Fillmore Auditorium emerged in the mid-1960s to meet the needs of the rock and roll community. It also met the fiscal requirements of Bill Graham who became not only a millionaire but also a mover and shaker in the music industry. Then he was killed in a plane crash. The Chef remembered meeting Graham, who acted like he was a God. Apparently, God couldn't stop the helicopter that killed Graham from hitting a power pole. It was late afternoon and the Chef still had to drive to the Fillmore.

Coffee was the next need. The coffee quickly came out of the Italian machine. He poured a cup of coffee and read about the war in Iraq. He needed to keep up on the news. His day job was a perfect cover for a murderer and he had to know the ins and outs of George Bush's presidency. What a miserable little bastard. Who would call himself W? He couldn't believe that the president was talking about Iraq in San Diego when New Orleans was flooded. Bush looked like Alfred E. Neuman and talked like one of the Beverly Hillbillies. Maybe they could put him on the cover of Mad magazine. The Chef focused his thoughts on driving into the city and completing his nefarious plan. He would poison another drummer tonight. It made him feel that he exacted the ultimate revenge.

He looked in the closet for his rock and roll clothes. It was time to dress up for the kill. He looked over at his picture. It was a photo of his basketball team at Everett High School in Lansing, Michigan. The Chef was in the last row. His famous teammate, Magic Johnson, had gone on to Michigan State. Then he had gone on to fame and fortune with the Los Angeles Lakers. The Chef went to the University of Michigan. He didn't want to be in Johnson's shadow. It had worked. The Chef was all Big Ten. He was a six foot five inch athletic stud. Then he hurt his knee and his athletic days were over. He was a former athlete who was frustrated. He also had a slight bit of deviant behavior. At least that's what his psychology instruction told him. No one knew that he was a cross dresser.

The Chef made a great deal of money. His real estate investments, his best selling cookbooks, his stock investments and his ghost writing of rock and roll songs made him a fortune. There was a numbered bank account in the Cayman Islands. He wrote songs under a pseudonym. The tunes were sold to major rock bands like Aerosmith, J. Giels and the Rolling Stones. He was angry that he had to sell the rights to his songs. The money was great but fame and fortune were more important.

When the Rolling Stones bought the BMI and ASCAP rights to his songs and put their names on the tunes, he was infuriated. He would get his revenge. He couldn't kill Charlie Watts. The Rolling Stones' drummer was too well protected. The beauty was that slowly, agonizingly getting ride of the drummers from the cover band, Start Me Up, gave the

Chef more pleasure. He never realized how much until the killings began.

When he started killing the drummers in the Start Me Up band, it gave him a thrill that was greater than scoring a basket over Magic Johnson. It was the ultimate aphrodisiac. He didn't kill for just the joy of it. The Chef believed that he was righting wrongs. He was killing for all the little people who had never achieved their dreams. He killed to equalize opportunity. The police believed that some of the deaths of the Start Me Up drummers were due to natural causes.

Police bungling humored the Chef. It allowed him to poison a drummer at whim. The police thought it was just another crazy rocker. When Bobby Fuller was found dead in Los Angeles in the 1960s the LAPD ruled that he had broken his arms and legs and then committed suicide. Bill "The Moose" Skowren was never indicted. There was no mention of the mobster's girl friend that he was bedding. Or the obvious sign that he was murdered. After all wasn't every body found dead in their car with a horse's head in the back seat.

The Chef had a moral standard. Never make money from imitation. Always remain original. That was the Chef's motto. Never copy anyone. Use your own skills. Use your own abilities. He was obsessed with dishonesty. He had morals. He had character. He had integrity. He realized few other people could match his personal coda.

Most of the Chef's songs were sold to the Start Me Up band. They were a Rolling Stones cover group replete with thirty-year old musicians who had plastic surgery to look like Mick and Keith. No one seemed to want to look like Ron Wood or Charlie Watts. The Ron Wood look alike and the Charlie Watts clones were a decade older than the fake Mick and Keith. It was a weird site to behold. When Keith Richards looked healthy something was wrong. The Start Me Up band had done everything possible to become the Rolling Stones. They only lacked one ingredient. Original talent.

The Chef didn't like the fact that the Start Me Up band was making money, millions to be exact, covering the Rolling Stones songs. They were the fake Stones. He collected Stones memorabilia. Each week at his post office box eight or ten items arrived as his Rolling Stone's collection took on an eerie religious persona. So he would get his revenge for the little people who paid fifty dollars at the local Indian casino to see the fake Stones.

He fantasized that this would destroy the Start Me Up band. The first drummer was already dead. It didn't make a difference. The next two were thought to be of natural causes. It only made the band a bigger draw and they went from playing small clubs to 20,000 seat arenas or the ballrooms in the Indian Casinos for an exorbitant fee. Not only did the Start Me Up band regularly sell out these small rock palaces, but their CDs, t-shirts and memorabilia sales rivaled bands like U-2. This made the Chef crazy. The immorality of making money off Mick and Keith enraged him. Even more irritating was making money from the Chef. His songs were a staple of the Start Me Up bands live performances.

No one had any idea about his identity. His apartment in the Castro overlooked the Chow Cafe. Sounded Chinese. It wasn't. The Chow was a marvelous place for a chicken sandwich or a spinach salad. It was his second home. He walked into the Chow bar for a quick drink. After polishing off a Heineken, he caught a cab to Fillmore and Geary Street. He got out and lit a cigarette. He didn't have any of these bad habits when he was an athlete. But that was in another life. It was also in another time and place. He looked at the Fillmore Auditorium. It had been a Jewish temple. He liked the idea of killing in a former place of worship. He worshipped at the altar of rock and roll. So killing was a religious experience. He always arrived early to savor the atmosphere.

He walked over to the nearby music venue, the Boom Boom Room. He stopped and looked at the huge Fillmore sign. Then he went into the bar for a scotch and soda. John Lee Hooker allowed his name to be used on the Boom Boom Room and he was rumored to be a part owner. The Chef knew that this was nonsense. Hooker's son and daughter were part of the ownership and the place jumped with the best in hip hop and rap music. The good old blues days were long gone. John Lee's name was the device to bring one into the club. He was now buried in a cemetery in Coloma and turning over in his grave.

The Boom Boom Room was a nondescript looking club previously known as Jack's Place. It had been a jazz joint. When Van Morrison finished a San Francisco concert, he came into the Boom Boom Room and jumped on stage with the band. One night a drummer, Big Bones, threw Morrison out the front door. So much for fame. At least Morrison had the fortune. Big Bones sold the bootleg tape of Morrison singing to a startled audience of African Americans who had little interest in his music.

When the Chef was young his mother brought him to San Francisco and he ate barbecue and listened to the blues on Fillmore Street. He had looked at the sign for Jack's Place. So going in to have a drink gave him a special thrill. Even if hip-hop dominated. Maybe it was a passing fad.

Times had changed. Stevie Ray Vaughn and Lowell Fulson no longer played the Boom Boom Room. Or most other blues clubs for that matter. Now it was a bunch of white guys with names like Papa Chubby. The blues were in a catastrophic downfall.

In this atmosphere the Chef was invisible. He was the kind of guy who fit in anywhere. So he enjoyed the drink in anonymity. He talked to the bar tender and found out that Jimmy McCracklin would play the club on the weekend. The cranky eighty plus year old blues icon was sitting at the bar. Glaring. Word was McCracklin didn't like white people.. Someone should tell him that they were the only ones buying his music.

The Boom Boom Room brought a major blues band in one night a week. McCracklin was this weeks star. The Chef loved McCracklin's "The Walk" but heard and witnessed the 85-year-old bluesman acting like a pain in the ass. What else would a bluesman be? The Chef finished his beer and left a five-dollar tip. McCracklin came over the pocketed it. Walking out of the club, the Chef tilted his head under the diminutive front door. His greasy palmade separated from his hair brushed on the top of the door. The grease was apparent to anyone entering the club. He still had some hair and the grease spiked it up to look like a full head of hair. So much for vanity. The Chef walked across the street and stood in front of the Fillmore. It was show time.

The Chef stood in front of the Fillmore Auditorium and marveled at the lack of a neon sign. Bill Graham made millions off the place but he never spent a dime to remodel it. The long and tedious climb up at the stairs at the Fillmore was a tiring walk. He looked out the bay window at the top of the Fillmore stairs. The San Francisco skyline had a red glow as the sky turned to dusk. The Chef stopped and looked at the skyline. It was beautiful. There was an esthetic touch to the city by the bay. He smiled. It was a good time for a killing. The Chef looked at his death venue. It was an appropriate one. Bill Graham's original concert venue at Fillmore and Geary was no longer an old Jewish temple. The Fillmore now drew a crowd that worshipped at the altar of rock and roll. The Chef mused that it was now the home of satanic music. There was an art deco feel to it. The Fillmore still had creaky wooden floors, a musty smell and a stage that was uneven. Coupled with an average sound system, it wasn't the world's greatest venue. It didn't matter; there was death in the air. The Chef smiled. He looked down. There were one hundred stairs made of wood and they were steep. It was not a climb for a middle-aged guy. When you are six feet five inches tall and haven't played basketball in twenty-five years you are out of shape. You also had bad memories. The Chef realized that he was a failed basketball player, then a failed musician, and then a period of nothingness and suddenly you are a financial success. He didn't want the success. What he wanted was basketball and musical recognition. Neither of which came his way. It was killing him. It was a crazy burden. It was one that drove him to kill. His profession was cooking. Now he had turned it into a deadly game. He killed with food. He had been to the Fillmore many times. Years ago he opened for Jimi Hendrix. His band, the Miscreants, was booed off the stage. Now the Chef wanted his revenge. He was sweating. Nervous. It was time to kill off the competition. The Rolling Stones didn't deserve some band that copied their material and made millions.

The Chef dressed appropriately. His white apron was full of sweat; he had a nervous tick that distorted his face. Soon he found the backstage kitchen. He had once been a member of the rock and roll royalty. A songwriter of note. He had to get his retribution. His white Chef's hat and carefully starched jacket was adorned with a pass "Backstage." He smiled. This would be easy. It took less than half an hour to prepare the ingredients. The pills were ground and ready to go to work. He always put the ingredients in at the last moment. Anyone could sample it and not get sick. There were no traces. Only a small amount of Tylenol.

The Chef looked at the seafood delight with a smile. It was the ingredients for his seafood salad. The rock musicians loved his cooking. He took extra time cutting the sole and mixing it with the divined shrimp. A little crab and lobster were added with some shiitake mushrooms and a mixture of Napa shredded cabbage, fresh bean sprouts and miniature carrots. Then he sautéed some grouper and the coconut shrimp was finished in a fryer. Now it was time for the seasoning. He took a small and special plate for the drummer. It was placed next to his drum kit. He could snack on stage. Drugs didn't kill, food did. The small dabs of poison were undetectable and the special salad was ready for the Start Me Up Band drummer. A platter of fish sautéed with fresh vegetables completed the buffet for the rest of the band.

A mega million dollar touring aggregation, the Start Me Up Band featured a career long retrospective of songs by the infamous Rolling Stones. With guarantees of $50,000 to $150,000 a night they toured three hundred plus days a year. When they played Las Vegas, Reno, Atlantic City, Miami, New York and the Indian casinos the guarantees were often $200,000 a night. All the band members had undergone extensive plastic surgery to look like their counterparts. Billy Williams, who was Mick Jagger, couldn't go out in public. The rest of the band gloried in the money and the fame. They each made a million dollars a year in salary. It was a business. So the band had medical insurance and a 401k plans for retirement. Rock and roll was a business and the Start Me Up Band was a corporate monster.

As their two tour buses pulled in outside San Francisco's Fillmore Auditorium, the Chef paused and looked at the large, rolling hotels. The band members got out and looked at Fillmore and Geary. It was a strange moment.

The Chef loved Geary Street in the heart of what had once been an African American neighborhood, and the street intersected with Fillmore Street where all the blues clubs existed in the 1950s. Now the Fillmore was full of white imitations of the blues. The old relic, Jimmy McCracklin, would talk shit about the blues and then he would play a Stevie Wonder song.

As the Chef surveyed a group of twenty-five or so groupies who held out CDs and other memorabilia, he was nauseous. What a bunch of losers. The band got off the bus looking disinterested. Typical rock stars. They quickly exited the bus and with ten bodyguards walked across the street to the Boom Boom Room. After a couple of scotch and waters and a few joints in the bathroom the Start Me Up Band strolled back to the Fillmore and quietly slipped backstage. There was an immense spread of food. The Chef had done his job. He prepared to leave the Fillmore satisfied that he would once again strike at this corporate monster which made real rock and roll a joke. He was killing for purity in rock music. The idea of a tribute show to the Rolling Stones using fake bands enraged the Chef. He put on his rock and roll clothes. He took his Chef's outfit and placed it in a sack. He would get rid of it. No sloppy evidence left behind. He was careful. Precise planning. He never forgot the lessons he learned from basketball. Play with passion and precision. So he killed with passion and precision. He had to be agitated to kill. The manner in which rock and roll concerts were presented drove the Chef over the edge.

It was the posters that the Fillmore Auditorium tacked on the wall leading upstairs to the music venue that drove the Chef crazy. The posters covered a different period in Stones history. The Start Me Up Band played a full-blown array of all the Stones songs. They always closed the show with "Satisfaction." The CDs, posters, t-shirts and small guitars sold in large numbers and netted the corporation between five and six million dollars a year. Another reason to hate the Start Me Up band. Their manager neglected to inform them of his immense profits. That was the way in the rock and roll world. The drummers were easy to replace and even easier to poison. The Chef laughed when he thought how little attention rock bands paid to their drummers. They were the blue-collar workers in the rock and roll jungle. The Pete Best's no one appreciated.

The Chef wondered if he had poisoned Pete Best or Ringo Starr if the Beatles would have remained in Liverpool. He doubted it. They had real talent. They were creative and didn't deserve to be poisoned. The Start Me Up band was a different matter. They were pure unadulterated scum. None worse than the new drummer.

Dean Moriarty, the drummer in the Start Me Up Band, was the last person to leave the stage. It wasn't his real name. He had read a Jack Kerouac novel and changed his name from Mort Bernstein. Probably a good move. He was considered the band's cute member. Ugh! For that reason, he would be the first to die. The other members of the Rolling Stones tribute band went to the bus where a gaggle of groupies were ready for drugs, sex and rock and roll. The drummer was hungry. Not for drugs or groupies. He was the consummate gourmet. Dean looked at his ample roll. A girdle hid his stomach. To hell with it, he thought. It was time to eat.

Dean went over to the private dressing room and picked up the special plate of the Chef's creations next to the drums. Why wait! The food was ready. The Chef was trying to leave the Fillmore. He bumped his head on the door. Despite his thinning hair, he used a gel that made it stand on end. The Chef stood stiffly as the drummer approached him. Dean Moriarty told him that he loved his hair. The Chef lied and told the drummer that he loved the Start Me Up band. They talked about rock and roll music. The stories the Chef told were legendary ones. The best one involved an LSD frosting he put on a birthday cake for Jimi Hendrix. Doctor Rock, a local San Francisco disc jockey provided the LSD frosting.

After Dean ravenously devoured a full plate of fish dishes and salads, he went to the bathroom. He died within an hour. The Chef left the scene of the crime. An innocuous figure. He vanished into the night. The next day the Start Me Up Band cancelled 285 dates and forfeited over $8 million in booking fees. The Chef smiled when he read the next day's San Francisco Chronicle..

He sabotaged the largest grossing tribute band in rock and roll history. It gave him a good feeling. The white Chef's coat was thrown in a dumpster outside the Fillmore. He created chaos for his rivals. Not to mention imminent financial problems.

It was time for a walk. The cook stopped on Fillmore Street at the Elite Café for a shrimp cocktail. He was still hungry. Killing made him ravenous. He ordered a large bowl of gumbo with a glass of Jordan cabernet sauvignon. The waiter stuck his nose up in disapproval. A white wine was more appropriate. The Chef ignored him. He left the Elite Café and continued to walk toward the Golden Gate Bridge.

It was a balmy San Francisco night. The Chef walked past the yuppie bars. He decided he needed a real men's bar. So he walked down to Union Street to the Bus Stop and a Miller high life helped him relax. Then he went across Union Street for a nightcap at Perry's.

When Perry's opened it became the unofficial hangout for the cool people. The Chef was there a little later in the 1970s along with the Irish bartenders, and he was known for his commitment to good scotch. The 12-year-old malt was his favorite.

The Chef sat at the bar. Everyone knew him. He was one of San Francisco's most recognizable and respected figures. That was in the financial community. He was a legend for his stock market investments. No one knew him as the Chef. He liked that mysterious side to his life. He could kill with food. No one ever suspected him. He could also be a man or a woman. Not necessarily a major feat in San Francisco.

When the Chef cross-dressed, he felt beautiful. Often he wandered from his apartment in the Castro, over to Polk Street or down to the Tenderloin. He loved to party dressed as a woman. No one paid any attention. San Francisco was the kind of town where this was not atypical. At six feet five inches he was not inconspicuous as a woman. It was San Francisco and no one cared. It gave him the freedom he needed to be himself. Magic Johnson didn't have that freedom.

For the moment he was a man. A tall, somewhat balding, middle aged man who looked like any other successful businessman. He was a happy figure in the big city. One whose face was known but his name often forgotten.

As the Chef wandered around Union Street drinking in a wide variety of bars, he thought of his dual San Francisco life. Tonight he was a man's man and it was time to drink in the local bars. He could talk about sports, politics or the latest movie. He could even talk hunting, fishing and Nascar racing. No one realized that he was San Francisco's rock and roll killer.

He wandered across the street from Perry's back to the Bus Stop for another drink. He talked football to Joe Montana who sat at the bar. Then he meandered down to the Matrix to search out a new musical act. The Matrix was home to Janis Joplin and the Jefferson Airplane in the early 1960s. He ended the evening talking about women. By this time, he was at the Balboa Café listening to Fat Jack and all the other losers. Then he took a cab to Broadway where he closed out the evening at O'Reilly's Irish pub listening to Van Morrison on the jukebox. It was rumored that Morrison ate there when he was in town. The Irish owner was from Belfast and a good friend of Van's. At each place the Chef fit easily into the scene. He was like a chameleon that was at home anywhere. This was the perfect means of being an undetected murderer.

The Chef had a strong sense of morality. He didn't like the cesspool life that was emerging in the city by the bay. Things were no longer what they were when Herb Caen wrote his columns, Joel Selvin reviewed shows, Vince Guaraldi played Charlie Brown songs at the Jazz Workshop or the San Francisco Giants played at Candlestick Park. Now the Giants played in a new park. This was the only place where the Chef didn't dress up as a woman. It was too cold. He never understood why women dressed as women in a baseball park.

There was still an hour of drinking time left. The Chef walked down to Vesuvio's. It was famous for Irish Coffee. The cable car whizzed by as he wandering into a bar with a singer-pianist and a bunch of lounge lizards looking like they had found religion. "Another Billy Joe song," a guy in a red sport coat with a white tie bellowed. The Chef smiled. The pianist was a friend. The pianist winked at the Chef. He was a weight lifter and a bigot. Alan from New York was a full time history professor who talked about himself. He had no idea about the Chef.

The Chef hollered: "How about some Jimmy McCracklin blues?" The pianist smiled and went into an instrumental version of "Just Got To Know." The Chef loved McCracklin's music. The pianist took a break and told the Chef that he was about to join the San Francisco Police Department. He was leaving academic life. They talked at length about serial killers. The piano player had studied serial killers and was going to work next work for a special serial violent crimes unit in the San Francisco Police Department. The Chef mused that he was as stupid as the rest.

The Chef left with a bad feeling. The people who controlled the city by the bay were not his type of folks. Mayor Gavin Newsom was a pretty boy with no brains. The police chief was an ethnic choice. The San Francisco Board of Supervisors was full of rich, old style Italians, a few Irish and some ethnics. Politically correct was the key to San Francisco politics. The Chef wondered how his bigotry got so well developed. No sense denying it.

As the left the bar, the Chef looked over at the piano man who was discussing San Francisco's eccentric characters. Not realizing that the most eccentric one was exiting the bar.

One San Francisco character that they talked about made him sick. The primary one was Don Gino Landry, a gay Mafioso, who was not only a prominent citizen, but he lunched weekly with former Mayor Willie Brown. Mayor Newsom had a standing dinner with him on Wednesdays. The Purple Don, as Landry was known, was seen frequently with Willie Mays in local restaurants. Even the reclusive Joe DiMaggio had coffee with the Purple Don. Herb Caen gave Landry this nickname because he affected purple clothing. He was the chairman of the Mission Delores restoration fund and a regular at the Mission District Catholic church. He was gay but would kill anyone who pointed it out. He was a crime boss who didn't allow drugs or prostitution in the Mission District. He made his money the old-fashioned way gambling, protection, loan sharking and legitimate businesses. Don Gino was in the grocery, produce and meat business and had a well-established dog food plant. Gino's Gourmet dog food was the largest moneymaker west of the Mississippi. The Chef hated Landry. He would take down the Purple Don.

He would also even his scores with the San Francisco Police Department. They had denied him musical permits. Bill Graham saw to that and a Detective Richard Sanchez was to blame. They would all bear the brunt of his fury.

Detective Sanchez was a handsome Latino in his late thirties who dated Sharon Stone after she divorced the industrialist Herman Gruning who was also one of San Francisco's richest entrepreneurs.

How Stone and Sanchez hooked up was a mystery. He was a right wing political nut and she was an anti-war activist. Testosterone had to be the answer. No one could figure the attraction. Stone and Sanchez were seen all over town. So Gruning bought the San Francisco Star and went after the police department.

When the San Francisco Chronicle broke the story of womanizing in the SFPD, Detective Sanchez' wife divorced him. Sharon Stone quit dating him. He stated that he forgot to tell Stone that he was married. He also forgot to inform the other girl friends. He was too busy fighting crime. The divorce followed and Detective Sanchez found his picture all over the newspapers. Sharon Stone was named as a co-defendant in the divorce. This made Detective Sanchez with deep blue eyes, Armani suits and drop dead good looks more popular than ever in San Francisco social circles. He was a regular at the best restaurants. He seldom paid.

Sharon Stone left town and went back to Hollywood. Sanchez was seen all over town with the most eligible women. All of whom seemed too rich for him. Most of these lovely ladies had numerous plastic surgeries and were millionaires. In the divorce Sanchez received his wife's Rolls Royce and the penthouse apartment on Nob Hill. His wife returned to Spain to live in her families' villa. He didn't appear heart broken.

There were others the Chef detested. Joyce Byers was a recently promoted detective second class. She had solved six murder cases the previous year involving serial killers. She and Sanchez were rumored to be investigating the Start Me Up crimes. The Chef laughed. The only crime was the band's lame music. He didn't worry. No one could catch him. He was too clever.

The most disgusting aspect of Joyce Byers' life was her boyfriend, Trevor Blake III. Trevor the turd as the Chef called him. He was a well-publicized private detective, who had yet to solve a major case. He was a newspaper darling because he played in a surf band. Whether it was music or private investigator work, the Chef hated the good-looking, blonde haired bumbler with dreamy blue eyes. Trevor was seen around town with not only Joyce Byers, but a host of beautiful women. Trevor was a serial dater. He never met a woman he didn't like.

The Chef had the knowledge and power. The way to kill people was fraught with careful planning, the proper ingredients and you needed to pay attention to detail. Gloves prevented fingerprints. The Chef shaved himself and wore a cap so that he didn't leave behind any trace evidence. He wore clothing that he discarded after each kill. His shoes were burnt. He wore a series of disguises. The more he planned the more confident he became. He knew that the problems would come after the killings. He was ready to fit into the background. He was a chameleon that no one would suspect. He was a master at killing people and getting away with it.

PART I

Chapter 1
THE ROLLING STONES AND ME

The sign read Blake Investigations. The office was empty. There was a desk and two chairs. Not exactly what Sam Spade envisioned. A large portrait of Janis Joplin hung behind my desk. Janis' breast showed in an erotic manner. I wondered do breasts often show in a non-erotic way? I purchased both of these posters from a collector in Seattle, McArthur Dee. Then this maniac hired me to find a Jimi Hendrix guitar that someone had stolen from him. I was able to collect $5000 from McArthur as a finder's fee. His twin brother stole the guitar. McArthur didn't press charges.

The Trevor Blake III lifestyle was a complicated one. I solved few crimes but I was well known for socializing. I invested heavily in rental real estate and had a side business helping amateur real estate investors. McArthur Dee never invested, he simply asked about it and he showed me properties. I bought them for myself. My other job was to advise Angelo Sangiacomo on his real estate investments. I received almost half a million dollars to invest. McArthur Dee was my point man. He found the properties. He was too stupid to realize his importance. He was too busy making wise remarks.

But McArthur Dee was harmless. He had a goatee, weighed 225 pounds and thought he was clever. "You're going to get a real estate wedge," he remarked time and time again to me. He was one of the few people who knew that my primary income came from rental property and not from solving crimes. Guys like McArthur paid the rent.

McArthur Dee drove a San Francisco bus. He worked night and day to pay for his girl friends eating habits. Selma weighted two hundred and seventy pounds and she was writing a book on San Francisco ice cream parlors. Weird! Yes! Mentally healthy! No! McArthur was a genius at helping me find cheap properties.

I needed the rental income to make my life work. So I used friends like McArthur. He would find a great rental. He couldn't pull the plug and purchase it. He was clever but stupid. Instead of investing his money in real estate or stocks, he invested in 45 records. He talked about turning his vinyl into gold. McArthur was typical of the nut cases who came through my door. He was not only a loser. He was a fool. Typical of what I dealt with everyday. I needed his retainer, so I played along. He paid me to search out private record collections. He was nuts.

My cases hadn't generated much money. Trevor Blake III is not exactly a household name as a P. I. I have never solved an important case. To find a well-publicized case, I had to use my expertise. I wasn't sure what I was most qualified to detect. I had a law degree. I passed the bar and decided I didn't want to practice law. I performed in a surf band, Blake and the Big Waves, every Friday night at Slim's in the South of Market area. Last week Boz Scaggs replaced us. He was trying out some new material. The album was a collection of blues songs for Scaggs, whose wife left him for a 250-pound fat guy. The fat guy was a billionaire. So it must have been love. Poor Boz. Maybe I was related to him.

I still played some basketball. At forty, divorced with no kids, I was able to survive on my real estate investments. I didn't want people to think that I was a failure, so I exaggerated my private eye experiences. I had money from other sources and a wonderful education. So I was a Private Eye. Not for the money. For the excitement.

I was the only private eye in San Francisco to be sued by the Rolling Stones. I devised a logo with the lips and teeth from a Stones album and I used it on advertisements for my surf band. My Private Investigation firm was known as Trevor Blake III, The Surf Investigator. It didn't bring in new business. I liked it.

I did have some musical success. The Masonic Auditorium is a magnificent concert all atop Nob Hill. An agent contacted me and my band, Blake and the Big Waves, opened for Van Morrison. The audience was full of celebrities. Halfway through the set Richard Gere stood and booed our version of the Ventures' "Walk Don't Run." I didn't care for Gere in "Pretty Woman." Mick and Keith were in the audience. The two Stones laughed until they saw the logo on the drums, it was their trademark tongue. They contacted their lawyer. The Stones' barrister sued for removal of the logo. We had already lost one lawsuit to the Stones. The Stones felt sorry for me and after they won the second case they paid my legal expenses. Unfortunately, my ex-wife represented me. So I couldn't stiff her for the court costs. They paid her and Mick Jagger took her out to dinner.

Jagger was shown smiling in the San Francisco Chronicle with my ex-wife Marilyn beaming. It was Jagger looking like he was ready for good sex. I hated to tell him the truth. Marilyn thought sex was a country in Eastern Europe. The publicity was great for me. I had twenty new cases the next day. None of them were exactly high profile ones. I solved them. What I did was to find over ten deadbeat husbands, a half dozen runaway children and four perverts. Not exactly high profile work. These cases paid the rent.

My office in San Francisco's Haight Ashbury is a retro one. The first impression would make Sam Spade smile. It's retro because I can't afford new furniture. I look out at the Haight Ashbury sign from my second floor window. Across the street the Ben and Jerry Ice Cream sign burns brightly into the night. The Haight is the perfect place for my detective agency. I can visualize the newspaper headlines: "Hip Detective Trevor Blake III Solves Major Crime." The problem was no one ever thought of hiring me for a breakthrough case. After one year I was the least known P. I. in San Francisco.

The irony was that I was making a living. Not a good one. But enough to survive. Rent was cheap. I did have some secrets. I owned some property and I was careful with my money. I also had a series of stock investments that brought in a nice income. It came in monthly and I could create any lifestyle I desired. The one I chose was that of a Private Investigator in the Haight Ashbury. I had just tacked to the wall a five-foot oil portrait of Jerry Garcia. A framed Janis Joplin hung next to Jerry. The walnut frames glistened as Janis and Jerry looking down on me. I was the only detective in San Francisco with Janis and Jerry on the wall. Kind of like two Picasso's.

My day finished late. I had to pay the bills. Clean out the old files. Create new files for the mundane cases. By the time I was finished, the Haight Street was dormant. The tourists had gone home. There were few signs of life on the street. The reason was that it was six o'clock in the morning. I had worked all night. Obsessive-compulsive behavior cost me my marriage. Marilyn screamed like a banshee when I converted our bedroom into a record and CD menagerie. She refused to sleep with me for two months. I didn't seem to notice. I found a sweet young girl at Henry Africa's. It was my favorite singles bar and our divorce went by without incident. I was now into sport fucking. That is sort of like sex dating.

My split with Marilyn was hastened when I brought home 324 Georges Simenon mystery novels and built a special bookcase in the front room. That was the final straw. She left. The second happiest day of my life was when Marilyn married me, the first happiest day was our divorce.

I looked out the window from my cool and retro office. As I searched the street below I saw apparition. It looked like Janis and Jimi were walking down the street. They were. Tourists. They loved to dress up like sixties icons. A homeless derelict was sleeping under Ben and Jerry's Ice Cream door. An organic hippie. So much for the Summer of Love.

I had a game plan. It was to become as famous as Sam Spade or perhaps Elvis Cole. How could a forty-year old Stanford graduate wind up in the Hashberry? The sun was shining through my bay window. Silver threads of sunlight pierced the wall. I needed to wake up. The coffee machine was handy and I named it for my favorite baseball player. I put on a pot of coffee in the Joe DiMaggio. and took one last look at the old mail. Nothing significant. Bills and a few advertisements. I looked at the CD racks I had built on the wall. All 10,000 plus CDs were in order. I was after all a collector as well as a Private Eye.

Generally, Haight Street is full of tourists. But not at six o'clock in the morning. I had on a pair of jeans, a tie died t-shirt that read Grateful Dead. Who could read it? The letters were in a psychedelic pattern that was incomprehensible to anyone not on acid. I loved the mornings. I changed into my jogging shorts and New Balance tennis shoes. Wandering out into the street, I was struck by the sunlight. The Haight was bright with sun and devoid of people. I jogged to Golden Gate Park. I ran slowly into the park and stepped in some dog doo. Welcome to San Francisco. I took off running in a brisk pace and stopped at the Japanese Tea Garden. It was beautiful with the hazy mist highlighting the plants.

When I returned to the office I felt better. I was bored so I ran up one flight up the stairs of my office building and looked down once again at the Haight Ashbury sign. I was depressed. There were no interesting cases. The boring and mundane is all I encountered. Runaways. Cheating husbands. Insurance fraud. Wife beatings. Lesbian beatings. These were some of my cases. I was sick of them. It was time for some fun. But first I had to take a nap. I snoozed on the couch until about three in the afternoon. I was now eager to go out. It wasn't five o'clock but I needed a drink.

I wandered down to the Haight Street Bar and Grill. It had a strange sign. Serving you since 2001. A glass of Merlot and a conversation with the bartender put me in a party mood.

I drove over the Bill's Place on Clement Street and had a Herb Caen Burger. Extra pickles and an extra sauce put me in a good mood. It was close to six in the evening and I was ready to think about going to the Oakland Coliseum and using my backstage pass to see the Rolling Stones. I drove over to Van Ness, turned right on Stanyan Street and passed the house where Rod McKuen wrote his poems. I entered my office. I quickly changed into a Keith Richards' t- shirt. I was ready for the chicks.

As I walked out of the office a midge was standing under the Haight Street sign dressed as Mick Jagger. It seemed like an improvement over the real thing. Then I remembered that I had left my wallet on my desk. I walked up the stairs and into my office. I picked up the wallet and found twenty dollars in the top desk drawer. The fiscal Gods were smiling on me.

I looked across the street in front of the Ben and Jerry's and another midget dressed like Mick Jagger smiled at me. I sauntered onto Haight Street and I walked by two midget Mick Jagger's. The taller midget sang a few lines of "Satisfaction." He kept mumbling "Can't get no, can't get no." I didn't think he was going to get anything any time soon. I thought of my bungled detective agency. Maybe I should hire a midget to promote me.

I thought a lot about my lack of decent cases. The results of my recent work are as follows. A missing heir was found, a runaway kid of thirteen refused to go home and a fifty-year-old drug addict, who had once been a lawyer, sued me for malpractice. There was a humorous irony to that case. The files for these cases sat on my desk. I looked at the larger stack of folders. These represented those who had not paid their fees. I had trouble collecting a retainer. At forty, I was the worst private eye in the history of San Francisco. Sam Spade wouldn't talk to me.

There are some strong points in my career. I am the most literate P. I. in San Francisco. Graduate degrees. I have three of them. I even have a law degree. I never practiced. I hate the law. The old joke was that the difference between a lawyer and a male sperm was that the sperm had a one in twenty million chance of being a human being. Bad joke. But true. Published books. I had written three novels featuring a Filipino private detective, Jose Rizal. Each book sold two thousand copies and the Mystery Press didn't renew my contract. They also didn't answer my letters. My personal life was in even worse shape. My wife was a ravenous blonde with big boobs, a 145 IQ and a killer instinct. She smoked and drank incessantly. But with big boobs who cares! I never used the phrase "big boobs" around her. It was a sexist phrase. I couldn't break my old habits, so I called her big boobs in private.

The divorce was a nightmare. It turned out the killer instinct caused her to get everything in the divorce. There was a rumor she was sleeping with the judge. I sued for alimony. The judge laughed. He awarded me the dog. Who promptly ran out in the street and was killed by a car. So I followed my boyhood dream and opened Blake Investigations. Trevor Blake III it sounded impressive.

My only problem is how to hide my money. Marilyn thinks I left the marriage broke. I did have my investments. This was a subject I had never shared with my wife. I was still able to do what I wanted. My rent is $1200 a month, my car is ten years old and I didn't eat much. When I get depressed I get away and have some fun. It is always music that was the catalyst to my good times. So I was off to retune my soul with some rock and roll sounds. The Rolling Stones would cure my ills even if they were old enough to be my parents.

I walked down to the corner near my Haight Street office and hopped a bus down to San Francisco's city center. I bought a $6 ticket on BART. Who said public transportation was cheap? The code letters for the Bay Area Rapid Transit were inspiring, the service was not. The letters make it sound like a modern transportation network, the reality is something different. I looked at a sign that Mayor Gavin Newsom had put up describing BART as "a modern version of the transportation of the future." Modern. Funny. Gavin didn't ride it. I though of his word modern. It isn't. BART has so many flaws that one is better off taking the bus. The future, there wasn't one for BART. My ticket stuck in the machine. Then I asked the ticket agent which gate for Oakland. She answered me in Chinese and slammed the window shut. I asked a security guard with a turban about my ticket. He simply smoothed it out and told me to use it again. I smiled at the Vietnamese janitor who was emptying the trash bins. His T-shirt read: "Mao is Back." What a sense of history. "Mao is Back." I wondered if he could find his way home with a map. Mao is Back sounded like the name of a punk rock band. Trying to get around on BART is not an easy task. BART has no signs and there are few people who understand where this nefarious transportation system goes. I don't ride it much, so I took some time to find the Oakland platform. I wondered if a Private Eye who couldn't find his way to Oakland could solve a crime. Probably not. Finally, I was on board the train and on my way to the Rolling Stones concert at the infamous Oakland Coliseum. I was the only American on the car. There were two guys talking in Farsi and a Chinese man listening to a CD player. A guy in a turban was reading a Hemingway novel. The Chinese man dropped his CD cover; I noticed it read Bruce Springsteen. So all was not lost. On another CD player I can hear the strains of drum music. Good old San Francisco, we are multicultural to a fault. I love it. At the end of my BART car I spotted a ragged looking guy. He was a wino and I watched him drink from a milk carton. The wino got off BART walked in front of me and began negotiating for a scalper ticket. Maybe he wasn't a wino. Perhaps just another 1960s hippie who was hoping to see the Rolling Stones. As soon as he bought his scalpers ticket, the wino pulled out a badge, two back up cops moved in and arrested the scalper. Welcome to the San Francisco Bay Area.

I love San Francisco. It is diverse. It is fun. It is also hard to make a living. The dot. com downturn took away much of my business. I wouldn't be hired to find that missing computer chip stolen from Bill Gates. My personal life is a constant and continual mess. After my divorce I decided to rent a small apartment on Chestnut Street. That was the good news. The bad news was that I rented it from Bennie and Bertie my ex-brother and sister in law. They liked to keep track of the family even divorced members. They had voted for George Bush twice and bragged about never watching the news unless it was on Fox, reading a newspaper, a magazine, a book or talking politics. "I know what I know and that's it," Bennie continued. "President Bush is fighting terrorism and I am behind him." I think Bennie and Bertie thought that the President was fighting terrorism on Chestnut Street. But cheap rent kept my criticism at bay. I did have an exclusive address on Chestnut Street.

Bennie was fond of calling Barack Obama, Osama. He watched Fox News and he also couldn't get enough of Rush Limbaugh. "Can you tell me what Rush looks like?" Bennie bellowed at me one day. I answered: "Yaw, a fat frog." That ended our political discussion. Bennie and Bertie loved to see me and hang around my Chestnut Street apartment. They were looking for girls I dated. I was the only single man on Chestnut that had to sneak his girls in the back door. The janitor never said a word. The reason is that Truong didn't speak English.

It was where all the swinging singles lived. I was suddenly a young single man on the loose. The ladies couldn't wait. I wasn't sure if 40 was young anymore and I wasn't having much luck with the ladies. I lied about my age. I told everyone I was thirty-five. Forty sounded old. What do you say to a twenty five year old? What's your sign? I am an Aquarius. That line sounded lame.

My social life was beginning to unravel; it was not yet in place after an acrimonious divorce. Getting back into the rock concert scene was the first step. As I watched the crowd wander into the Oakland Coliseum, I wondered if Geritol was sponsoring the gig. Maybe Jagger had false teeth. I had never seen so many old people. I noticed two fifty-year-old guys in Armani suits trying to light a joint. Nothing amazes me more than old people trying to be hip.

I wondered what the Rolling Stones must look like. Keith Richards was getting blood transfusions. Mick Jagger had opted not to have plastic surgery. He needed it. Ron Wood was working on the lung cancer. Charlie Watts looked like a banker. He had been one, so that was typecasting.

Once inside the Oakland Coliseum, I wondered why I showed up. It was May and the weather was in the fifties. Mark Twain's comment about the coldest winter he ever spent was a summer in San Francisco was one that I lived. I wondered if Mark Twain would go to a rock concert. Finally, the Rolling Stones ambled or should I say staggered onto stage. Their costumes were great. They looked tired but once the music kicked in, I noticed that they still had some oomph. Whatever the hell that is. They also had another ten musicians helping them create their sound. Or at least what used to be their old sound. I saw Chuck Leavell on stage and I remembered recording with him in Los Angeles. A great keyboardist who never made it. Now he made a half a million dollars a year with the Stones. Not bad for a failure.

Mick Jagger, looking like an old man in his sixties didn't appeal to me, but since I was in my forties I had noticed my own declining sex appeal. Perhaps Mick could teach me something. Then again maybe I'd wind up looking like Keith Richards. As Keith played his guitar with a cigarette dangling from his mouth, he looked like he was dead. Maybe the cigarette was stitched to his lip. He wore an old and tattered coat that looked like a Japanese kimono. They did remember the lines to their songs. The music was another problem. Ron Wood played like he was on another planet. It seemed that Wood had lost his guitar riffs but who noticed? Would I get as old as the Rolling Stones? Would I look as bad? Would I go bald? I probably wouldn't. The family had hair cards. Most of my family was overweight. I was aghast at the prospects. So I ran in Golden Gate Park every day.

I looked on the stage with amazement. There were so many other musicians that drummer Charlie Watts looked lost in the shuffle. Nostalgia. I was caught up in it. The concert began with Jagger jumping around the stage singing "Jumping Jack Flash." I had my fill of nostalgia. It was time for reality. After two hours the Rolling Stones were ready for an encore. I loved the concert and left in a good mood. But, as I prepared to leave the Stones came back for a second encore.

But before they finished performing "Start Me Up," there was a commotion in front of the stage. I ran up to the front and found Charlie Watts lying dead with a sausage hanging out of his mouth. There was a guy standing over him squirting a mysterious liquid on him, as he appeared to die. It was a water pistol laden with poison. The other Charlie Watts was a prominent member of the Rolling Stones cover band, the Start Me Up group. I wondered if he was really dead. At least he looked dead. How could anyone die by choking on a sausage in front of 60,000 people? I looked up and the real Charlie Watts stood on the stage looking at the dead Charlie Watts. At least it wasn't a dead Mick Jagger impersonator.

I hadn't taken any drugs or drank any booze. But I was seeing two Charlie Watts. I wasn't a rocket scientist but I realized one was an impersonator. It was none of my business, so I exited the building with a lot of people who thought it was part of the show. Rock music fans are not known for their sophistication. Or for their powers of detection. As a trained private eye I knew a murder when I saw one. No one choked on a sausage. At least not at a rock concert in front of 60,000 adoring fans. I looked at the body with my superb detection powers. He wasn't breathing, so he was dead. Not my problem. I needed to go to a singles bar and find a woman. I had trouble finding the right woman. I had trouble finding any woman. My personality and looks were still there.

The problems of the single life began when I was married. I had given up on socializing and allowed Marilyn to set our social schedule. My wife, a graduate of the University of California Boalt Law School, made over a million dollars a year I had trouble bringing in $50,000. So she ran the fiscal as well as the social show.

We went to one lawyer party after another. We hade nothing in common. We had no children. It was hard to get your wife pregnant when you couldn't stand to have sex with her. So we divorced after two years. I got the dog, Chaka, and she died. So I became a Private Investigator. I loved the romance of my new profession. It was the only romance I had at the moment.

My time was taken up getting my fledgling detective agency off the ground. We had only been in business for a year. The Haight Ashbury was not exactly the center of private eye offices, but the rent was cheap. I thought about my partner, Guitar Jac, and our nickel and dime cases. The thought of our small number of insignificant cases depressed me. But I had a great partner.

Guitar Jac is not only part of my newly established detective business, he is an old friend. He comes from a wealthy Palo Alto family. His earliest California descendant, William Leidesdorff, owned much of the Embarcadero in the mid-1840s during the last days of Mexican California. The family lives on San Francisco's Nob Hill in with a summer home in nearby Mill Valley and a pied a terre in Palo Alto. I met him while I was in law school. After graduating from Stanford, Guitar Jac completed a PhD. in comparative literature but didn't like college teaching. He found the professors stuffy and pompous, so he left a tenure track position at Brown University. He moved back to San Francisco where he purchased a penthouse condominium on Nob Hill. He vowed to become a blues musician.

The irony was that he worked in the blue-collar music world. He performed as a blues musician and used his trust fund to help set up our detective agency. He is not only a gifted musician but a writer and a hard-core intellectual. He is an African American who has an eye for cultural history. His first book, African American Intellectuals Since the Civil War, was nominated for a Pulitzer Prize. He wasn't impressed. Over the years he gravitated to the Republican Party. No sense letting those damned Democrats take away your trust fund. He is also one of the most politically incorrect people I know. I can never forget his description of BART.

To hear Guitar Jac tell it, BART is the "Negro employment network." He has evolved into a man who thinks Clarence Thomas is a liberal. Although we have known each other for almost twenty years, I hadn't been able to convince him to abandon the use of the word Negro. I wince, as I am a classic liberal. Somewhere along the line, Guitar

Jac left the family home and became something of a redneck. Only in San Francisco could an African American with a comparative literature degree from Stanford work as an assistant to San Francisco's least successful detective. That would be me, Trevor Blake III. My battle with weight continues, my hair is not thinning, and my personality wows the young ladies. The body is still muscular and the mind taut. My divorce gave me little in the way of a settlement from my lawyer wife Marilyn. I did inherit her brother and his wife. I need to remain on friendly terms with them. Bennie and Bertie own the Chestnut Street apartment that I rent. I had to remember that fact.

Bennie has a large real estate empire and is one of the most knowledgeable slumlords in the city by the bay. He charges a five hundred dollar key deposit to his tenants and always finds a way to keep the money. They are typical middle class people who seldom read a book, only watch Fox TV News and they have all sorts of political opinions. This is possible only in America. They like me at times and at other moments Bennie bursts out at me. He blames me for the divorce.

There had been a crisis in Bennie and Bertie's marriage. So I hadn't seen them for some time. Bennie collected Barbra Streisand records and Bertie banned them from the house for political reasons. Bertie saw Barbra as a dangerous left wing radical. "I think anyone who leaves the a out of Barbara is a Communist," Bertie smugly remarked. I tried to break the news that there were no longer any Communists. No luck on that end. I knew they had solved their musical-political problems when their Cadillac SUV parked in front my apartment. I snuck in the back way so that they wouldn't see me. Troung smiled. He doesn't say much. He handed me mail. I saw a few new file cases and snuck back out to my car and drove up the Haight Street office. I needed to avoid Bennie and Bertie at all costs.

Bennie and Bertie usually showed up at my Chestnut Street apartment unannounced. It was usually about the time I am making my move to bed a young lady. I think that they have a form of radar. Bennie's sister, Marilyn, who is also my ex-wife, told them time and time again to leave me alone. They didn't. Their camper was often seen on Chestnut Street. Even a not so bright private eye knew that they were in the neighborhood. I still had a fondness for Marilyn. We didn't have kids because I couldn't stand going to bed with her. Her girl friends were another matter. Marilyn knew how to get to my weak points. She did it with gifts.

The gifts didn't include her girl friends. I felt that sleeping with them was a bonus. It was a bonus that caused my divorce.

Marilyn also gave me the statue of Jimi Hendrix that stands on my desk. I prefer the Janis Joplin-Jerry Garcia wall hanging. The two-framed portraits of Janis Joplin were picked up due to her diligence in searching out rock and roll memorabilia. It is a reminder of past times. Some of the times were wonderful. Then there were the dinners at Bennie and Bertie's. Not exactly fun times. Bennie Junior was in this tenth year at Chico State and Bennie, Sr., loved to talk about what he had learned from his son. He kept telling me that the apple doesn't fall far from the tree. Bennie Jr. was an expert an gambling, womanizing, drinking and his hobby was the Rolling Stones. He made ten thousand dollars a year as a General Contractor. He spend half of it on the Rolling Stones. His dad provided the rest of his living expenses. Bennie, Jr., had a large collection of Stones memorabilia that took up two rooms in his house. It made a two-bedroom house inconvenient for modern living. Each day Bennie, Jr. received a package from somewhere in the world containing some oddball Rolling Stones tape, CD or who known what else. His collection was featured in Rolling Stone. I was envious.

Bennie Sr. bragged about his life. He was rich and well connected. He was also connected socially to the owner of the local RV Park, where he washed while telling anyone who would listen that it cost more than any other RV in the park. Bennie had money and he let everyone know it.

He had made his money the old fashioned way. He inherited it. Bennie Sr. kept talking about his son's economic enterprises. He was a contractor who never seemed to have a contract. I sat in my Shadow Morton chair and laughed about the good and bad memories from my marriage. Marilyn had purchased the Shadow Morton chair at a Los Angeles auction. He was a legendary early 1960s producer who turned out most of the girl group hits by the Shangri Las. Every time I heard the Shangri Las I thought about Shadow Morton, sitting in his chair.

As I looked around the office, I was proud of myself. I am not the most organized person in the world. But the office looked great. Clean. Well maintained. A private eye with few cases had time to think and organize. It didn't pay well but I was open for business. I have also practiced acting like a private eye. I had a black fedora that comes down over my eyes. A raincoat in the closet put me into a Sam Spade mold. A three-piece suit hung in the dark recesses of my closet. Never know when you need that retro look. I twiddled my thumbs and the doorbell rang.

When I answered the door I barked into the intercom, “Welcome to Blake Investigations.” It sounds nice smiled and looked out the window all the way to Golden Gate Park. I buzzed the door open. I heard heavy footsteps heading toward the office.

“Trevor Blake,” a booming voice cut in.

“Ya!” It helped to sound like a private eye.

“Sign here.”

I signed and looked at a summons. “What?”

“You are served and you are sued.” He smiled.

“Agh!” I didn’t have a more intelligent response. I looked at the summons. It was from my landlord. He wanted to evict me. Fat chance.

In the 1960s the neighborhood was different but today we have an abundance of tourists. Not to mention retro hippies. A collection of dot. com yuppies and even a few old Italians from the neighborhoods early days. There used to be twenty-one bars in the Haight. Now there were three. They call that progress. Or is it urban renewal?

Our office on the second floor of a building at the corner of Haight and Ashbury is offset by a huge psychedelic painted sign that reads: “Blake Investigations: More For Your Investigative Dollar.” Unfortunately, few people can read the sign as its painted like a rock and roll poster from the Fillmore. Stanley Mouse did it for me as a favor. He was the fellow who invented purple LSD for Jim Morrison and the Doors. Few people know that he was an artist. Those who read the bright sign still don’t believe that Stanley Mouse has artistic talent. The price was right. It was free. Somehow the 1960s continue to haunt me. I put out a slick brochure with our skills as investigators listed in great detail. None of this seems to do much for business. We may get six cases a month with people who skip bail, a few divorce investigations and a lot of missing young persons. I would love a murder case. That doesn’t seem to be in the cards.

Everything is mundane and routine. The life of a private eye is not a glamorous one. What happened to the babes that Mickey Spillane gave to Mike Hammer? What about the humor of Richard Prather’s Scott Shell, not to mention the babes? I went into this business for babes. There are no babes. The closest I have come recently to a babe is a movie about a pig. In the office, I spend an inordinate amount of time listening to Guitar Jac play his guitar. In addition to being my investigator, he continues to moonlight at local blues clubs. The fact that his band is all white doesn't go over in the ghetto, so he plays white blues clubs. Guitar Jac and the Blues Express are a well-received act. Everywhere except the ghetto.

Sometimes I look into the mirror and pretended that I am Scott Shell. A thirty-year-old private eye living in a nice three room Hollywood apartment complete with babes and a swimming pool. I have babes on my mind a lot. That is because I haven't met the right one. In fact I am having trouble meeting anyone. I know that I have a long way to go before I become Scott Shell. Maybe I can become Red Diamond. This fictional character was a mild mannered cab driver who would hit his head and became a 1950s P. I. Red Diamond. His creator was so frustrated with lack of acceptance for his character that he became a Portland based psychiatrist. A scary thought. I had to remember that I was Trevor Blake, III. College educated. Sophisticated. A man of the world. I was also a music lover. Maybe it was the music that prevented me from being successful. I spent an inordinate amount of time building my CD collection to its almost 10,000 level.

There is a forensic anthropologist I intend to use if I ever get a real murder case. He is a world-renowned authority on bones. So one day he would help me. His name is Walter Malland. He is a renaissance man who also plays piano professionally in some of San Francisco's finest venues. Malland is a multi-tasker known for anthropology, writing and music.

So far we were good friends as we have music as a common passion. I wanted to be as successful as my good friend Walter Malland who had a cottage next to his Mill Valley home filled with CDs. It was a strange collection. His collection included Beethoven, Brahms, Brecht, Bukowski, Chuck Berry, Bo Diddley, Bob Dylan and the Rolling Stones. He also had the largest Kinky Friedman collection known to mankind. I never saw the connection. He also had more than 10,000 classical CDs and 5,000 books on all forms of music. He was too busy to put his collection in order. He was a photographer who traveled world wide to take portrait type photos of dead musicians graves. His small house was an odd place but what a shrine. I was jealous. There was no wife.

In his other life when Malland is a lounge lizard, he dresses like a 1950s jazz buy complete with beret and a cigarette dangling from his lips. He plays a classical, blues and pop piano at some of the finest supper clubs, sleazy bars and honky tonks in San Francisco. Malland is an obsessive compulsive on the musical end. He played at times with saxophone virtuoso Oppenheim Bennett. They spent most of the night picking up young ladies and offering to give them music lessons. Somehow the music lessons never materialize.

Walt Malland was also the world's foremost authority on Guitar Jac. He had his records, his CDs, his early guitars, as well as 2000 in-concert photos, more than a 1000 studio and home photos. I was in two of these photos. Malland had also written six articles on Guitar Jac for small rock magazines like Blue Suede News, Rolling Stone and Rock N Blues News. He was a strange man. But a great guy. He continually lectured me on my weight as well as my eating and drinking habits. When you are 6-2 and weight in at 180, as Malland did, you could lecture people. He also sent me Guitar Jac blues tapes he made from concerts and I loved them.

When I listen to Guitar Jac, my world seems to fall apart. His lyrics and themes often sound like Strom Thurmond or George Wallace. I have to remind him that he is African American. He is intolerant of everyone in and around San Francisco. He dislikes gays. He thinks women are too pushy. His language is that of the Southern red neck. His appearance is that of a college liberal until he opens his mouth. Where did Stanford fail him? Maybe it didn't. He could be a typical Stanford graduate. He is my investigator and Blake Investigations couldn't function without him. He is literate, intelligent, writes well and has a nose for investigation. He has one other use. He is a karate expert, can come into a crowd without being noticed and seems to be around at any crisis. His physical skills are such that you always feel safe around him. It is the personal Guitar Jac that worries me. His continually use of racial slurs offends everyone. Mayor Gavin Newsom has officially banned such words as faggot, dyke and queer. Guitar Jac hasn't gotten the message. I have been trying to get Jac to replace these phrases with liberal, domestic, feminist, partner and who knows what else. He ignores me. He also reminds me that all his degrees are from Stanford. Enough of Guitar Jac. I have other concerns. Namely me.

My main problem is my personal life. It is rotten. It's not easy being a forty-year old San Franciscan. I can still hit the bars and find a young girl. I am now lying about my age. I am thirty-five. Hope I can pass for it. After passing my fortieth birthday, I suddenly became thirty-five again. I am also trying to get my bar room banter down. It isn't easy talking to young girls. Particularly when you have to listen to Guitar Jac on a daily basis. What do you say to the girl in a bar? Guitar Jac's commented: "What's your sign?"

Try this Trevor, "Wanna go to the gym?"

"I don't think those are the best lines."

"Consider this Trevor, do I have some great looking ladies?"

"Yes, you do," I added grudgingly.

"Then go to the health club, the gym whatever you honky folks call it," Jac continued, "the new bars are the gyms. Buy some good looking work out clothes."

I wondered what my babe future had in store for me. Who knows? Guitar Jac continued to babble on about women and how to please them. I looked around my depressing office. I looked out the window and I noticed the midget dressed as Mick Jagger was playing an air guitar and holding a tin cup. I smiled at him from the window. I waved. He frowned. Midgets weren't know for their sweet dispositions. Looking out my office window I assessed my life. I didn't come to a positive conclusion.

I am a musician with minimal talent, and a private investigator who hasn't solved a major case. I thought a lot about the Rolling Stones. What did they have that I lacked? I couldn't begin to answer that question. I thought long and hard about the concert. Nothing seemed to connect. Primeval urges took over.

After spending the night watching Mick Jagger prance around the Oakland Coliseum stage, I was hungry. I drove down Haight and turned onto to Irving and headed for Park Chow for a ham and chess sandwich on a French roll. I drank a giant Budweiser. Only the worst beer for me, none of that low carb yuppie crap. I smiled at the cocktail waitress and she looked the other way. The waitress winked at me as I left. I wonder if it was the 25% tip or my animal magnetism.

I returned to my Haight Ashbury office, and got ready for another day at Blake Investigations. Guitar Jac and I had been in business for a year and we still didn't have more than a handful of insignificant cases. I also had my real estate and stock investments to keep me afloat

I thought a lot about my ex-wife. I seldom saw Marilyn anymore, unless she wanted a pot of Chicken A la Trevor. She was too busy. Money was her constant companion. The problem was that I hadn't divorced her brother. He showed up when I least wanted to see him. He continued to be my landlord. I stayed in our apartment on Chestnut Street and Bennie, and Bertie supervised my sex life. Their answering machine stated" "We're in the hot tub." His fat ass wife with her short gray hair talked continually of her private college education and her continual reference to herself as "the Bertie" made me ill. But they charged me so little in rent, I had to be nice. My ex-brother in law, Bennie, was in his late 50s and just retired. He had grey hair, an aggressive personality and he was always right. He was a former businessman who bragged that he had never lost a card game, a contest or a sales event. He also had a magic show. He called himself "Bennie The Beautiful" or "Magic Bennie." He was the kind of guy who has games all over his house. They are games that he has mastered. When I beat him at pinball, he stayed up for two days until he mastered the machine and could beat me. He did magic shows for people, whether they liked them or not. He was fond of quoting Italian businessmen who said they loved his magic. They also loved the fact that he bought them expensive dinners. They also didn't understand English, so they could smile and drink the expensive wine he ordered while Bennie prattled on about his various magic tricks. He was the kind of guy who was the ultimate truth. But I needed cheap rent so Bennie and I were at least civil with each other. It was hard on me. He had a large Afro with almost white hair and wore psychedelic shirts. Not exactly in fashion. So the apartment on Chestnut was the bachelor pad that Bennie never had and he reveled in my sexual exploits. Most of which were made up. I told him tall tales of my sexual prowess as he alternately smiled and frowned. Viagra frequently came up in my conversations. I had a prescription for 499 refills in a year, it was an error on my doctor's part but I loved it.

When my girl friends met Bennie and Bertie they invariably remarked that Bertie, looked like an overweight sorority girl who had once been a cheerleader. When I described her as "a fat Eskimo who had gone to finishing school," my ex-wife agreed. Marilyn had no more use for her brother than I did. The bad news was I saw more of him than my ex-wife.

It was Bertie who drove my ex-wife crazy. Since Marilyn was a tall and beautiful blonde with a body from heaven, Bertie kept asking when she was going to have children. Marilyn endured the barbs. Then one day Marilyn was out with Bertie and they went to a hair stylist. Marilyn had the usual shampoo, manicure and pedicure. So Bertie decided to have her hair done. Marilyn paid for everything and when they left to get the car from the valet, there was a humorous incident. Bertie had cut her hair so short that someone hollered to her: "Say, sir, can we get your attention?" Marilyn laughed so hard Bertie didn't talk to her for six months.

Bennie and Bertie live in Sausalito across Golden Gate Bridge in a beautiful home that overlooks San Francisco bay. They have completely redone the kitchen. Bertie spent over $100,000 to have a special set of French ovens. Their furniture came from China, London and Paris. They had the most expensive set of silverware and dishes I had ever even. They often pointed that out when we had dinner. They ate a low fat, low carb and non-sugar diet. On the refrigerator in the kitchen a list of foods that were not allowed in the house were displayed prominently. When Marilyn and I left their house we raced into Starbucks for the biggest cookie and a large Mocha. It wasn't easy being around health Nazis who loved George Bush.

When we went to their house I used the bathroom and left the seat down. My ex-wife lectured me constantly about inappropriate behavior. Then she gave me an ultimatum. Be nice to them or else. So I changed my ways and pretended I liked them. Marilyn became nasty and insulting. So at least one of us was nice. My fondest memory of Bertie was one Christmas when she refused to put on her Santa Claus hat. She claimed it would mess up her hair. She had the shortest haircut possible and it was so grey that the young clerk at Safeway thought it was a hat. But she loved her hair.

"I don't want to mess my hair," Bertie smiled. "It is perfect, I am now retired and can do what I want. I don't have to look pretty." I hated to tell her she had never looked attractive. Pretty wasn't even an option. Ugly was a constant.

I introduced Bertie to my friend Herb Gold. He is a famous writer and he used her banter and physical appearance for one of his character in his novel, He/She. Then her character continued on in Gold's next two books. He loved her character and called her a literary cliché. Gold remarked that her short haircut that made her look like "an endomorphic Eskimo."

Bennie hated him. "I don't want you to bring that Herb Gold around anymore, Trevor, he gives me the creeps. He looks at my hair in a strange way." She combed her hair to emphasize the point. I tried to look sympathetic. Maybe there is something I could do to make her feel better.

"You can't tell if your hair is messed or not, Bertie," I smirked. "You always look beautiful in the same way." I hope God didn't strike me down. She was insulted. Herb Gold once remarked to me that she looked like a guy in drag. I recounted Gold's remark and assured her she didn't look like a guy in drag. She looked like a woman in drag. I liked to pour intellectual gasoline on Bennie and Bertie. It wasn't the reason for my divorce but a contributing factor. Bennie and Bertie were the ultimate American dream. Or was that nightmare? They loved George Bush and they had little flags on their porch. A Rush Limbaugh poster hung in the bathroom. Taking a shit in front of Rush is not a pleasant task. When New Orleans flooded Bertie spent a week knitting small socks. She talked about sending them to "Needy Negroes." Wouldn't want the people in New Orleans to have cold feet while they were homeless. They also made little American flags with various symbols. The most popular American flags were the ones with pictures of Karl Rove in the corner. They identified with his double chin. Newsweek magazine did a story on Bennie and Bertie and called them the ultimate patriots. Herb Gold cashed his checks as Bertie's fictional character had a brief television show, the adventures of Patriot Bernice. The show was cancelled for low ratings on the Lifetime channel.

Marilyn and I were divorced a year ago. She hadn't seen her brother and sister in law since the marital breakup. I saw them weekly. Something was wrong with this picture. I needed a divorce from Bennie and Bertie. It wasn't going to happen. Once the local lovelies found that I was on the market they showed up for a date. When I did find one who interested me, I cleaned the apartment and brought her back after dinner. Invariably, Bennie showed up at my door. It was as if he had personal radar for my women. If I bring a young lovely into my place, Bennie shows up. He is prone to saying things like "I only want to be around people like myself." I am not sure what that means. I shudder at the thought. So as I arrived at home from the Rolling Stones concert, I was extremely depressed. Divorced. Broke. Unsuccessful. This was balanced by the fact that I am still attractive to women. I even have a sometimes or quasi girlfriend, Joyce Byers. Like the others she likes me for one reason. It's my gift of gab. The next morning I headed back to my office.

The Haight Ashbury is an altered landscape. Whatever happened to the Hippie dream? It died with Jerry Garcia and Janis Joplin. Or perhaps the dream never existed. Maybe a guy who is looking for work in the Haight is not mentally balanced. Could that be me? Who knows? If I were Elvis Cole I would have plenty of high profile cases and a bevy of young ladies. Joe Pike would be around to beat up the bad guys. I had an African American redneck, Guitar Jac, who played the guitar and quoted Nietzsche. I needed a Joe Pike.

When I look out my office window it reminds me that the Haight Ashbury is a constantly evolving tourist cesspool. I pine for the old days. I can still remember meeting the girl in the fringed leather cowboy coat who spent a week in bed with me. I never found out her name. She didn't ask for mine.

I am not even sure I remember the old days but they have to be better than the computer age. I watch as a girl walks by the Haight street sign with two mouse ears glued to her head. What would Walt Disney say? I longed for the drugged out hippies. Where is Charles Manson when you really need him? But, then again, the Haight Ashbury is so different today. Nothing like in the past. Maybe Richard Brautigan will come back from the dead and we can all go fishing.

Chapter 2
THE HAIGHT ASHBURY TODAY

Why is the Haight Ashbury nothing like it was forty years ago? It begins with the shops on the street. Why are they now high fashion boutiques? It doesn't make sense for London and Paris designers to vie with New York and San Francisco designers as old hippies light up a joint on the street. The Haight is filled with high-end designers. Jimmy Choo has a shoe palace; Barney's of New York is constructing a high-rise emporium and Neiman Marcus is up and running. Proof that God does not exist. Pictures of Jerry Garcia are everywhere and Ben and Jerry's sells hundreds of scoops of Cherry Garcia ice cream each day. Proof that God does exist. Everything is driven by the economy. It costs money to dress in style. The Haight is now largely an upscale woman's clothing boutique. No wonder the landlord is suing me to get me out of the ironclad five-year lease. I wonder what his grounds are? Incompetence! Lechery! Having an African-American partner! Attracting midgets dressed like Mick Jagger.

All is not lost in the Haight. There are some businesses reminiscent of the past. A huge old bowling alley is now the home of Amoeba Records. It still has records. It is also the source of my enormous CD collection. So I love the place. There are a few seedy bars, a couple of coffee shops that need the floors swept, my favorite donut shop with Emilio and Jo the blonde manning the counter and a real Mexican restaurant. A real Mexican restaurant is one where only the owner speaks English. So all is not lost. The Haight is a neighborhood going through an identity crisis. Or as they say in yuppie land a gentrification.

The language on the street is different. When I use the word "woman" people holler at me. My girl friend, Joyce Byers, calls me a "dinosaur with words." She tells me women are persons, people or significant others. As I walk down Haight I notice that the displays in the stores are like Telegraph Avenue in Berkeley. All the clothes seem to be fashioned in black with safety pins and there is a distinctive Generation X tone to the clothing. Then the $250 price tag stares out at me and that is on sale. That is until you get to the upscale boutiques. Then the price tag jumps to a $1000 an item. Maybe I need to get with these times. Other things depress me. The price tags are enormous on the clothing for everything made in Asia. The best example of this is the French Connection Store. The tee shirts sell for $50. They have a huge "FCUK " label on them. I thought it was a dirty word spelled incorrectly. It turns out it means the French Connection United Kingdom. I am really behind the times. What can I say? Nothing. A sign reading "No Hate" catches my eye and I realize the 1960s did have an impact. I have to learn not to degrade the fashion revolution. It is one that I can't afford, so why not hate it? I am continually ridiculed for my clothing selections.

When I need to buy some clothing, I go to the least expensive place. I am off to the T. J. Maxx, a downscale store where I can still buy a pair of Armani jeans. On sale the Armani jeans from the discount rack run only $80. What a bargain. But when I went looking for men's shoes, I found a brand called Campers and the shoes cost $200. They were made in Spain. I went to the Discount Shoe Outlet and paid $30 for fake Campers. It isn't easy being 40 in the Haight Ashbury. I'm not sure which generation I identify with. Was I a latent hippie in training? Or was I just a loser? The Haight was now a smaller version of Berkeley. This was insulting as Guitar Jac continually reminded me. My history and law degree hadn't prepared me for modern life. I dreamed of being Sam Spade and solving crimes. I felt more like Red Diamond. I had hit my head and woke up as a bumbling private eye. I was sick of my cases. Runaway kids. Philandering husbands. Tax cheats. These were my cases.

I sit in my office at the corner of Haight and Ashbury looking at my record collection. I keep one thousand blues records in the office. It's the only way to keep Guitar Jac on the job. We often wander down a few blocks to Amoeba Records where I spend fifty bucks a week on vintage vinyl. I may be the only person on the planet who still collects records. I just sold the first Kinky Freidman and the Texas Jewboys LP for $500 to pay the office rent. "They Don't Make Jews Like Jesus anymore" remains my favorite Kinky tune. I don't play "Put Your Biscuits In The Oven And Your Buns In the Bed," it is sexist. I am after all a liberal. Hope Kinky isn't upset. Near Amoeba, a Mexican restaurant sits on the corner. It is my favorite place for a pork burrito. In between there is a yuppie coffee shop. No wonder Janis Joplin and Jerry Garcia are rolling around in their graves. The Haight is in the midst of a consumer explosion. Bring money. The fashion, food and good times are expensive.

Corporate capitalism is everywhere. Four blocks from these new businesses I constantly look at the Ben and Jerry's ice cream store sign. It is in four colors and shows the two fat guys who invented the ice cream. They look rich and happy. It is right above the Haight Ashbury street sign and seems to denigrate the ambiance of the street. The Ben and Jerry building is a strange one. It has a bright front with the two goofy guys who founded the company staring at you from a big billboard above the sign. They are painted on the door, they are painted twice inside on the walls, they are painted on the cups and the cash register has a painting. They are painted on the wall of the men's room. Money creates bad taste. They look like they have eaten too much ice cream and made too much money. I say this because I am unable to do either. The druggies still haunt the streets but they fight the tourists for a part of the sidewalk. The only old drugs available appear to be alcohol and caffeine. Trendy boutiques not only sell hippie clothing but hash pipes, bongs and other assorted drug paraphernalia cover the counters. A car drives by with a bumper sticker reading: "Kill All Hippies." A loud set of speakers boom something out about killing cops. The ghost of Ice T. Who would be left if the hippies and cops died? Probably just Karl Rove.

In the old days in the Haight Ashbury booze not drugs was the stimulant of choice. The darkened dens of alcoholic abuse have given way to fern bars, decorated cocktail lounges and fine restaurants with cocktail lounges. Piano bars have sprung up with Billy Philadelphia playing like he actually enjoys it. Mark Naftalin, formerly of the Paul Butterfield Blues Band, played for years in these dives and then fled to Maine. He wanted to see where Stephen King lived.

Cocktail is no longer the operative word in San Francisco. A martini is a forgotten religion. Bands like Steve Lucky and the Rhumba Bums play to crowds of people under thirty. They play old time music. I feel left out. Many of the new bars have turned into one-window affairs with tourists gawking out the large, luminous windows in search of a hippie while they swig on a shot of Jack Daniels. Where is Jerry Garcia when you really need him?

I walk into my office and look around. Blake Investigations has a coffee maker, a file cabinet, a Macintosh computer, two chairs, a couch and a toilet. A small CD player constantly features Van Morrison singing "Brown Eyed Girl." There is also a television set hooked to cable for sports events. It is black and white and never on when clients arrive. It seems the black and white set drew more conversation than our fees. I had to special order the black and white TV from a Japanese company. All this is placed in one room. It is a budget affair. Only the paintings on the wall save the office from total boredom. Clients usually sniff when they come in the room. It seems that an air freshener never quite kills the coffee odor. Business is slow.

My only real cases involve the predictable and mundane. No one wants to hire an unknown P I without a reputation. As my friends remark, I may be without a life. Things have not gone well for me at age forty and the private eye business is not glamorous. The prosperity end of the business is equally depressing.

When I became a private eye it was by accident. I graduated from the University of California in the early 1990s, then I went to law school at Stanford, passed the bar, got married and settled in Mill Valley. Ten years later I am divorced, I have quite practicing law and I am struggling to keep a private investigator's office open. I did work for a time as a paralegal for a large law firm. That was just before I passed the bar. After I passed the bar I had twenty interviews. I made the wrong choice by going to work for a Jewish law firm. I was the only Gentile. It was an affirmative action hiring. One of the partners was a Chinese Jew and like the others from Stanford. They hired me for my Stanford background.

Then I was set up. The law firm of Irving, Schwartz, Liu and Isaacs had forty partners and more than two hundred associates. An incident took place that soured me on the law. I worked on a case that saw a client awarded ten million dollars in an industrial accident suit. When the case concluded the lawyer in charge lost the money entrusted to him in a divorce case. He told the press that I stole it to purchase real estate. I didn't and he could never prove it. I did have a bit of real estate investments and I found my private life in the press. It attracted the local gold digging ladies, who I bedded but didn't marry. I was already married but still dating. Maybe that contributed to the divorce. I left the money in our office safe and it was gone the next morning. Our client refused to press charges. I was blacklisted by every law firm. Most people assume that I used the money to open Blake Investigations. I would rather have them believe that little fact than the truth. When a wife writes a check for $50,000 she wants out of the marriage. I didn't ask for spousal support. I wouldn't have gotten it as I had some hidden money. I am a sly little bastard.

I did have one other asset, Guitar Jac. His real name is James Jackson Wellington, III, an African American with a sizeable financial inheritance and an advanced degree in English literature from Stanford. He works on commission. He gets a cut of my case money. By day Mr. Wellington, as he is sometimes known, is a sleuth, but at night he turns into Guitar Jac, consummate San Francisco bluesman. He is also a black belt in karate and an accomplished street fighter. It is not easy being African American in San Francisco's richest neighborhood.

Guitar Jac lives in a four-bedroom condo worth in the neighborhood of two million dollars. It is located on Nob Hill. His previous condo was across from the San Francisco Giants ballpark. He made two million dollars on it and moved up to Snob Hill, as he calls it, near the Fairmont Hotel. He paid cash for his new place. Guitar Jac is an accomplished person. He was a Pac Ten All conference outfielder and after signing with the Atlanta Braves, Guitar Jac was shipped to Double AA ball in Shreveport, Louisiana. He didn't like the food or the city. He retired after playing five games. He also didn't like the travel and the South. Jac remains a baseball fan. He walks down to Pac Bell ballpark and takes in most San Francisco Giants home games. He is seen with Barry Bonds in the best restaurants. They work out together and Guitar Jac has bulked up considerably. I hope steroids aren't in the mix. He is an integral part of the Blake Investigations summer softball team. Naturally, we are undefeated. Guitar Jac's life is in sharp contrast to my own. He dates the most famous and best-looking women. I date whoever is available. I live in less than an upscale apartment on Chestnut Street on the edge of the Marina. I have a couch in my office and often sleep there. I have Bennie and Bertie to watch over my sex life.

On the days when I sleep in at my cramped Chestnut Street adobe, there is generally a cluttered atmosphere. To save money, I often take a bus to the agency. Before I go to work I have a cup of coffee and a donut. Each morning as I stop in Emilio's Latin Donut Shop on Haight, I notice a new group of tourists. Jo the blonde courteously waits on them. Jo's last name is Marichski so the nickname Jo the blonde. She is thirty, drop dead gorgeous and finishing a PhD in comparative literature. Hope there is a professor job for her somewhere. Emilio immigrated from Vietnam to open a business that serves Chinese food to go, Mexican food and donuts. How he got the name Emilio remains a mystery. His real name is Phuong Nguyen. He is a compact man with a body that is like steel from various karate exercises. He is soft spoken and a wonderful man.

Rumor is that Emilio was a Vietcong solider who talked his way onto the last helicopter out of Vietnam. He is in his late-sixties but looks like a man of forty. He came into San Francisco washed dishes for five years on Haight Street and wound up purchasing the donut shop. It became an immediate moneymaker. Emilio's personality is a grandiose one. He is overly friendly and loves to talk about American literature. He remains a walking contradiction. He is educated but doesn't talk like it. I walked into Emilio's for my sugar fix. There is a shrewd nature to Emilio and he loves to play to stereotypes.

"Hello, bossee," Emilio remarked, "You likee some chocolate donut," Emilio continued with a sly smile. "I makee just for you."

Jo the blonde comes over and sets down a cup of decaf and a buttermilk donut. So much for nutrition. Emilio stands over me smiling.

"God damn it, Emilio, speak to me like a human." He smiles. I quickly finish my first cup. He pours another decaf and shakes his head.

"No blood pressure problems for me," Emilio smiles

"Kiss my ass." I open the San Francisco Chronicle. How can a forty year old have a blood pressure problem? Genetics. With decaf, I still drink ten cups a day. I am often reminded that Frank Zappa died after a ten cup a day habit. But Frank was in his fifties so I have time to burn. I smelled the donuts. Man do I love that smell, I cut the buttermilk donut in half and slowly ate it. I was in heaven. It didn't last long. Emilio had no way of knowing that I wanted quiet. I had to think about my life. No one knows when I want quiet; the result is people talk to me night and day.

Emilio stands over me smiling. A bad habit. "Come on, Trevor, my degree in American literature at San Francisco State prepared me for very little. Maybe hanging out with you, that's it." Emilio continued: "You see the tourists like you to talk like you just got off the boat, that way they can tip you and feel good. It assuages their white guilt. "

I looked at Emilio and tried to be nice: "I don't need a lecture on political correctness, give that one to Guitar Jac."

"No, no," Emilio looked on in horror. There was no hope for Guitar Jac. "He thinks Barack Obama is a terrorist," Emilio continued. "Jac calls him a Negro. Can you believe it?" I could.

Emilio continued talking for another ten minutes, I had to say something. As Emilio prattled on about Edmund Wilson's life as a critic,

I tried not to look bored. Not exactly a subject that I was prepared to discuss.

"I need a job as a professor, Trevor, this donut shop is shit."

"We all got it tough Emilio," I sighed. "At least you are making a living."

"A living that doesn't provide much," Emilio remarked in the perfect English that generally eluded him in front of Madge and Blanche from Iowa when they were purchasing donuts. I could tell he was about to slip into Emilio jargon.

"Have you seen Bennie and Bertie?" I asked.

"Yes, yes, I was at their house in Sausalito having dinner last night, quality people, how did they wind up with you as an in-law, you are an asshole, a womanizer and a turd," Emilio laughed. "Get it, Third, Turd."

I didn't laugh. "Ah, the educated immigrant. A dangerous man in America," I laughed.

"No like us immigrants, no got advantage, end of conversation." Emilio curtly remarked.

"I don't think your professors at San Francisco State would pass you after that little spiel," I laughed, "it's time to face up to it, you love suburban bores like Bennie and Bertie." He turned and walked into the kitchen and began splashing little pieces of dough into boiling oil. I recoiled with terror. Those splotches of grease would turn into my donuts. I remembered that he told me eating a donut was like eating a cup of mayonnaise. Not exactly the point to make when you sold donuts for a living.

Harold Wheat walked in the door. He is a handsome forty nine year old investment banker who lies about his age and his marital status. "Hello asshole," he smiled. I have known Harold through all three wives and he still thinks my name is asshole. He is wealthy, a retired CIA operative and one of my drinking partners. If you want women hit the bars with Harold and get laid. He sat down and began going over his financial statement. Harold carried a hand-strengthening gadget and he was a marital arts legend. No one messed with him.

I read my paper for another half an hour before walking across the street and back to the agency. The lazy morning was a relaxing one. So I picked up the San Francisco Chronicle for one last look. The local political news suggested that the gays in the Castro were supporting Gavin Newsom. I guessed they thought he was cute. Guitar Jac walked through the door.

"Well Trevor, my man, you see the rump rangers in the Castro are putting up signs for Gavin Newsom." I blanched. There was no controlling Guitar Jac.

I had never used the term rump ranger, perhaps as the French would say the "rump de rangers." Guitar Jac used it daily. Remarks like that about gays were forbidden in Frisco. As was the word Frisco, the pompous literati preferred the use of the term, the City. Finally, at ten in the morning, I settled into my office for a long session of filing papers, bringing cases up to date and hoping for some business. I also hoped for some good coffee. Cup number five went down smoothly. A new Sumatra roast from Starbucks that was exquisite.

"Here Jac. A big case, we have to repossess a BMW Z4. The owner forgot to make her payments. It's over in Sausalito. Have lunch on the deck at Sam's in Tiburon and charge it to the repossession company." Guitar Jac usually refused to repossess. A lunch on Sam's sunny deck overlooking the San Francisco Bay changed his mind.

Guitar Jac left to repossess the BMW. He was eager to get out on the job. I wondered if he would have been as eager if it was a Ford Probe. Maybe it was the lunch at Sam's. When I could talk him into it, he loved to hot wire-repossessed cars. It gave him a feeling of power. The latent juvenile delinquent.

After four hours of paperwork, coffee, no phone calls, no business and no hope for the future I was wondering if I had made a mistake. Maybe detective work wasn't my forte. Maybe I could be an intellectual, read books, and write books.

At two o'clock on a San Francisco day that suddenly turned cloudy, I looked out the window of my second story office and watched a long, stretch limousine pulling up into the bus zone in the front of my building. Out of the limo a slinky, beautiful woman in her late twenties stepped onto the curb. She had long legs, designer clothes, Jimmy Choo shoes and a strong case of bottle blonde hair. One look and I decided that she could have me. A longhaired young man followed her out of the limo. I couldn't believe my eyes. It looked like Brian Jones of the Rolling Stones. Then I remembered that he had died in 1969. I stood transfixed at the window. I looked at her and she could have been Marianne Faithfull. That is the 1964 version of Faithfull. The Marianne with the white virginal dress, the blonde hair and the pouty lips is the one I remember. Not the one we see today with a cigarette, wrinkles and a drug induced stupor. Maybe it was the coffee. I was seeing things.

A few minutes later the office door opened and Brian Jones walked in. He looked at my Janis Joplin-Jerry Garcia poster and remarked: "I balled her before a gig, man, at least it was someone who looked like her." He laughed. "I want to hire you man." What an asshole. I didn't want to tell him that she had been dead for forty years. Maybe he did ball a dead woman. He might not have realized it. I looked at him in disgust. I hated being called "Man, Buddy, Pal" or any other generic term used by familiar assholes. Particularly those I don't know. I did admire this Brian Jones look a like disguise. Maybe I should get a face and hair job. I could look like Elvis, it wouldn't hurt my business. I could see the sign now: "Elvis Blake III: Private Eye."

I smiled. The girl looked at my crotch. Suddenly I realized that my fly was open. At the age of forty I wondered if I was losing it. Then again maybe I was something special, what Mick and Brian lacked, I might have. Maybe I was a middle-aged sex symbol.

"Can I help you?" I gave them the Trevor Blake smile.

"God damned, Samantha, he can talk." The Brian Jones look a like laughed at his remark.

` Suddenly I wasn't smiling. "Nice seeing you asshole," I remarked. Turning and walking into my office bathroom I slammed the door. I washed my hands and came out. They were staring at me. A standoff. At that moment Guitar Jac came through the door. He looked well fed.

"Hello Folks, I'm James Jackson Wellington, III."

"Damn a spade, Samantha, and one who can talk." Guitar Jac didn't smile. He was a spade with a PhD., a trust fund and a penthouse apartment. He was also a karate expert, not to mention a practicing red neck who hated rock musicians. Not your average spade. Guitar Jac looked angry. Not a good sign. He has reached the ultimate level in karate training and he also has a low tolerance for rednecks and assholes. The only redneck he likes is himself. If anything, he is a walking contradiction.

Suddenly, Guitar Jac grabbed the guy by the collar, walked out the door and threw the Brian Jones look alike down the stairs. That was a move not good for business. The girl screamed and ran down to pick him up. They hustled out onto street, dumped themselves into the limousine and left Blake Investigations. I guess they weren't going to hire me.

"What in the hell was that?" I asked. "They were here to hire us."

"I think it was one of your musical brothers," Guitar Jac replied. "We don't work for assholes."

"He is an ugly white guy but a potential client," I lectured Jac.

"Nobody talks to me like that," Jac remarked.

"Let's not fight, Jac, business is not good enough for it. You may have thrown out our only client this week."

"You're right Trevor." We didn't talk much for the rest of the day. I typed up three insurance fraud cases. After our brief argument, business picked up. We found one client had bilked three different companies out of new cars. We caught him. Then Guitar Jac busted a guy collecting workingmen's compensation after we photographed him in a tree cutting the branches from a twenty-five foot Cyprus. He was listening to Van Morrison's classic tune "Cyprus Avenue" as he cut the tree. Ah, retribution.

An insurance fraud trial was pending and jailed awaited him. The last case was an alimony one. The husband failed to pay, and he had relocated to San Lorenzo. I drove over to this small suburb in the East Bay south of Oakland. San Lorenzo had tree-lined streets, small mom and pop markets and I expected to see Ozzie and Harriet walking down the street. Instead I saw some divorced guys walking down the street who looked like they couldn't afford the rent.

Moving to San Lorenzo was not a smart move as it was only thirty miles from San Francisco. The husband also left a forwarding address with his San Lorenzo post office box. I found his home address by taking the Post Office clerk to lunch. Not only am I a brilliant private eye but a sex symbol.

I found the divorced guys house. His name was Clyde. The postal clerk gave me a piece of his junk mail. I walked up to a small white stucco house with cute little blue gables on each side of a big picture window. A fifteen-year-old kid who looked like Ricky Nelson answered the door. Maybe Ozzie and Harriet were home.

"Hello," I smiled.

"Can I help you?" The kid smiled drinking a large Starbucks. Whatever happened to kids drinking Cokes?

"I have a mail delivery for your dad." I smiled.

The kid looked confused. "I don't have a dad, you must want my mom's boy friend." This was getting complicated.

I need to speak with Clyde, my name is Hieronymus Bosch and I have a check for him from the California lottery."

"Clyde!" the kid bellowed in an unnaturally loud voice.

A small man maybe 5-2 with beady eyes and a hawkish nose stood behind the kid. He was maybe 120 pounds and dressed in a jogging outfit. He had a twenty- pound weight in one hand. He looked bent over carrying it. Behind him stood a woman who looked like Angelina Joie. I understood the divorce. If you had an Angelina Jolie look-a-like, no sense keeping the wife around. Sometimes it is better to move on.

"The games up pal." I smiled and handed him a summons. He looked blankly at me. After reading the summons he looked at me again.

"This says I owe $5000." He looked confused.

"That's right and jail is the next step." I smiled.

"I've been paying her in cash." He looked honest. He sounded honest. He looked not too bright.

"Nothing I can do.? I replied.

"If you drive me to the Bank of America, five blocks away, I will give you a cashier's check." We drove and I got the check. I took it over to the city and stopped at his wife's apartment on Union Street. It was a toney, high priced two-bedroom place with designer furniture. Sitting on the couch one of San Francisco's best-known lawyers smiled at me. The wife took the cashier's check and thanked me. Poor dumb Clyde. Maybe not. His new woman was beautiful.

I left Union Street and turned left on Fillmore and drove to the Haight where I turned right and parked on the street. It was six o'clock and I didn't need to feed the parking meter. The evening sun hung over the Ben and Jerry's sign. The two fat guys looked happy. They should. They were millionaires.

Inside the office, I put on a pot of coffee. Looking up at the Janis Joplin-Jerry Garcia wall hangings, they seemed to smile at me. I got out the company profit and loss ledger. Time to up the profits. I finished the cases added up the books and found that he had made $1500 in the last month. After paying $1200 rent, a $59 light and heating bill and a $119 phone bill we had the magnificent sum of $126 profits left over. I wrote a check for $63 to Guitar Jac. I took home $63. Who said the private eye game is not a lucrative one?

At this precise moment, Guitar Jac made his appearance.

"Trevor, my man, I need to pick up a few things. I have a gig at Biscuits and Blues tonight." He smiled. Ah, the life of a bluesman. Particularly a rich one. The sixty-three dollar check wouldn't cover his Starbuck's bill for a week.

In a quiet and reflect mood, Guitar Jac cleaned his desk off and bid me good night. Another routine day at Blake Investigations. No profits. No fun. No interesting clients. No future. We still loved it. I am not sure why.

I looked at the clock. It was seven o'clock. Outside a lazy, dusk settled over Haight street. I was eager for my first adult beverage. A nice glass of Merlot at the Haight Exchange, the last real bar on the street. Then home to watch the Golden State Warriors lose once again. Ah, the life of a forty's bachelor. Wine, basketball and detective work.

Suddenly the door burst open and two of the biggest, nastiest guys I had ever seen in my life stood in the doorway. "Hey you," the biggest one hollered. Since there was no one else in the room, I wondered about my visitor's mental condition. Before I could say anything, he lifted me off the ground and his garlic breath hit me in the face. I'm six feet two and two hundred pounds, I was understandably frightened.

"Yes," I meekly called out.

"Are you an asshole?"

"If you want me to be, fine."

"Smart guy huh. You know why I'm here!"

This type of question befuddled me. I had left my crystal ball at home. So I took a wild guess. "To help you solve a case."

"You're a rocket scientist, Trevor, I can't believe it." He knew my name, not a good sign. Then again my name is on the door. Maybe he is a rocket scientist.

"Can you solve any case?" garlic breath asked.

"I don't know," I replied. "Is there something I don't understand? What case? I don't even know who you represent." Always use private eye lingo on them, it confuses them.

"You bet your ass, white boy," the smaller mobster with an equally foul garlic breath screamed. "You just pissed off Mr. Jones." Garlic seemed to be all they had in common.

"Mr. Jones," I asked incredulously. "You mean Brian Jones of the Rolling Stones?"

"That's right, asshole."

"I hate to tell you gumbas but Brian Jones died in 1969." They clenched their fists. Suddenly I was frightened. The truth does not sit well with steroid induced morons.

"He's our employer and he's Brian Jones," tall garlic breath added.

"Fine, fellas, he can be Bill Clinton or Socrates for all I care."

"Hey man watch it, Socrates Solina is one of the best known local hit men, you asshole," short garlic breath bellowed. "What's your name again you little cunt." Now I was worried, the little mobster had already forgotten my name.

"It's Trevor, pal." I reflected on my gender.

"Ok, Trevor Pal, we are going to educate you. What kind of name is Trevor Pal? It says Blake Investigations on the door." I knew I had to be careful. They were too stupid to explain anything to.

"Trevor Pal is a pseudonym," I smiled.

"What the hell is a pseudonym?" Big Garlic Breath bellowed.

I asked Big Garlic Breath his real name. "You wouldn't believe it you asshole, but my name is George Smoot and I graduated from Wichita State. I was the only mobster in the business administration degree program. So you can see asshole that I am not some moron. I am a dangerous psychopath with a college degree." I looked scared. I was. I couldn't help my sarcasm.

"Whey don't your guys leave and look me up on the phone book later under P. I. That is if you can read." The small one slapped me across the face. It hurt. They looked upset. I looked scared.

I couldn't resist further comment, even if it meant another slap: "You need to get your gender id system in order you malevolent misanthrope. " I shouldn't have said that. Misanthrope was a loaded word. They couldn't spell it and they didn't know what it meant. A dangerous combination. Big Garlic Breath slapped me across the face again. He smiled and looked like he was going on a date. I swear the slap gave him sexual energy. Shell Scott wouldn't stand for this. Scott was a 6-2 Marine. I had to remember that he was a fictional character.

Well, little man," Big Garlic Breath intoned, "we are taking you for a ride."

"Are you sure?" I realized how stupid this remark sound as they hustled me out to a big, white limousine. In the back seat sat another Brian Jones or at least someone who looked like the dead Rolling Stones guitarist. He was taller than the first Brian Jones. Well how many people meet two plastic surgery induced Brian Jones? Not many. I never did drugs. Was this my comeuppance? I could hardly wait for the ride. Then again everyone needs a spare Brian Jones. Maybe we were going to hang out with Elvis and John Lennon. I didn't mention this as the two gumbas squeezed into the front seat. Then a thought struck me. I might need plastic surgery after this ride.

Chapter 3
MURDER BY THE ROLLING STONES

"Hello asshole," Brian Jones remarked." My name is Warren Johansen." I looked at him with disdain. A Norwegian who'd undergone plastic surgery to look like one of the Rolling Stones. But then the surprises came in many forms. I needed to say something.

"You do have a name. What about the other Brian Jones?" I didn't look happy.

"Call me Elliott Shonestein." The other Brian Jones remarked. He smiled and lit a cigarette. There was something strange about him. Elliott lurched forward grabbed furtively at his head and took off the most expensive mask I had ever seen. Now he looked like an Elliott Shonestein.

"Let me guess, you both are comedians," I remarked. In the front of the limo, little garlic breath reached back and started squeezing my arm. I suddenly became silent. I thought that my elbow was going to explode. Tommy John surgery appeared to be an option.

"I want to hire you on a very delicate matter." Shonestein smiled. He took a long drag on his cigarette. He took the mask and stuffed it in his pocket.

"You are nothing but delicate," I continued. "As soon as I get out of here I'm gonna file a nice law suit." I was a brave guy. Maybe stupid too. No one had ever accused Trevor Blake, III of having the ability to keep his mouth shut.

"Suit yourself," Elliott Shonestein remarked. The other Brian Jones, the one who really looked like him began to explain. "Listen to my offer. We have a $50,000 fee for you. He unfolded an envelope filled with hundred dollar bills. Inside was $25,000. "Half today and half when you finish." Shonestein ground out his cigarette in the limo ashtray. Yuck!

I was listening. Speechless.

The other Brian Jones continued: "It's a simple case. I am an entertainer who impersonates Brian Jones of the Rolling Stones in a Las

Vegas-Reno cover band that travels all over the world. My friend Warren is the alternate Brian Jones."

"Why two Brian Jones?" I smiled and cleverly remarked: "Is there a vacation plan for impersonators?"

Ah, a smart ass," Shonestein remarked.

Brian Jones said: "He is also the manager. His company, Shonestein Enterprises, manages the band. We do very well."

I remarked: "Sounds like a union job, guys." A glare from Little Garlic Breath silenced me.

Shonestein continued: "We gross more than eight million dollars a year."

They had my attention. "How does an imitation band featuring the music of the Rolling Stones gross that much?" I was shocked.

"We play all the casinos, Las Vegas, Reno, Atlantic City, the Miami Clubs, the Indian casinos, and in the last year we have booked 10,000 to 20,000 seat arenas. With the Stones on tour we are making more money than ever."

"So what's the problem, you guys too rich? You want to hire me to advise you on how to spend your money." I was nothing but clever.

"The band has had three members killed—-all of them are drummer, Shonestein lit another cigarette and continued. "Dean Moriarty is the most recent one. We can't go on without the right drummer. So you see we are being sabotaged and losing millions."

"Let me guess, Jack Kerouac is the replacement drummer," I smiled. I continued to be clever.

"This is serious, Trevor," Shonestein paused. He was looking for the right words. "No other private eye can handle this case. You have a music background." Elliott Shonestein pensively punched his finger in the air. Maybe he was like Socrates, he was thinking. Garlic breath one and two glared at me, I let Elliott think.

I couldn't contain my clever nature. "Maybe it's Pete Best, he hasn't had a gig since the Beatles," I chuckled. Big Garlic Breath grabbed my elbow and squeezed. I went silent. Pain is the one thing that I recognize.

"Now where was I," Elliott remarked. "You're one of those guys who talks and doesn't listen." My teachers said the same thing.

"Are you interested in the case?" I was afraid to say no. I also liked the thought of $50,000. Big and Little Garlic Breath cracked their knuckles in unison. Maybe they weren't stupid, just musical.

"I think you were talking about a dead drummer. I need to know more. A dead drummer or drummers and what about the case. What does it involve?"

Elliott looked at me blankly. A thinking stare. "Yeah, the dead drummer, well we think that the Rolling Stones have hired someone to murder our drummer." Elliott Shonestein looked angry. So did the two gumbas. I looked frightened.

"Why would the Rolling Stones even care about the Start Me Up Band?" I paused and looked at Elliott. "Explain," I added.

"Well we have a picture of someone who looks like a Rolling Stones roadie poisoning our last drummer." Elliott produced a picture of a guy in a Rolling Stones tour jacket serving a pasta dish to Dean Moriarty. The picture showed the back of a tall guy with a bad haircut. Greasy kids stuff was all over his hair. The Stones had two hundred people on tour with them who had bad haircuts and were tall. I looked at the picture and was horrified. It showed Moriarty's face and he was in agony as he died. I guess everyone is in agony as they die. I also wondered how pasta could kill you. I looked at the picture again. It frightened me.

I looked at the picture pensively, I recognized the guy. Before the gumbas twisted my arms or legs I decided to speak. "I saw this guy in front of the stage at the recent Stones' concert. He was dressed up to look like Charlie Watts. I thought he was dead."

"Food poisoning," Shonestein commented.

How could Dean Moriarity escape a poisoning at a Stones concert and then die at the Fillmore? There was no explanation.

Elliott continued: "He does dress like Charlie, asshole, he even looks like him. Dean had no enemies. This is too weird, asshole." Two assholes in one sentence was grammatically unacceptable. I had to remind Elliott that my name was Trevor Blake, III. Asshole was not a name that I liked. I looked at the gumbas and accepted it.

A look from Little Garlic Breath prepared me for Elliott's continued remarks: "By day our drummer looks like a character from a Jack Kerouac novel, but by night he became the Rolling Stones' drummer." This explanation frightened me. How would I find a killer who looked like everyone else?

I blinked in amazement. "You mean the real Mick and Keith fear the competition, so they have to silence your guys," I paused and thought. Maybe they are finally ready for a Las Vegas lounge residency.

Big Garlic Breath spoke: "It's the competition, asshole?" He cracked his knuckles. Little Garlic Breath jumped in. "It's them, those long hairs." I tried not to laugh. It wouldn't be good for my health.

"You guys are truly amazing. You might need some stronger evidence. You know a piece of something pointing to the Stones camp. Some idea how the poison got there. What type of poison. You know guys, the simple things."

You are complicating it, asshole," Big Garlic Breath screamed.

"You guys are morons. Anyone can buy a Rolling Stones tour jacket and poison someone." I realized my mistake when Little Garlic Breath pulled out a small knife. I was hoping that he wouldn't cut my tongue out. Maybe he wanted to peel an apple. The look in his eyes suggested he wanted to peel me.

"Listen asshole," Shonestein man remarked, "we can simply threw you out of a speeding car or you can listen and cut the wise remarks." Maybe I should have cards printed up: "Trevor Asshole III, Private Investigator." It sounds kind of romantic. Then again, maybe not.

I decided to listen as I looked at Big Garlic Breath. He pulled out a gun and began loading hollow point bullets into it. A knife and a gun have a way of grabbing your attention. I realized that I had made a mistake. It was time for diplomacy.

"Faced with your explanations, I'm listening," Then I fell silent for the next half hour. Shonestein took me through the business affairs of the Start Me Up Band. The band had an excellent corporate structure with a strong profit line. He pulled out accounting sheets that showed the positive financial results. Costs were low and revenues high. The explanation of the fake Rolling Stones business activities intrigued me. At least I had the background to understand what was going on.

"I need a list of people who want the Start Me Up band to fail."

"The way I see it Elliott is that booking agents, managers, musicians, rock critics and fans might want to kill the Start Me Up drummers."

I thought that rock critics might be first in line after listening to their lame version of "Satisfaction." What is my role?"

"I need you to find out who in the Rolling Stones management is sabotaging our act." Then Elliott pulled a paper out of his pocket. He read from it. "The Rolling Stones are touring America with the Bridges to Babylon tour and performing all over the country." For another half hour, Elliott wove tales of problems with the Start Me Up Band and suggested that someone wanted to undermine their financial success. I could guess that garlic breath one and two didn't endear themselves to everyone by shaking their head in agreement at everything Shonestein said. Maybe it was the Holy Grail. Shonestein style.

"We have $50,000 for an investigator. Naturally, you get it by the hour." I thought I may have just lost some money.

"Elliott I can't take any more explanation, I get a hundred dollars an hour. So pay up for this lengthy and often inarticulate explanation. For the ride and my time you owe me $200." He laid two one hundred dollar bills in my hand. I was pissed. I had decided not to take the case. I knew I had made a mistake. Big Garlic Breath pointed his gun at my knee. I wouldn't die but my over forty-basketball league would lose a star. Elliott smiled put up his hand and Big Garlic Breath moved to the side of the room. I knew that we had a deal.

"You will take the deal," Shonestein smiled.

I reconsidered. "We have a deal." So much for my integrity of a minute ago.

Before I took the job I asked the obvious question. "Why not go to the police?"

Elliott looked at me like I had lost my mind. "We tried that and they laughed at us. They claim the guy in the jacket was holding a water pistol."

"What guy was holding a water pistol?" I inquired.

"The guy they arrested for attempting to kill our drummer at the real Rolling Stones concert at the Oakland Coliseum. You attended it. Your picture was in the paper standing next to the dead guy. That guy was our drummer. Someone shot him with water, he died." Shonestein continued. "Is this too difficult for you to understand?"

"Maybe the drummer drowned." I am big on jokes. Big Garlic Breath squeezed by elbow. He didn't like my humor. I shut up. I guess the way that my arm felt meant that eighteen holes with Tiger Woods was now out of the question.

"Do you want to know how he was killed," Shonestein asked.

"Surprise me," I smiled and continued, "how in the hell do you know how he died. I am the private eye, I have this type of knowledge."

Shonestein smiled: "Read the autopsy asshole. He was poisoned." He threw the autopsy in my lap. I looked at it. The death came from accidental poisoning backstage at a Start Me Up concert. They found a vial of poison. The drummer was dead by the time he hit the ground. Just another drugged out rock musician. Who cares!

Suddenly I understood. "The police thought it was accidental," I asked

"You got it superstar, now find the killer." At least he hadn't called me asshole. I liked superstar better.

"Why do you need me?" I smiled and knew how to ask the tough questions.

Shonestein stared at me: "Are you hard of hearing. Do you have a brain malfunction, Trevor."

I was baiting Shonestein. Now for the obvious question. "What local promoter hates you?"

Shonestein looked perplexed. "What one doesn't?

"Then run by me again, what my role is."

"You are the only P. I. with any knowledge of the music industry. It is you or no one. You need to listen I have already told you that once." Elliott continued: "I'll give you a $25,000 retainer, an expense account and money for that spade who works for you to investigate. Guitar Jac never liked being called a spade but for $25,000 he was known to make an exception.

The assignment seemed a simple one. Find the person sabotaging their act. "I'll take the case with $25,000 up front and the promise that the police are brought into the case." I knew that I could find the murderer and that there would be complications. At a hundred dollars an hour that was 250 hours. Little more than six weeks of work. Not bad for a starving P. I.

"I have a contract for you to sign," Shonestein remarked. He was a businessman.

"Fine." I remarked.

"It's a deal," Shonestein continued. "I want this kept confidential." He was nervous. I had the feeling that Shonestein would give up even more money. After all Sam Spade wasn't available. Maybe Bono could help. When the hit records stopped he would need work.

I needed some internal help and looked to the San Francisco Police Department. They had the information that would help me solve the case tout suite. The new SFPD building was located in the mini slums in San Francisco's south of market neighborhood. It looked like an up ground fall out shelter. The Iraqis would have trouble mobbing it, as the neighborhood wasn't even safe for the police. The inside of the SFPD was painted in a grey hue and there was a tile that looked industrial. It was not a friendly place. The neo industrial look, the smell of disinfectant and stale coffee made the criminals comfortable. I needed some police help and had a friend in the bowels of the SFPD fortress.

My old friend Detective Richard Sanchez was among San Francisco's finest police detectives and my sometimes girl friend, Joyce Byers, also had a strong interest in helping me with my cases. In his late thirties, Sanchez was San Francisco's youngest homicide detective and he had the highest rate of cleared cases in SFPD history. He was destined for management. He also made the ladies swoon with his Castilian Spanish accent, his Armani suits and his well publicized social life. He drove a BMW Z4 and was frequently seen around town with Sharon Stone. He never mentioned that she was ten years older than him. A night on the town with Detective Sanchez usually meant free drinks, a sumptuous dinner and a pick of the ladies. I had helped him solve a number of cases. He owed me.

Joyce Byers was a Ford model in police clothing. She was tall, lean, beautiful, smart and picky about men. She was my sometimes girl friend. Unlike Sanchez, she had a private and prickly side. She was so beautiful that men were afraid to approach here. I met her at a Gay Freedom Day Parade, and we had dated for a year. She thought I was cute and gay. When she found out I was straight it took her some time to get used to me. She did. We dated. She was helping me forget my wife. That is when I didn't have another date. Every girl I know was helping me forget my wife. Both Sanchez and Byers were happy when I leaked criminal activity to them. They solved a number of cases due to my expertise. The only problem was that I had trouble solving a major case.

So we cut a deal. I would help Sanchez and he would help me. Byers would also assist me. Joyce would not only help me but sleep with me at times. She was secretive about her life. I didn't even know where she lived. But she gave me all the investigative help I needed. Usually, while we were in bed after furtive sex. Not a bad deal. Fortunately, Detective Sanchez had no interest in sleeping with me. In San Francisco that was a rarity. Little did I know the crazy adventure that awaited me in the music underground?

I walked down to Sanchez's office. "Hey bro."

"Trevor, how's your sex life?"

"Not as good as yours."

"To what do I owe this dubious visit?"

"I need some info on the Start Me Up killings."

"Ah, yes, that is a mystery. The suspects are many and varied. Who cares? They are just a bunch of drugged out musical assholes."

The problem with Detective Sanchez was his San Francisco State philosophy degree. He talked and thought like a philosopher. That is except when he was referring to rock musicians. They ranked just above cockroaches with Sanchez. "Can I get what you have on the three drummers who were killed?"

"Sure, sit her." In half an hour three large folders sat on the desk. "I am going for coffee, Trevor, see you in an hour." He left the room. I spent an hour taking notes. He returned.

"Is that enough?"

"Thanks." I got up and left. I put the notes on 25 napkins. I had some ideas. I walked out front and hailed a cab. It was time to talk to Elliott Shonestein.

The cab took me to 870 Market Street. It wasn't an upscale building. When I went inside everything changed. Shonestein Enterprises had money. The floors were Italian marble; the walls were painted with art deco murals. The elevator was state of the art. There was a cute girl with a uniform, low cut I might add, who asked you what floor you wanted. A nice touch. Shonestein's office on the sixth floor office was filled with contemporary furniture and a group of secretaries who looked like models. That is if models had breast enhancement. I remembered not to use the term models. It was a sexist definition.

"Hi," I said to a young women who looked like Madonna. I guess that means she is an old young woman.

"Can I help you?" She smiled.

I put one of my cards in her hand. "Tell the boss his secret agent is here." She frowned.

She picked up the phone: "Elliott there is some asshole out here who thinks he is James Bond." She listened.

"Your name, sir."

I couldn't believe it. "You read don't you? The name is Trevor Blake III."

She barked into the phone, "Mr. Shonestein, some asshole named Trevor the Turd demands to see you." She looked at me with a glaring hatred. Suddenly she smiled. "Go in, sir."

As I walked toward Shonestein's office I heard a faint word: "Asshole." I guess everyone knows my name.

Shonestein came out of his chair with a smile and a firm handshake. "Trevor, progress?"

"None so far, I do have some questions." I continued. "Have you seen the autopsy?

"Why would I care about the autopsy, they are dead, all three drummers."

"There was no sign of foul play, they all committed suicide, according to the autopsy."

"So, Trevor, we hire maladjusted drummers." Shonestein lit a cigarette. A nasty habit. I needed to do some yoga.

As Elliott droned on about his business misfortunes, I looked up as garlic breath one and two entered the room. I decided they were not only stupid but extremely dangerous. After he repeated himself a dozen times, old Elliott came to the crux of the issue. I thought that he should be a college professor. He explained himself in twenty sentences that all said the same thing. Finally, he got to the point. The death of the drummers, Shonestein continued, was bad for business. It was even worse for the drummers. The replacement drummers were increasingly skeptical about joining the band. It seemed like a piece of cake. I knew all the musicians in town and could find out what was going on. I also had experience in the food industry.

For five years I had taken courses at the California Culinary Academy. The object wasn't to learn to become a gourmet Chef. It was to meet young ladies. I met my wife and then we got divorced. I became a private detective to lower my income. If Marilyn tried taking me to court, there wasn't much she could be awarded. A CD collection of almost 5000 featuring Van Morrison was it. But who cared about a cranky Irish midget with a bad personality.

All I had to do was to find a guy who murdered drummers for cover bands. Then again the Start Me Up cover band was rivaling some mid-level rock groups in earnings. Suddenly Journey, Reo Speedwagon, and Foreigner had to worry. The Indian Casinos might not hire them, the Start Me Up band drew more people and cost less money. Suddenly every over the hill rock group was a suspect.

The problem was that the drummers were killed at a Fillmore West concert. I needed to find out how security was breached. I decided to call on my old friend Larry Watlin. He was one of Bill Graham's original blue coats. These were the guys who beat you up if you tried to get backstage. He also was a Start Me Up fan and a consummate concert professional.

I dropped over to Watlin's house on Fillmore Street. He lived two blocks from the original Fillmore shrine to rock and roll. He was home and working on his computer. Watlin's flaming red hair made him look like a run down version of Jerry Garcia. He is fifty years old. He looks like he's eighty but he has had more fun than the rest of us. He ran through the security procedures that Shonestein used and laughed at their inadequacy. He told me to get Guitar Jac and run my own security survey.

Certainly not a hard task. I called Jac and he met me at the Fillmore. We went backstage and mapped out the rooms on ten napkins. He laughed as we went through our plan to watch the Start Me Up drummers. I was surprised at how exciting P. I. work could be in the rock and roll world.

I was ready to find my first real killer. I could just imagine the headlines in the **San Francisco Chronicle**. "Private Eye Finds Killer, Lauded As Hero." It didn't quite work out that way. I was doing the grunt work to find a killer. I needed another trip to the San Francisco Police Department.

I parked my car on 11th street and walked over to the SFPD. I asked for Detective Sanchez. He came through the door with a glare in his eyes. I wasn't sure that he was glad to see me. "Hey Sgt. How's it hanging?"

"Trevor the Turd," he smiled, "what can I do for you? These visits are getting a bit too commonplace." Never talk to a detective with too much education.

"Start by getting my name right, Trevor the Third."

"Cut the crap, asshole," Sanchez smiled. I wondered if he had been talking to Elliott Shonestein.

"I need the case files on the three Start Me Up drummers."

"Why would I do that? I just gave you the three autopsy reports."

I looked perplexed. "What can you do with an autopsy, Detective Sanchez?"

"You can read it and draw some conclusions," Sanchez remarked.

"Well, Detective when I solve the case you get the credit. I will come to you with the killer on a silver platter." Sanchez looked at me for a few minutes and left the room. Ten minutes later he returned with three small manila folders. "They all were accidental poisonings. Rocks stars are not known for their brains. Death by accident. Poisoning by stupidity," Sanchez continued, "the files make it clear that the guy ate some tripe or some other fucking Italian type sausage and died because he was too stupid to keep it in the refrigerator. They all had drugs on their body. Not your average death. Just another rock star croaking of lifestyle. The meat was contaminated but that wasn't enough to kill them. There was no known poison. There was no trace evidence. There were no fingerprints. There were no signs of forced entry to the well-secured entertainment room. We kept their drug dealers out. The security was so tight that it was impossible to penetrate the inner crime scene. So, asshole, there is no crime. The drummers simply ate some bad sausage and took some drugs. But here take the folders. They contain all the relevant facts." I nodded and reminded myself to lecture Sanchez on vocabulary building.

As Detective Sanchez walked away I noticed the nice Armani suit, the expensive Italian shoes and a tie that would pay for a months rent in my place on Chestnut Street. Maybe the tie was worth two months rent. A nice touch for a cop making $60,000 a year. Rumor had it that detective Sgt Sanchez inherited his money from a Spanish uncle. The truth was that he was for some years a successful real estate speculator. He also had stocks and bonds. He remained a good friend, even though he continued to berate me. The autopsy provided me with my first clue. Sanchez had overlooked an important fact.

Chapter 4
GUITAR JAC IS ON THE CASE

It was time to enlist the aid of my trusty assistant Guitar Jac. He remains not only a great tracker of people but he is a consummate human being. The translation is that he gets along with everyone. He is also a force in the music business. He is the only San Francisco bluesman to live in a penthouse. He is so articulate that everyone trusts him.

I arrived at Jac's penthouse on Nob Hill. The doorman sneered at me. I took the elevator to his penthouse and marveled at the view.

How does a Stanford graduate, who is black, afford this?" I smiled always the comedian.

"Black, Trevor, last time I looked I was African American."

"Ah, finally we are politically correct." We laughed and left the building sneering at the doorman.

We drove downtown to talk to some of the booking agents. Someone had to know how a Rolling Stones cover band with the name Start Me Up got so popular and so profitable. It was a rock music phenomenon beyond my scope.

We took his Lexus and parked at the 5th and Mission garage. It was city owned and cheap. I was paying. We wore our dark suits and broad brimmed hats. It made us look like real detectives. Or at least prosperous ones. Rock music must pay well. When we got to the concert promoters headquarters, his corporation owned the entire building. The sign read: "Bill Raymond Presents." It was garish in psychedelic electric lights.

Bill Raymond Presents was the major West Coast rock and roll booking agent. He had come out from New York in the 1960s and opened the Avenue Ballroom and became a millionaire. If you wanted to play rock and roll in San Francisco Bill Raymond Presents was the only booking agent. We ascended to their plush corporate offices and asked for Louie Di Salvo. He was the head of everything and a good friend.

"Trevor," Louie belched. "How's the rock band? No, I don't have any bookings for you. I loved you at the Saloon, you did 'Louie Louie' three times and got it wrong each time." That is my charm but Louie wouldn't understand. The trouble with talking to Louie is that you might not be able to get a word in edgewise.

"Hello, Louie the Lip," I continued: "We need to find out who is killing the Start Me Up drummers."

"In case you haven't heard," Louie remarked, "the drummers all died of food poisoning. It was accidental. They also were hoarding drugs. Get it Trevor? Death by lifestyle." Louie continued. "Whoever killed them did everyone a favor. They're assholes, They are bad musicians. They are greedy bastards." Louie smiled. Not a good sign, I suspected that he and Elliott Shonestein didn't get along.

"What!" I remarked with surprise. " I bet that you don't book them."

"Smart ass. How did you know?" Louie looked perplexed. He was reminded that I was a private eye. Sam Spade at work. I could deduce all the subtle nuances of a crime. The problem was I didn't know what was going on.

"No one told me a thing." I replied smugly. Deduction after all is the backbone of the detective world.

"Well, Trevor, the health department ruled it was poisoning by salami."

"How do you know? Maybe it was a meatball."

"No, Trevor, you are the meatball. Those bums never refrigerated anything. You know modern science. Keep the food from bacteria. E-Coli you ever heard of it?"

"How do you know that," I replied.

"Read the newspapers. The health department investigated and there was no killing. Joel Selvin wrote about it in the San Francisco Chronicle. Spend fifty cents Trevor and solve your crime." Louie laughed again. He loved to laugh at his comments. The police then showed that some guy with a Rolling Stones jacket had fired a water pistol at all three drummers. He was a quack and had nothing to do with the deaths. They died of stupidity. Then the guy with the water pistol died of food poisoning Poetic justice, Trevor"

What could I say. It was a strange set of circumstances. "Maybe they all died of some crazy affliction with the Rolling Stones' hit records." Louie smiled. He thought I was clever. He was the only one so far.

"Trevor, give it up. It was all accidental."

"Thanks Louie," I left dejected.

When we got out on the street I realized that I was a private eye without a single clue. There was something wrong. But what was it? I was missing something. I took out a napkin and made some notes on what might have been. Guitar Jac was mute during the entire exchange. He was thinking. I had to find out his take.

I walked outside with Guitar Jac. Things were not going well. Jac hadn't said a word. That was unlike him.

"You know, Trevor, we are missing something." Guitar Jac looked up. He was thinking. "It is someone who is like a chameleon, he or she fits in too easily. There is no suspect who stands out."

"I agree, so I need to talk to that dirt bag."

"You mean Shonestein."

"You got it, Jac."

So we drove up to see the man. Elliott Shonestein was in his office. Garlic breath one and two were nowhere in sight. I walked in. Elliott looked surprised. We had just talked to him. It was obvious we weren't being social.

"I hope that this doesn't become a habit. I just saw you guys."

"Well asshole," I exclaimed with courage as the two hoodlums entered the room. I was visibly deflated. "Let me rephrase that, sir, I have some suggestions."

"Continue Trevor," Shonestein looked quizzically at me as the two hoodlums cracked their knuckles.

"Death by food poisoning," I screamed.

"Ya, so what." Shonestein glowered at me. Garlic breath 1 and 2 began sharpening small knives.

"Don't you buy my conclusion," I retorted.

Shonestein looked at me incredulously." I don't believe you, do I look like a dumb asshole. I am paying $50,000 for this crap."

I didn't answer. It would not be good to tell him the truth. I didn't know a damn thing. Either did he. "I am thinking," I remarked.

"Let me make it real clear for you shamus," Elliott remarked with a sardonic smile. "What do you think the odds are of three guys in the same band dying of food poisoning? The cops never looked at it. Remember when Bobby Fuller died. He had broken his own arms, beat himself and then committed suicide after dicking some Mafia broad. Trevor has it dawned on you that the police may have missed something?"

"I think I said that." I felt pretty strange. It was time to investigate. "I have one question."

"Yes, shamus."

"Who provides the food and the catering?"

"Jesus, Trevor, the police have grilled those guys, gone to the supplier, talked to the trucker, the Chefs were subjected to intense questioning and nothing of value was found. Capice?"

I wasn't sure. My Italian was confined to va bene. "I'm on the case, Elliott," I remarked, "Come on Jac, let's get out of here."

We walked out to the street. It seemed I was doing a lot of that these days. I had no clues, no leads and no idea what I was doing. So I drove back to the office. Guitar Jac left for his Nob Hill apartment. He probably was having a fondue party. He was ready for some brie and a glass of Chardonnay. I had a Budweiser cooling in the office fridge. A dead end on my first important case and no leads in sight. It was time to think. But I didn't have much to think about.

After parking on Ashbury Street, I walked up the stairs to my office. No one was waiting for me. A relief. I unlocked the door. It was cold. I had to remember to pay the P. G. and E. bill. I sat at my desk and looked at those two fat guys eating an ice cream on the sign across the street. Ben and Jerry were generic names. They were probably Bernie and Alfred in real life. I was stymied. Maybe I was in the wrong business. All I knew was death by salami.

I needed expert advice on the case. It was time to reconsider my options, so I headed out for fresh air and to think. I retrieved my car from Ashbury Street and drove out to Clement Street to Bill's Hamburger Place. I ordered a bacon cheeseburger and sat out in the open-air backyard. Another Budweiser put me into a proper thinking mode. I took out several napkins and made diagrams of what I knew and where I was going with the case. I had extensive notes for two Brian Jones and three murders. I had a napkin with cooking ingredients and I drew circles around the key facts. I was getting some ideas. Things were now a bit clearer. I did see a pattern. It was time to get some expert criminal opinions and I knew just the person to consult. The purple don, with the moniker, Don Gino, was my next stop. But first I had to go back to my office and get ready for a meeting with San Francisco's most notorious gangster. I called him on the phone and he agreed to come to my office. That in itself was a miracle. He seldom left the Mission District. I had saved his life when a group of gangsters cornered him in the Mission and I drove up to rescue him. He owed me. I had an hour to put my thoughts together. I put the diagrams down on the desk. The napkins cluttered my desk. Sam Spade in action. There was a mystery person somewhere in my napkins. I just had to find him.

Chapter 5
ENTER THE PURPLE DON

Driving down Haight Street to the office, I noticed that Haight Ashbury sign was being repainted. A big picture of the Mayor was prominently displayed under the garish new paint job. Mayor Gavin Newsom never met a tourist dollar he didn't love, so the Haight Ashbury looked like a picture postcard neighborhood. Just don't look a block behind the Haight at the urban ghetto. It is not a pretty picture. I parked the car on Ashbury. It is my usual spot, a night worker leaves and I pull in. Walking to my office I am frustrated.

I climb the stairs to my office. I peek inside. No one is waiting. No bill collectors. No hoodlums. No young ladies. My desk is cluttered so I sit down to catch up on the paperwork. As I sat looking out the window I didn't think that things could get worse. They did. The door opened and a five-foot dark haired hoodlum entered followed by a six feet tall crime boss known affectionately in San Francisco as the Purple Don enter my office. The hoodlums name is Gino Walker. He wears a purple suit, a purple hat, a white tie and a purple shirt. He also sports a white handkerchief. The purple suede shoes were the final touch. Gino Walker's real name was Garfield Kinderhoven. Not exactly an Italian name and to compound matters he has blonde hair. But who would tell a cold-blooded killer that he wasn't an Italian. Not me. He looked and acted like a rock star. Gino had the market cornered on the sale of illegal liquor, cigarettes and coffee. He owned a dog food factory and assorted other businesses in the Mission District. Over the years, Don Gino increasingly opened legitimate businesses. He was fond of telling me it was more profitable than crime.

The Italian don controlled business in the Mission District as well as the Mexican American section of San Francisco. He was also known for keeping drugs and prostitution out of the Mission. He made his money the old-fashioned way extortion, loan sharking, protection for small business and gambling. Prostitution and drugs were not a part of the streets that Don Gino controlled in the Mission. Rumor had it that missing gangsters wound up in his cans of dog food. He was also gay and a staunch Catholic.

Don Gino was a man of many contradictions. He dated some of San Francisco's most beautiful women. He was seen in the Castro. He loved the gay bars. The Opera was his favorite hangout. He was a regular lunch guest with Mayor Newsom. Willie Brown, the retired San Francisco Mayor, held a monthly investment meeting with Don Gino. The San Francisco Chronicle reported that Brown's wealth increased ten fold since the Purple Don became active in Brown's investments. It was Don Gino who convinced Willie Brown to build the San Francisco Giants ballpark on Third Street just off the bay. Not surprisingly, Don Gino made more than thirty million dollars from land he owned in the area. So money was never a concern with the Purple Don.

He donated half the money to restore the Mission Dolores. Not only was he a regular at San Francisco's oldest Catholic church, he was chairman of the Wednesday night bingo sessions. Not exactly your typical gangster.

He was also the only person supplying food to the cocktail lounges. He had a lock on the hors d'ouvres trade in the city by the bay. Don Gino had a major deal with the local unions and his company, Gino's Chicken Wings And Assorted Goodies, fed the after work cocktail crowd. If you had free chicken wings, salami, some barbecue, cold cuts, little vegetables and other bits of nibbling food it was due to Don Gino. He loved talking about the carrots and celery that he supplied to the bars. They were his biggest moneymakers. The rumor was that nothing was built in San Francisco nor was there a license for a bar or restaurant without Don Gino's opinion. Or perhaps his consent.

His favorite lounge piano player was my old friend Walter Malland. Not only was Malland a magnificent pianist but a forty-year-old prodigy who played a variety of instruments with the San Francisco Symphony. Malland was six feet two and 180 pounds with a trimmed beard and the looks of a matinee movie star. He was not only Don Gino's favorite piano player but he guaranteed him top paying positions. Malland had a residence at the Fairmont Hotel that pulled in a quarter of a million dollars a year. The rumor was that Don Gino ponied up some of the money. Lounge piano players weren't Don Gino's only interest, he was a supporter of the San Francisco arts in general. The contradictions continued with his religious fervor.

He showed up virtually everyday at the Mission Delores near the Castro District. He took confession from his priest once a week. Don Gino confessed his criminal sins. The routine was always the same. The priest would tell him to say twenty-five Hail Mary's. Weird. Then the priest would tell him that he would see the Don at bingo night. Go figure. The church loved him. He donated more than a million dollars a year to various Catholic charities.

Don Gino was politically connected. Gavin Newsom praised him to the press. The mayor appointed Don Gino to a number of city commissions. He also was seen at lunch with Senator Barbara Boxer. Senator Dianne Feinstein had him over for dinner. At society fundraisers, Don Gino was photographed with the beautiful people. The San Francisco Chronicle regularly featured articles on his charitable deeds. He had a five-foot tall valet who followed him everywhere and a group of eight Samoan bodyguards. All were dressed in purple. Only in San Francisco.

What was crime coming to? Working for Don Gino the eight Samoan bodyguards provided a high level of protection. All were karate experts. They also didn't have a sense of humor. If you owned a restaurant, a nightclub or a grocery store, Don Gino made sure his company supplied your needs. If you didn't do business with him, there was a fire, a gas explosion or an order from the health or fire department to cease and desist due to city regulations. The norm was for your business to burn to the ground. While word on the street was that he was gay, the subject never came up in polite conversation. No one interested in maintaining the status of their health ever talked about Don Gino's personal life. He walked into my office with a smile. For some reason I was one of his personal favorites. It had to be my detecting skills.

"Trevor," Don Gino smiled. "You look like you have some worries." He sat down and his trusty aide stood behind him. No sign of the Samoans. They were always around in an invisible way. How one hides eight Samoans who weigh three hundred pounds remains a mystery.

"Don Gino," I said as I stood at attention. Better to stand at attention than to have the Samoans on you.

"Sit down, Trevor, this is business."

Monkey business I thought. "Well what is it?"

"We have a problem and I need you to fix it."

"Wait, wait, wait," I stammered. "I asked to see you, it's me who needs information."

"In time my son." Don Gino had been hanging around the Catholic clergy so long he talked like the priests. "I need your help, so for once listen." Don Gino lit a cigarette. He took a long drag and smiled. He always smiled.

"Let me guess you can't control the cream and sugar trade in San Francisco, Ben and Jerry's won't play ball," I remarked with a sly smile. Always the clever guy. Out of nowhere I spotted one of the Samoans. Thank god for my peripheral vision.

As the Samoan moved toward me I realized my mistake. Don Gino raised his hand. The Samoan stopped. Maybe garlic breath one and two could be trained the same way. I didn't see the Samoans come into the office. But that was the beauty of their training.

"Sorry Don Gino," I continued. "Too much college."

"Ah Trevor, I have a simple job for you." He laid down twenty $100 bills. I was all ears. I had more money on my desk in two days than the whole time the office had been open.

` "We need you to look into our salami source. It's killing people."

"Don Gino, may I humbly point out that you would do a better job with your people investigating."

"Ah, Trevor, you don't understand business. I have to stay out of these matters. It could prove to be delicate. I lunch with the mayor, union officials and the beautiful people. I had lunch with Danielle Steele last week. I can't read her books. Lunch is another matter." He paused. "I have to retain a certain distance. Discretion, I believe, is the word. But you my friend can be my eyes and ears in the salami world."

I shuddered at the thought. I looked at the stack of one hundred dollar bills. That changed my mind. "What is the salami problem?"

Don Gino reflected for a moment: "It has killed three musicians, I have come to believe that there is more behind this than meets the eye."

Suddenly I realized my good fortune. I may be able to solve my own case and pick up another two thousand dollars. "You got it Don Gino. I am on the case." I was after all an equal opportunity P. I. I could work for gangsters as well as drug addled rock musicians.

He stood. "Trevor you might like a lead."

"Sure, what is it?"

"You can start by going to the Irvington Salami Company."

"You got it, Don Gino." He left; I smiled at the Samoans, the five-foot valet glided out the door giving me the finger. No only was the valet a little swishy, he always smiled at Don Gino. I had to remember to be politically correct and not use swishy or faggot as terms of endearment.

Hey, I'm a liberal. I could care less. It was an awful private thought. I also remembered that the last guy who insinuated that Don Gino batted from both sides of the plate was found floating in McCovey cove. Fortunately, Barry Bonds hadn't hit a bill in the water that day. Or for that matter all year. No one signed him to a contract. Proving that being an asshole is a problem. I had to think. There was a way to solve this little crime twice. To collect two fees was a P. I.'s dream

After two hours with Don Gino my office smelled of cigarettes and expensive cologne. I was hungry. Walking out on Haight Street I was besieged by tourists. The price of cheap rent. A parking ticket was on my car and I threw it away. Civil disobedience feels good.

I left the Haight and drove over to Bill's Place for a hamburger. I go there a lot. Bill's Place is on Clement Street on the outer edges of the Sunset District and has a beautiful garden out back. It is a place for reflective thought. It was still the best burger in town and it was located in an old Italian neighborhood. The only change is that 90% of the people living there are Chinese. Oh, well, I am a liberal.

I had the Herb Caen burger. It was named for the fabled newspaper columnist and hit the spot. With my stomach full, it was time to solve the case. Although I had no idea how the solve the case. I took out my napkins and looked at the clues. There was something I was missing. The Chef was the culprit. It was something about his hair. There was a subtle nuance I was missing. Maybe it wasn't a subtle nuance. I looked for the obvious and found nothing new in my notes.

I went home and reflected on the strange direction of the day. I had $27,000, in the bank that Marilyn didn't know about. I also had two clients, no leads and no idea how to catch the killer who had iced three drummers. I had two clients who would ice me if I didn't come up with results. Sam Spade never had these problems. I needed Chestnut Street's safe haven.

I drove home and turned on the television. I fell asleep as David Letterman had two Indian guys running around New York asking stupid questions. I didn't think you had to have television to do this sort of thing. You could hail a San Francisco cab and get the same show.

Don Gino's lead was a good one. He had given me a piece of the tainted salami. It was time to see the Irvington brothers.

Chapter 6
OUR SALAMI IS THE BEST: THE IRVINGTON BROTHERS AND MR. LARUA

San Francisco's warehouse district is on Third Street. There are very few warehouses left. The neighborhood now sports the San Francisco Giants baseball stadium, a myriad of yuppie restaurants and the requisite trendy clothing boutiques. No self-respecting longshoreman would be found dead in this formerly blue collar area. I hadn‘t been there in years. I was shocked by the coffee shops, the fine restaurants and enough new bars do destroy your liver. Now with the Pac Bell baseball park, the success of the San Francisco Giants and the invasion of dot.com yuppies, it is hard to find a Teamster who admits to being a warehouse man. There is a 12-step restaurant that serves liquor. Am I missing something? Why they still called it the warehouse district baffles me. You can find a lot of yuppies hanging around with designer clothes and opinions on everything from the Giants to world peace. Where is Charles Manson when you really need him?

The Third Street Warehouse stands out as an exception. It is a dreary, unkept four-story building housing various liquor distributors, food wholesalers and a raft of foreign importers who bring in cheese and other delicacies. The Irvington Brothers are so successful they have an entire floor. This is big business. So I was ready for the challenge. I dressed in my best suit. It wasn't an Armani but the Men's Wearhouse is still a class operation. Detective Sanchez laughs at my descriptions of suits for the up and coming executive. As Sanchez remarks: "Success is not only a state of mind, it is the way a man looks." I walked through the door confidently. The Irvington Brothers were about to be charmed into giving up their culinary secrets.

"Hello sweetie," I remarked to the receptionist, "I need to see Joe Irvington." She looked at me with cold dagger eyes. If she could have uttered asshole I wouldn't have been surprised. Her blonde eyes were clear and precise. She was reading a Gloria Steinhem book. So much for my "sweetie" comment. As usual I was a little behind the times. She was six feet tall with a beautiful body and expensive clothes. I didn't see a future with her. I smiled. She didn't have a ring on her finger. Maybe I did have a chance.

She responded: "Fuck off, you sexist pig," she smiled and rang a buzzer. Joe Irvington was a six foot five inch hulk who still worked out at the gym.. He squeezed my hand trying to turn it into orange juice. I smiled. I noticed a bad hair do with a lot of grease. Oh well, it fits his demographics.

"Good to meet you Joe."

"Well, to what do I owe this visit?" He looked at my card like it had a fungus on it.

I smiled. It seems I do this when I am nervous. "I need a little information." I showed him my P. I. license, and mentioned that I was looking into the matter for Don Gino. He looked frightened. Don Gino's name did open doors. He sneered at my P. I. license.

"Come into my inner office, we have a dining room." Joe walked me into a plush and very private dining room where another good-looking young girl was setting two places. "We have a cook, sit down. I'll do the ordering." No sense arguing with the boss.

After a small salad with goat cheese, fruit and a low fat dressing, we dived into lasagna that was perfect and it was followed by crème Brule. There was no sign of Irvington salami. Just as well. After we ate he talked. It was all platitudes about the wonderful salami business. I needed to find a real question. I couldn't think of one as he never stopped talking. Then we walked back into his office. The cook entered the office served us a Spanish brandy and a cappuccino. I could get used to this fare. It was time for the detective to detect.

"Information is what I need," I reminded him. "I am trying to find out where the salami came from that killed three musicians in the Start Me Up band."

"Fill me in," Joe Irvington continued, "I think they died from lack of talent." He laughed. He loved his own jokes.

I told him about the deaths and it jogged his memory. Or maybe it was the specter of Don Gino waking in and asking for his help.

"Remember I am Don Gino's emissary."

"What the hell is an emissary?"

"Sorry Joe, too much college." Always the intellectual.

Joe Irvington thought for about five minutes. "All I know is we shipped the salami to Elliott Shonestein's residence. His house is in Twin Peaks. I had to pay the Union guy extra, Elliott wanted the salami delivered early in the evening."

"Why late at night," I continued, "I don't get it, what did it matter?"

"Elliott says it was picked up by a Chef who had a day job, some financial guy somewhere who moonlights making food for the rock stars." Joe thought for a moment. He continued: "Elliott said something about preparing the food backstage. The concert started at ten at night and this Chef brought the food in around eight." Joe was still thinking. He paused and lit a cigarette. He looked at the wall. Obviously, he was deep in thought.

"Is there a point here, Joe," I am after all an inquisitive P. I.

"We are being sued by Shonestein. The son of a bitch probably had something to do with the deaths. I sold the salami to Don Gino, he sold it to Shonestein and that fucking Jew bastard is suing me."

"Do I need to point out, Joe, that suing Don Gino might not be good for your health."?

"You have a point, Trevor."

"Back to the salami, why would Elliott Shonestein provide salami to his group, if he knew it was killing them?" A good question from the detective.

"This is beyond me, Trevor, you are the fucking detective, solve the crime."

I had no comment. I wish I smoked or had a cup of coffee. I just put my hands in my pocket and thought. My client killing his breadwinning drummers, so he could hire me to find the killer. I didn't think so.

Joe stared at the ceiling. He took a drag on his cigarette and in a low voice remarked: "We are contacting our insurance company and Shonestein has a settlement check waiting for him. The son of a bitch is suing us for emotional distress." Remind me to tell Joe to get a new attorney and insurance company.

"Any suspicion of funny business?" I asked quizzically.

"The police couldn't help. Can you?" I picked the lasagna out of my teeth. I smiled. Everyone was smiling. We all did that when we were nervous.

He walked into his outer office. When you are a multi-millionaire you have an inner and outer office. You also have a secretary with big tits and no brains. Joe beckoned me to follow with a wave of his finger. I stood and he pointed to a chair. I sat. "Do you mind letting me know what this is about in some detail?" Joe Irvington looked nervous. I would be too if Don Gino was interested in the matter.

I explained as best I could about the drummers in the Start Me Up band dying of poisoning. I continued that it was a good bet that Don Gino was somehow involved in the business of the Start Me Up band. He didn't tell me that he was but the Don was a secretive guy. I think we all needed a good detective. I was missing something. Maybe I was missing everything. Don Gino thought that someone didn't have his best interests at heart. I pointed out that this made Don Gino unhappy. This caught Irvington's attention. No one likes it when Don Gino is unhappy.

"Let me get this straight kid," Joe continued. "You want me to tell you that the salami I provided Don Gino was defective. Maybe it poisoned someone."

"Yah," I stated.

"Ok pal, let's go to our scientific control center."

"What?" I couldn't believe this, some sort of health lab. Joe looked like a reject from a bad restaurant.

We walked up one flight of stairs and came to a small room filled with three scientists. Joe introduced me to Pam D. She was about thirty, had long black hair, breasts like small melons and a warm smile. Maybe selling salami turned you into a sex symbol. No one was ugly in the Irvington Brothers employ. That is except Joe Irvington. I had to remember that I was an investigator not a horny bachelor. Pam D. showed us around the lab and then went to a row of six filing cabinets. She bent down. Now I know why they call here Pam D. She pulled out records on all the salami provided to Don Gino. It was clean. At least that's what the records said. There was no question that the salami passed a rigorous inspection. It even had a USDA stamp.

"Trevor, is that your name?"

I must not make much of an impression. "Yes."

"I'll give you a little demonstration."

"Sure!" I was hoping she would take her clothes off. No such luck, she went right to science.

Pam D. proceeded to place thirteen separate salami's on the table. "What we have here Trevor is comparison sampling."

"Which is?" I stuttered.

"Look at the texture of the salami, see how it differs, that tells you if it is close to causing health problems. There are six different types of salami. We have a machine that radiates each salami and it is yanked from the line. The ones in question all passed. The tampering took place elsewhere."

"I see." I didn't know what else to say. I kept looking at her breasts.

"Does this help on the salami end," Pam D. inquired.

"Shows how little I know," I smiled. I thought that there was one kind of salami. She took out a Mortadella and cut off some pieces. I ate them.

"This is a fatty sausage made out of finely ground pork." Pam D. knew her salami. She continued. "Here we have a Toscano salami which is a Tuscan style that is dry cured and made from coarse cut pork, red wine and whole black peppercorns." I smiled as I ate it.

"What other interesting salami's are on the premises?" I ate another piece of Mortadella. No sense wasting good salami.

Pam D. looked down the long table. She picked up a piece of Milano salami. This is a mildly spiced chunk of meat with garlic and white wine. Not bad. Then came the prosciutto, which was a salty piece of salami. I passed on the guanciale, which is a dry cured pig cheek. I finished up with the Sooppressata. This is a coarsely chopped pork that is highly seasoned. It was also very thin and extremely spicy. Pam D. gave me a glass of Chianti. I burped as I washed down the last traces of sausage. I belched. Not cool. I smiled. Total satisfaction.

`"Well pal," Joe intoned, "does that do it for you?"

"I still need an explanation of how salami can kill." Joe Irvington looked perplexed. He lit a cigarette. He was quiet for a moment. Obviously thinking.

"Well, Trevor, we put out a plate of salami. By that I mean that it is a platter of Italian style cured or preserved meats. Most people expect salami but they are often served mortadello, prosciutto and lardo."

"What the hell is lardo?"

"Lardo, Trevor, is back fat cured in salt and dried." He smiled.

"Yuk!" I looked green.

"It is quite good." Joe Irvington lit another cigarette. Lung cancer was on the horizon.

"What does the word salami mean?" I thought I had him with that brilliant question.

"Salami is a general term for sausage that is dry cured and salted."

"I think I got it. It looks to me Joe that it would be difficult to poison via salami."

"Oh, no, Trevor, you could easily add a number of very subtle poisons." Joe pulled out the "Food Poison Journal," and he read statistics that showed that there were 272 cases of salami poisoning in forty-four states and the District of Columbia.

"Where can I go to try a salami plate?" I needed to see what types of salami made up a plate.

"I got just the place for you Trevor, It's the Zuni Café at 658 Market Street right here in good old downtown San Francisco."

"Joe, thanks for your help. I have a handle on the Chef and his methods." Pam double D smiled at me. Joe Irvington grabbed my arm and bid me goodbye. Joe led me down to his office. As I left the secretary handed me a huge bag. It was filled with salami and special breads. The investigation hadn't been a waste after all. I wasn't getting anywhere and wondered about the next step. But at least I could eat.

After leaving the Irvington Brothers factory I walked back up Third Street to Harrington's Bar and Grill. Michael wasn't in so I had a large glass of Merlot. Anyone who drinks wine in an Irish beer bar is suspect. Mr. Larua, the bartender, had served in World War II and was now approached his mid-80s. He poured himself a gin and tonic and stood looking at my glum countenance.

"Trevor, what is it pal?" he asked.

"Mr. Larua I can't seem to get a handle on the case."

"Let me get you a cheeseburger and fries on the house and we'll talk about it." A good idea and I quickly wolfed down the burger. I only ate a couple of the fries. Mr. Larua ate the rest. Then I gave a portion of the salami and bread to Mr. Larua. He had smoked four cigarettes and finished four drinks as we talked. He would probably outlive me.

"What you need Trevor is to find the bootleg salami guys. You do know who they are, a private eye like you?"

"Bootleg salami guys?" I hope it didn't sound like a question.

"That's what I said," Mr. Larua poured his fifth drink. He could drink on the job and never feel the effects. I had the feeling that I was being kidded. "No, I don't know shit about bootleg salami. How about a bootleg Jimi Hendrix CD."

"Never heard of him." Mr. Larua took a long drag on his cigarette and poured us both another drink. I think that was his sixth but who was counting.

"Go down to Mission and nineteenth. The Mexicans knew all about this."

"Might there be a Mexican I could look up?" I asked Mr. Larua in amazement.

"Sure his name is Ricardo Diaz. He stands on a street corner in front of the El Chollo Bar."

"Jesus, there are a dozen guys on that street corner and they are all Mexicans."

"You won't have any trouble Trevor, he looks like Carlos Santana."

"Great," I couldn't believe it. I have to depend upon a Carlos Santana look alike to solve my crime.

I caught a cab to the Zuni Café and walked into the bar. I ordered a glass of Dom Perignon and a platter of salami. The bartender looked on with disapproval. He didn't have Dom Perignon. I settled for a Gallo jug red. The salami came instantly.

I made a serious mistake by asking: "Is there any thing I should know about slicing salami?" The bartender looked at me like I was a moron.

"Slicing is everything." He finished his sentence with a "Umph."

"What?" I didn't get it.

"Well," the exasperated bartender continued, "we have a Berkel."

Huh!" I had never heard of a Berkel.

"For the uninitiated a Berkel is an old fashioned hand cranked antique model. They coast $25,000." I was sorry I asked. Salami was getting complicated.

"I still want to know what is a Berkel?"

The bartender looked at me like I was nuts. "It's a slicer, moron," At least I was no longer asshole.

"What if I wanted to poison someone." The bartender looked shocked. I placed one of my cards on the bar. He eyed it suspiciously.

"Trevor the III," he replied.

"In person." I smiled

He was thinking.

"Well anything is possible." He looked uncomfortable. "Our Berkel came from Florence." This was more than I needed to know about salami.

"How would you poison someone?" He looked at me like I was his next candidate.

"Simple, don't cure it, don't smoke it and lightly coat the meat with a colorless poison." I suddenly understood the importance of salami. I left a twenty-dollar tip and left the Zuni Café. Unless I was mistaken, I caught a glimpse of my sometimes girl friend Joyce Byers in the corner. She was smoking. No one smoked in San Francisco restaurants. But she was a member of the San Francisco Police Department. She was probably on a stake out. So she was smoking.

I needed to go back to my office and make some notes. Unfortunately, I continued to drink. Soon a beautiful young lady was sitting next to me. She introduced herself as Chastain Johnson. I was uncomfortable. Joyce couldn't see me from the bar. I kept looking at Chastain's breasts. They were beautiful. We talked and found out that we had a lot in common. We were in the midst of a great conversation when I looked in the back of the restaurant. Joyce was gone. So I did what any gentleman would do. I asked Chastain over to my place. I told her that we would listen to some Janis Joplin. She had never heard of Janis, but she got in the cab with me. We ordered a plate of salami di Felino that is a lightly cured meat made from very lean pork to go. I stopped and bought a bottle of classic Chianti. It was from my favorite spot Habib's Liquors on Chestnut Street. Chastain entered my apartment pretty drunk. She promptly passed out. We spent the night together and it was a total surprise. No sex. Just sleep. In the morning she was nervous.

"Was it good?" She looked embarrassed

"If it was good for you, it was good for me." I chuckled.

"Asshole."

"We both drank too much, so I guess it was good, the drinking that is."

She smiled. Chastain realized that we had collapsed and nothing happened. Why she looked relieved I had no clue. I felt guilty as Joyce Byers was my steady girl friend. When Joyce left the bar I became Casanova. Chastain was too good to pass up. She was a typical California blonde built right in all the right places and she seemed enamored with me. The only thing we forgot was sex. But I guess you can't have everything. I left the next morning with a smile on my face. Chastain had fallen back to sleep. No sense bothering her. I decided to go down to Starbuck's and get us some coffee and scones. When I returned a half an hour later, I found my apartment in a shambles. Betrayed by a wonton woman. Chastain was nowhere in sight.

What I didn't realize was that Chastain had not only searched my apartment but put a listening device under the bed. I didn't find this out for some time but considering my recent sexual conquests this was the last place to secure a listening device. There would be total quiet for some time. I looked at the mess and decided to clean up later. I had bigger fish to fry. I drove back to 19th and Mission and miraculously a parking place turned up half a block down Mission. Maybe that was a sign that I should convert to Catholicism. Then again maybe some higher power knew that I was looking for Carlos Santana. Or at least someone who looked like him. The Mission District is Hispanic to the core and finding someone who looked like Carlos Santana among the hundreds who walked around looking like Santana was no easy task. Maybe I should just ask for Ricardo Diaz. Or for that matter Ricky Ricardo. I forgot Ricky was Cuban.

Chapter 7
ARE YOU CARLOS SANTANA?

It wasn't hard to find Ricardo Diaz. He was standing on a street corner signing autographs. As I approached him, a young girl asked: "Are you Carlos Santana?" Ricardo simply smiled. I bet he got a lot of girls with his Carlos look. Then again maybe not. Carlos is in his fifties. Carlos is bald. He is also rich. Rich and bald appeal to young girls. I couldn't wait to get there myself. Maybe I would look as good as Santana. Only if Matchbox 20 sang in front of me. My surf band could use some help.

I cried out: "Ricardo." He looked at me stunned. "Mr. Larua sent me"

` "Hey man, I don't sell illegal liquor anymore." He tried to walk away. He had on this funny hat. Maybe Ricardo was bald.

"Wait," I said in a soothing voice. I have some Lincoln's and Jackson's here for you." Carlos smiled, stopped and shook my hand. It's a good thing I didn't offer any Washington's he would still be moving and the Lincoln's and Jackson's were in a wad.

"Good to meet you brother." He smiled and I wondered if I had become an honorary Chicano.

"I need to find out some things about the salami you sell, I am not worried that it is, should be say, from another source." I smiled.

He smiled. "I don't know what you are talking about, asshole." Maybe he knew Elliott Shonestein. Everyone seemed to call me asshole. Carlos reached inside his pocket. I reached inside my pocket. He probably had a gun or knife. I had a pack of chewing gum. It looked like a Mexican standoff. Carlos pulled out a little cigar and lit it.

Then Carlos smiled again. If nothing else, the man was all smiles. So was I. I smiled. Now we stood looking at each other smiling. A mental health worker might wonder about us. He fingered the gold cross around his neck and spoke: "You know man, this is strange. You are some foreigner coming into my turf with this self-righteous horseshit about stealing. Is there a reason for this? Is there something I am missing? Explain asshole?" That was two assholes in one conversation. Carlos needed a vocabulary builder.

"Where do I start," I continued. I told the Carlos look alike about the Start Me Up drummers, the meeting with Joe Irvington and my suspicions that something was amiss. The drummers had all met their fate after eating a big salami sandwich back stage or some form of pasta with some kind of Italian meat. I was told that the band loved Bresaola, which is a dry cured beef. Salami was becoming too complicated for me. Then I told him about the Mick Jagger look alike. He listened to me and then he smiled. I was getting tired of the smiles. He knew something.

"Once again Trevor you need to play detective. Get back stage and you will find the killer." I wasn't keen about being lectured by the Carlos Santana look alike. I didn't have a choice, he had some answers.

"What do you mean back stage?" I asked. "Backstage where? What venue? What band?"

The Carlos look-a-like smiled: "Word on the street is that someone is going after the cover bands. It's big money now, pal." I hated to be called pal.

"Ok, I'll look on the streets."

"Are you stupid," Carlos called out. "Look at the Fillmore." He walked away looking like I needed guidance. Perhaps I did.

I walked away and went down Mission Street to the Foreign Cinema. This restaurant shows cheesy foreign films while you eat an overpriced dinner. I am a sucker for a gimmick. The food was good, so why not. There was also no salami. As soon as I sat down, I noticed a beautiful girl and I heard the mellifluous voice of my erstwhile assistant Guitar Jac. He had his back to me and was romancing a young lady. At least it seemed that way, not too many people brought a guitar into the Foreign Cinema and quietly sang a song. When I complained to the waiter, he threatened to throw me out. They loved Guitar Jac in the strangest places.

"Ju know jat Mr. Guitar is our favorite singer." So much for a French waiter. I walked over to the table and tapped Jac on the shoulder. He waved me away without looking up. I stood my ground. He turned. Surprised. "What in the hell are you doing here, Trevor. Carmelita, Trevor."

I looked astonished, "Carmelita! "

"You have trouble hearing, Carmelita." Guitar Jac did not look happy. We exchanged some banalities.

I asked Jac: "Could I see you in my office?"

"Your office," Guitar Jac looked confused. I pointed to the men's room. I wondered what he had learned at Stanford. We walked to the men's room. There were no urinals. Not my kind of place. It was the men's room, it was just hard to tell.

"Well, Trevor, let's have it. As you see I have a date. Something I notice that you eschew."

I always like it when Stanford grads used words like eschew. "We've got a problem. I am running into some dead ends on the salami." I proceeded to tell Guitar Jac about the Irvington Brothers, Mr. Laura and Carlos Santana. He didn't look perplexed. Jac was thinking.

"Come on, let's take a walk." He walked over kissed Carmelita and ordered another round of drinks. I couldn't believe it. He had a beautiful date and he wanted to take a walk. I followed Jac outside.

"What happened to your date?"

"She is the owner, cook and chief financial officer at the Foreign Cinema. She teaches a French cooking class that I have taken seven times at the Culinary Academy. I am also a, shall we say, a quiet investor in the business."

"You are also a pompous ass."

"Wealth, brains, sex appeal, it's not an easy task being me." Guitar Jac popped a breath mint in his mouth.

"Some guys will do anything to get laid." I smiled and considered taking a cooking class. We walked down Mission Street with its smell of burritos, the blaring of Mexican music and the colorful dress of the Latinos. There were also the poseurs who pretended to be Latino. So it made for a fun walk. After a couple of blocks, Guitar Jac turned into a seedy bar.

"I thought that Stanford education made you pick out better drinking spots." I looked around. Seedy bums. Smokers. Hippies. A few druggies. A couple of transvestites. Just another day in the Mission. What a clientele. The only weird thing is that there were no Hispanics. The Mexicans wouldn't come into the place. I looked around like I didn't belong.

Guitar Jac glowered: "For once Trevor shut up and listen. Follow me." We sat down and the blaring with the sounds of early Santana filled the bar. Nothing like the strains of "Black Magic Woman" to make you feel Chicano. As least they had that right. Now they had to import a couple of Chicanos to make the atmosphere work.

"Ola," Jac hollered. Ola I thought. What in the hell is going on? Just then a Mexican who looked like a Samoan linebacker showed up. Maybe he was really Junior Seau. He moved toward Guitar Jac and hugged him. I couldn't wait to have my backbone crushed.

"Trevor, meet the man."

"Hello," I said with an almost speechless intonation. The man was that a name?

Guitar Jac continued: "The man knows everything and he is going to set us straight." We ordered double Tequila chasers with our beer and sat down to get a headache. After two beers and four tequilas I was ready to go home. We told the man our story. He looked like a Greek philosopher. You know the guy with his hand on his face as he hunches over. Finally, the man spoke. Liquor will do that to you.

"Your problem is a simple one. It is not the salami you need to look at, it's the music business. Your client is not telling you the whole truth. You need to ask Ricardo Diaz some more questions." We shook hands and walked into the street. I was getting a headache. I didn't feel like I was talking with Socrates. Or even for that matter with someone informed. But I had to take the leads where I could get them.

"Where do we find Ricardo Diaz?" I asked.

"Follow me," Jac said and he started striding up the street. We walked over to Valencia Street to the Elbow Room and sure enough there was Ricardo Diaz. He had on a yellow sport coat, crème colored shoes, a yellow tie and a bad white shirt with black pants. Always the urban hipster.

"Ricardo are you auditioning for a job selling ice cream in Beverly Hills?" I laughed at my joke. No one else did. No one told me that Ricardo was a former golden gloves middleweight champion. As I watched him it was obvious that he was one without a sense of humor. He glowered at me.

"Asshole, I have said everything I have to say to you." Ricardo smiled. I knew that I had made a mistake.

"Sorry," I smiled. "My humblest apologies." At least I understood the meaning of asshole.

"You are a typical Anglo asshole," Ricardo smiled, "a typical Anglo asshole."

Repetition is the mother of invention. I think Frank Zappa said that. I said: "The redundancy in your language doesn't get you off the hook." He looked at me perplexed. I have some questions." Ricardo looked at me with disdain and got up and jumped onto the stage. It was Amateur Comedy Night. It turns out he was pretty funny. So we sat and listened to his half hour spiel. I laughed like hell. The guy was great. Finally, Ricardo came off the stage.

"Can we talk?" I asked. Guitar Jac had bought a pitcher of beer, a plate of chicken nachos and a tray of tacos. Ricardo smiled and looked at our table. He started eating the tacos.

"You laughed with genuine enthusiasm, I couldn't believe it," Ricardo smiled and put out his hand. I shook it. Brothers.

"Ju are funny," I intoned. He didn't laugh.

"Well Mr. Private Eye what are you after? I got a call that you were coming." I hoped the call was from the man. Ricardo was working in the chicken nachos. The tacos were history.

I ate the last taco. "The salami is still a problem. I need to find out why it has a connection to the death of the three Start Me Up drummers."

"Trevor, for a college educated guy you don't know shit. Who hired you?" Ricardo smiled. It seemed that was all he could do.

"That's confidential." I smiled. Nothing like using the other guys weapon.

"Think about it. Do you know anything about Elliott Shonestein?"

"Ya, he hired me and paid good money up front." Ricardo smiled. He knew that I was missing something. I knew that I was missing something.

"Did you check his credentials?" Ricardo asked. I looked at him in wonderment. Was it possible for a private investigator to check his client's credentials? I hadn't considered the possibility. I thought for a moment. He had a point.

" I didn't usually investigate my client, Ricardo."

"What?" he said in astonishment. "I'll draw you a picture, Trevor, you are a patsy." Ricardo got up and walked out. I wondered if Guitar Jac was suddenly mute. He got up and went over to the bar. Shots of tequila soon appeared at our table. He was nothing if consistent.

"Well, Trevor." Guitar Jac sipped his tequila. "I think we have a line on the killer. He is someone who has easy access backstage and is generally one who is a chameleon. We have missed the obvious." Stanford grads always talk in riddles.

"Ah, Jac, the great Spinks speaks." I hoped that it made more sense than Leon Spinks. "What do you mean that we have missed the obvious?"

Guitar Jac said: "We've got a problem. It's an inside job. We haven't found inside suspects."

"Really." I looked at Guitar Jac like he had lost his mind.

Guitar Jac knew he had a point. "You are just getting hip to the difficulties of our case."

"Jac, we have a list of possible suspects that is never ending. We need to tie the salami to someone."

"Trevor you haven't figured out what we need to do to solve this crime. You can start by looking at the key players. Start with the key figure."

"Ya, really. We need to talk to those who work around Elliott Shonestein." I volunteered. The three of us continued to drink shots of tequila. Ricardo and Guitar Jac looked like they were enjoying themselves. I looked like I was going to get sick. I couldn't get it out of my head. I wondered if Elliott Shonestein was the key. Maybe I was the patsy. I was too busy to think clearly. We were having a great time. Suddenly things got better. Women will do that to you.

A beautiful young girl came up to the table. "Hello, I'm Pam Wong." She smiled. We all smiled. There was silence. "Aren't you Trevor Blake?"

"Yes, I am Trevor Blake III at your service." I smiled. We all smiled. Famous private eyes always attract beautiful women.

"Well, here's my phone number." She handed me a card it read 925-555-6439, I couldn't believe my good fortune. My sex life was looking up. Maybe I was really a private eye. Had to get a hat and a trench coat. I also had to drink less, I was getting sick. She vanished. I wonder what the old time private eyes would do. I filed Pam Wong's card in my to date file. It was the only card there.

We left the Elbow Room, I felt like I'd had my fill of Mexican food, tequila, beer and Carlos Santana look a likes. I wondered home with the notion of calling up a beautiful Asian lady. Pam Wong, what a nice name.

Chapter 8
DON GINO AT THE PANCAKE HOUSE AND THE SEARCH FOR MICK JAGGER

I drove through the Mission up to the Castro and down Divisidero Street and made a left to my humble office on Haight Street. I wandered up the stairs to find the door ajar. I pulled out my pepper spray. I walked in and four of Don Gino's Samoans almost fell on the floor laughing.

"Hey man you gonna spray us." One Samoan said, as he continued to laugh.

I put it away. "To what do I owe this dubious pleasure?"

"The boss wants to see you."

"Guys, it's two thirty in the morning." Each one grabbed me by the arm and I was in the limo. An old limo from the 1960s, it made me feel at home. Somehow I knew that I was on my way to see Don Gino. We arrived at the International House of Pancakes on Van Ness Avenue. I bet that John Giotti and the boys didn't hang out as places like this in New York. Don Gino was in the back with the breakfast special. Eggs sunny side up, two sausage, two bacon, two hot cakes and a side of fried potatoes. I think he had just passed his cholesterol test. I smiled. What else could I do? I couldn't call the Don a cheapskate for ordering the early breakfast special.

"My boy, my boy," Don Gino exclaimed as a piece of sausage hung from his lip. A red suit replaced his standard issue purple suit. Consistency is part of being a good Godfather. His assistant, the horrible midget, smiled and cracked his knuckles. He also had on a red suit. Midget style. Actually he wasn't a midget but a five feet tall gnome who looked like one. Then I remembered his martial arts skills. Best not to piss off the midget. Silence was the prevailing mood. I looked at each of them. There was dead silence. So I broke the tension.

"Va Bene," I cried out in my accented Italian.

"Sit, Trevor, sit."

I felt like I was being treated like the dog. Then again maybe I asked for such treatment. The minute I sat down a fresh breakfast special was placed in front of me. After the beer, the tequila, the tacos and the huge plate of nachos, I wasn't hungry. I ate. No sense pissing off a don.

"Do you wonder Trevor why you are here?" Dino Gino scratched his nose.

"It's the breakfast special Don Gino, I never miss it. The International House of Pancakes is my favorite." I hoped that I had lied convincingly. I looked at my runny eggs and hoped that I didn't throw up.

"We have a problem. It seems your esteemed client, that Jew you work for is in the rackets." Don Gino never had a sense of propriety. Political correctness was not in his vocabulary.

"Am I missing something, Don Gino?"

"As usual Trevor you are missing all of it. The word on the street is that our good friend, Elliott Shonestein is making a fool of you."

I was beginning to see the picture, what the picture actually was I had no clue. "I'm looking into it, Don Gino." The Samoans were hovering over my shoulder. Nothing like four nasty Samoans to make you feel uncomfortable. I almost wanted garlic breath one and two back. I hoped that I had given the right answers. We stared in silence. The meeting was not going well.

"You're a P.I. Trevor, who needs to look beneath the surface," Don Gino paused and lit a cigar. I wasn't going to tell him that you can't smoke in any California eating establishment. No one else imparted that knowledge and Dino Gino wistfully blew smoke toward the ceiling. I suspected the health Nazis would burst through the door and arrest him. The waitress brought Don Gino an ashtray. He continued: "I am going to increase your retainer on this case, here is another $5000." Now I paused. I hadn't found out anything. I had taken money from Elliott Shonestein and now money twice from Don Gino. I had to confess to Don Gino my transgressions.

I looked fearful and spoke: "Now I have multiple clients for the same case. Am I right to assume that is a conflict of interest?"

Don Gino scowled: "You are looking into what I call a peripheral matter. It is sensitive." Don Gino ground out his cigar. He took a long hit from his coffee, drank half a glass of orange juice and continued: "Your task is simple. I want you to discretely find out who killed the Start Me Up drummers."

"I think you have got this wrong. The police are looking into the murder. They have concluded there is no evidence of foul play." I paused and drank some coffee.

"Trevor, Trevor, there is more here than meets the eye."

"So what am I looking for?" The private eye usually finds out what he is looking for. Not in my case.

"Trevor I do have some leads." He took out a long knife and cut the end off a new cigar. I wondered if that was all the knife did. He continued: "I have an interest in should we say the box office receipts of some of the lesser known rock concerts."

"You mean you are the guy behind the tribute bands?" I was missing a lot. Somehow it was coming together.

"Bingo, Trevor, once again you amaze me."

I felt like kicking his ass. As I looked at the Samoans and the midget, I reconsidered. "Let me get this straight. All I need to do is to find out where the receipts are going or what is happening to the money?"

"Remember Woodward and Bernstein during Watergate, follow the money." Don Gino waved his hand and two waitresses with red hair brought more coffee. The gangster of the week getting good service.

I stood up. "I'll see you in a week, Don Gino." I threw five dollars on the table. The midget picked it up and shoved it in my shirt pocket. The look on his face suggested that he hoped to shove it somewhere else. He was about the right size to do it. I walked out of the International House of Pancakes and onto Lombard Street. The sun was coming up. I could see the edge of the Golden Gate Bridge. Birds were singing. Coffee and pastry odors punctuated the air. The only bad smells were the ones I left at Don Gino's table. Now I was confused. I had a case that paid me more money than I ever suspected. I seemed to be working for everyone who might be the murderer. After driving back to my Chestnut Street adobe, I mentally filed away everything I knew. I still didn't have a clue.

I woke up the next morning. Looking at the clock it read one o'clock. I guess that I missed lunch. Looking in the refrigerator I noticed mayonnaise and taco shells, a quart of milk, one month past the expiration date and a box of fig newton's. Not exactly the breakfast of champions. Somewhere in the back of the refrigerator there was a subway sandwich. I threw it away. After I dressed, I headed out for a donut. I drove up to the Haight and parked at a meter. A miracle. After feeing the meter three dollars, I was ready for coffee and donuts. The donut shop was healthier than my refrigerator. Emilio's Donut Shop is exciting. You have druggies, hookers, cops, lawyers, students, tourists and the homeless all at once. It was hard to tell who was who.

"Bossee," Emilio shouted. He put down a chocolate covered donut and a cup of decaf coffee. Since Emilio arrived from Vietnam he had acquired an MA in Asian studies from San Francisco State. He was a novelist but made the same amount of money as Dominic Stansberry. So he bought a donut shop. He did very well with his tourist friendly accent. He loved to play to stereotypes. So I always got the greeting "bossee." It was annoying.

As I sat eating my donut I contemplated my life. It seemed in my early 40s I already had blood pressure problems. It was probably due to my life style. It couldn't be the daily habit of two donuts. I bet that Shell Scott never had those concerns. Then I remembered that Shell was a fictional detective created by Richard S. Prather. He was thirty and in more than thirty years of exciting books he had never aged one day. He had a crew cut, muscles and liked the chicks. He also had a Hollywood apartment. He paid fifty dollars a month. So it was an old book. My thought was that Shell Scott would be unemployed today. He had the wrong hair, incorrect clothes and a bad line with the ladies. My thoughts were interrupted. Emilio was ready to talk.

"Somebody lookee for you this morneeing," Emilio smiled. "Girlee is cuteee." He loved to talk improperly. After three novels he was an underground cult favorite. Emilio's latest novel was about Annabel Chong, a Chinese girl at UCLA, who bedded 600 guys to get into the Guinness Book of World Records. The reviews on Emilio's book, Annabel, My Annabel, were generally negative as Chong bedded 70 guys 250 times. Some didn't wear condoms. I was surprised the new book was literate and exciting.

Emilio had a raw intelligence. No one was around, so he talked to me normally. A relief. "Some good looking girl come in, you know the kind with big ones." His background in Vietnam was one where he hid his thoughts from the Communist government. He continued to do that with his friends. Someone sat next to him. That changed his conversation. "Girlee, me no like her. Too much makeup and a cunning look. She looked and acted like a hooker."

"Political correctness, Emilio, learn it," I exclaimed. "She is a person not a girlee.

"She leave a cardee." He walked into the back room. A few minutes later I was looking at Chastain Johnson's card. I had forgotten about her, but I remembered her body. Talk about being politically incorrect. The card shocked me. It read Federal Bureau of Investigation, 550 Golden Gate Avenue, San Francisco, Ca. I knew that I was a sex symbol but sleeping with the FBI was not one of my main objectives in life. Maybe I was a real sex symbol. Then maybe Chastain was simply horny. Probably the later.

"Thanks Emilio." I wondered outside holding my coffee cup. I left the donut half eaten. Some things don't add up. This case was my toughest one. Then I remembered it was also my first real case. The surprises that had come my way created problems. Was I really a detective? I guess so. It was time to do some more detecting. What was Chastain Johnson's interest in me? I came to believe that it wasn't going to bed. But, then again, maybe I underestimated myself. It was time to do some female detecting. I drove down Haight Street to Fillmore and turned left and then I turned right on Geary and drove past the Fillmore Auditorium. With bands like the White Stripes playing there I felt like a dinosaur. Only because I was one.

I was looking for someone inside the music business. That made everyone but Don Gino a suspect.

Chapter 9
ENTER CHASTAIN JOHNSON

I drove downtown. After parking the car I had another cup of coffee and looked at my notes. Then it was off to see The FBI. At 550 Golden Gate I looked up at the twenty-story building, which housed an entire floor reserved for the local FBI. For San Francisco it was a modern building. After taking the elevator to the 15th floor I asked for someone to help me. I had a story to tell. After sitting for half an hour a tall, dark haired young woman who looked like a terrorist came out and beckoned me to a small room. I went in and sat down. The door opened and in walked Chastain Johnson. I looked in disbelief. A night at Harrington's and a roll in the hay and here I was looking at her. She showed me her FBI badge. She was wearing a gun. She was beautiful. Now was not the time to remind her of her good looks.

"Hello, Chastain, you were on my list to call."

"Shut up," she smiled. Chastain sat down, opened a manila folder and lit a cigarette. I thought FBI people didn't smoke. She looked like she wanted to speak. Anger was in her face. Maybe I wasn't so good in bed. The silence was deafening. She was reading. I took out a nail clip and began to cut my small pinkie finger. Not exactly the behavior of a macho man. Then I looked at them and remembered that I was a habitual nail biter. I had no nails.

"Trevor, let me introduce myself."

"No need, I do remember you." I smiled. She didn't.

"I'm a special agent in the white collar fraud division. My specialty is money laundering, drugs and of course murder."

"Are you looking into the salami poisonings?" I asked. I knew that this would throw her.

"You mean your talk with Joe Irvington, Miss Double D's who cut you salami while you drooled on her and then there was the would be Carlos Santana." She smiled. "We have been following you. You can't seem to find your asshole."

"Well then you know I haven't gotten laid lately." I smiled.

"You got lucky, Trevor, it won't happen again."

I was nervous, she knew more than I thought. "I think we have to get on the same page, Chastain. I mean on the same murder page."

"I will show you mine, if you show me yours first," she said. A smile came over her face. She had to quit smiling, it was making me nervous, and her big breasts didn't help my concentration.

We sat and talked at length about the case. It was more complicated than I imagined. I was horny looking at Chastain. She had a figure that was a knockout. I overlooked the excessively muscular body. At least the muscles were all in all the right places. Her cigarette breath was another matter. I hadn't noticed this the night that I picked her up. I wondered why she had gone to bed with me. Was she on the case? I needed some answers.

"I think we need to get some things straight," I said.

"Like how bad you are in bed." She smiled. I hated that. We weren't getting anywhere. What would my detective idols do? I imagined that Kinky Freidman would light a cigar. Shell Scott would stroke a beautiful babe. Mike Hammer would simply beat the hell out of her. Red Diamond would pursue the killer in his cab. Elvis Cole would bring Joe Pike along to beat up the bad guys. These weren't my options. I had no options. Guitar Jac was nowhere to be found and he had no idea what was going on. He was also probably drinking a cappuccino. Shell Scott wouldn't be caught dead with a cappuccino.

She said: "Can we quit the verbal sparing." I didn't smile. Chastain continued: "Ok, here's the story. I have been following you. The reason is a simple one. Every one of your clients, if you haven't picked up any new ones, is a suspect in the Start Me Up murders."

"What, murders." I asked. "Since when is poisoning a murder. And how does the FBI get involved in this?" It was now my turn to smile.

"Trevor, did you take anything in college which remotely resembles real life?"

I didn't, what could I say. Silence was the key I glowered. She stared. "My heart is broken," I continued. "Not only did I think I was good in bed but I did learn a little bit from my history courses and at Stanford Law." I said "Stanford Law" with a slow cadence. Throw law school at them if all else fails.

"Stanford Law," she smiled. "Your class graduated 191 students and you were 190." She laughed.

It was my turn. "What do they call the last person to graduate from Stanford Law?" I asked the question and she looked perplexed.

Tell me, asshole."

"Lawyer." Now it was my turn to smile. I said: "Shouldn't we talk about the case? We needn't say anything more about you in bed."

Not a bad idea, I thought. We spent the next hour, as some guy brought us coffee and I noted that the FBI was politically correct, the men continually brought fresh coffee as we discussed the case. I was beginning to see that I had stepped into deep dodo. Is there any other kind? After we talked, I left Chastain's office more confused. I tried to look like a serious private eye. Mike Hammer leaving the scene of an investigation. Red Diamond going to the cab and driving to the bad guys house and beating the hell out of him. The problem was that I didn't know where the bad guy lived or who he was. I needed to buy a detective hat and maybe a trench coat. I walked out onto Golden Gate Avenue and saw a familiar sign, it read, Ratskeller. It was time for a drink. Maybe some German food. Maybe a new woman. Maybe getting my mind on the case. Or better yet off the case.

In the old days, the Ratskeller was full of young girls. I hadn't been there for almost twenty years. I walked in and saw a bunch of old guys, my age, playing cards, I guessed times had changed. Maybe forty was old. The long wooden bar, brought around the horn during the California Gold Rush, was still intact. I walked up for a drink. The Chinese bartender walked over. "What'll it be, Mac?" I guess that was better than asshole. I ordered a glass of Merlot and some chicken wings. Sitting at the bar and eating the honey baked wings brought me back to earth. That ended quickly. A tug on my arm caused me to turn around. Chastain Johnson stood smiling.

"You can't take advantage of me." I said.

"This is business, asshole."

That word made me feel better. My last asshole of the day. Chastain explained that she had followed me to the Ratskeller. Maybe she wanted to get laid. Calling me asshole wasn't a way to get into my pants.

"Well, let's see," I said. "We have a manila folder, a case and no leads. I do have some ideas."

"We aren't interested in your dumb ass ideas. Just do as I say."

She sounded like my ex-wife. Attila the Hun or Marilyn as she was known. My ex-wife was a Russian who came to this country as a sweet young girl. Together with her brother and sister in law she built a real estate empire. She also finished law school and went to work for a high powered Montgomery Street firm. Her brother and sister in law, Bennie and Bertie, were retired. They were millionaires who bought their clothes at Mervyns. They also liked to go camping. They called it life with the real people. They were my landlords. Their twelve rentals made them slumlords. Rich ones. When my ex-wife left law school, she became a tenacious attorney for the district attorney. She didn't become an instant millionaire, so she became the nastiest attorney in San Francisco. I came home one day as she was throwing my surf records into the garbage. Jon and the Nightriders was my favorite surf band. Their record was broken and twelve Jan and Dean's lay with ripped covers. My Al Casey's 45's were broken. Divorce followed.

I became the ex-husband. I had to keep these memories of my past life out of my subconscious. So Chastain suddenly looked like the wicked witch of the west. She could be Marilyn. Or at least a version of my ex wife. I wasn't sure which one was worse.

I said: "Elaborate." At times I am succinct.

"We need you to keep investigating. I am going to assign another agent as a tail."

"Make it a piece of tail." I smiled. She didn't. We talked for another hour. I still love to be seen with a good-looking young lady. She told me she would shoot me if I called her a girl. Even one who said I was the worst lay in San Francisco. We walked out together. The next night I was once again sitting at the Ratskeller. A young woman walked up to me. Asked me to buy her a drink. "Only if you're not an FBI agent. She told me that she was a secretary for a rental car firm.

"I can get you a discount," she stated.

I hoped that I didn't have to be good in bed for the discount. We talked and she was in fact a rental car secretary. "Why are you here with me," I asked.

"Simple, you left here with the best looking girl in the place last night. So you have to be good in bed." We left and had a nice night. I walked slowly out of her Pine Street apartment the next morning. I hoped that I was good in bed. Now it was time to get back to the case. Once again I was a bachelor who conquered the young girls. It was a great feeling. Maybe I would see Chastain again. Then maybe that was a bad idea.

Chapter 10
BACK IN THE HAIGHT AND THE MIDGET ARRIVES

My car was parked on Pine Street and I needed to get to work. I drove up California Street turned left on Divisadero and then right onto Haight. It was 8:30 in the morning as I wandered into Emilio's Donut Shop. I sat down with a French cruller, a decaf coffee and began making notes. I used up ten napkins. I couldn't figure out where I was going or what was happening. I needed help. I also needed to sort the napkins. I had almost a hundred of them for this case alone. I also needed time to think. I also needed to get laid. I wasn't Shell Scott. I looked out on Haight Street, a city water truck sprayed the street. The sun caused the water to glisten off the payment. A rainbow rose over Ben and Jerry's. They would probably name an ice cream for it.

"Donut noee good for you," Emilio said.

"Think about it, Emilio, a donut shop. You're Vietnamese and we are in the Haight. None of this makes sense. You have a degree in literature. Nothing makes sense."

"I'm the only donut shop in the Haight, Trevor, I get a subsidy of $50,000 a year for it." When it came to money Emilio spoke perfect English. Emilio continued: "I am a minority businessman. I am also a wealthy man. So me all right. Me no speakeee English." I frowned. I couldn't take much more of Emilio's humor. Or lack of it. He spoke and wrote English better than I did.

"The federal and state governments that subsidize you might not approve of you fracturing the language." I continued: "Especially when they find out that a Vietnamese mercenary owns it."

Emilio said: "Look out front, Trevor, what do you see?" I knew it was something serious he was speaking in perfect English.

The only car on the street was a gold Lexus. It was Emilio's. It was about to be sprayed by a street sweeping truck. I smiled.

Two tourists wearing T-shirts that read "Jerry Garcia Lives" walked in and sat down. "I go move my car," Emilio said. "Lots of donuts buy nice car." I got up and served the tourists donuts and coffee. Emilio ran out the door, started his car and gunned the engine. A second later the car was flying into a side street. Then Emilio jogged back behind the counter.

"Let me guess, a gift to your self."

Emilio smiled: "You got it."

I knew that from time to time, Emilio took on should we say side jobs. He was a cat burglar. He offered protection to people. He was what one might call a security consultant. He also stole from common criminals and returned the goods to society people. That is after they collected on the insurance. A cat burglar for hire. Once he burglarized a safe in a house next to Danielle Steele and then broke into her house and took all her first editions. He doesn't have level literary tastes. He remarked that he would rob her but couldn't stand to read her books.

At night he could sneak in and rob select clientele. Maybe a dowager on Nob Hill had missing jewelry. Emilio's specialty was jewelry. The police visited him regularly. They never came close to catching him. I waved goodbye and crossed the street to my office.

As I climbed the stairs I smelled food. It was ten in the morning. I saw my door ajar. I was prepared to take out my gun. Then I remembered that I didn't carry a gun. I peeked into my office and saw a table of food set up next to my desk. I walked in and there stood a midget in a cooking uniform. I stood in the door with my mouth open.

"Hello, I'm Chef Fred."

I looked shocked. "Chef Fred?" I guess I stammered.

"Yes, I'm the executive Chef for the Foreign Cinema."

"I know it, I was there recently."

"Yes," Chef Fred remarked "with Mister Jac. He is a culinary genius." Chef Fred then went into great detail on the cavernous restaurant that featured a foreign movie along with some of San Francisco's best French food. The table set up in my office had abundant hors d'ouvres and a trio of burners kept a shrimp, a lobster and a chicken side dish hot. It smelled good. It was inviting. But why?

"You don't mind if I ask what is going on?"

"No, No." Chef Fred smiled.

I hated people who used double negatives. "Well explain."

"Sit Trevor and eat and I will tell you the story." Why not, I thought. It beats donuts. I took a plate and filled it.

Chef Fred pulled a small bottle out of a case. "No Fred, no alcohol, it's almost 11 in the morning.".

He looked bewildered. "It's pure French apple juice. The sparkling kind."

"I certainly wouldn't want impure French juice."

Chef Fred continued: "I have a side job. It is a lucrative one. I prepare food for the larger rock concerts. It is all very exclusive backstage stuff."

I hated people who used words like stuff, not to mention exclusive. "Is there a point, Chef Fred?"

"The point is that I work for Elliott Shonestein and I'm convinced that he was behind the Start Me Up murders, the startling death of the drummers is only the beginning."

"Well, Chef Fred, why don't you just solve this little crime for me." I smiled. I liked being a smart ass. "Elliott is my client, why would he hire me to find his killer. When he is the killer. It doesn't make sense. Unless of course I am the worst private eye since Red Diamond." I shouldn't have said all that, there may have been an element of truth in it.

"Tell me what you see, Trevor," Chef Fred stirred a strange looking concoction.

"I have talked to the police at least six times since the death of the Charlie Watts look-alikes. I have interviewed the illustrious Don Gino." Nothing came of any of this."

Chef Fred looked anxious and spoke nervously. "The police have talked to me six times, I'm the chief suspect. I was the sous chef during all the killings. I am connected."

"What is a sous chef?" I hated to show my ignorance.

"It is the second in command." He lit a cigarette. Bad health habits were everywhere.

"Why are you telling me this?" I was lost in the case. No clues.

"I want to hire you to find who set me up and framed me for killing the drummers." I looked at Chef Fred in astonishment. "I want to hire you to find out why and how I killed the drummers." He smiled. "I really didn't kill them."

"You would be my third client, but what the hell, there is no conflict of interest."

"I know, I know all about your other clients, I'm about to take a fall for a crime I didn't commit."

"Tell me more, Chef Fred." I smiled.

"I keep having a dream that I killed the drummers. Why is that?" Chef Fred looked frightened.

"I'm a private eye, not a shrink."

"You know everything about the case." He looked nervous and guilty.

I said: "You're the killer? I think that you need a psychiatrist not a P. I." I looked at him like he was nuts. He smiled. He dished up a fresh piece of the lobster and poured a light colored sauce over it. I ate it. A man needs nutrition when he thinks. I was not sure that I could take on another client. Particularly one who thinks he committed the murders. Then in the next breath says he's innocent. It seemed like everyone involved in this little crime was hiring me to find the killer. But the killer hiring me to find the killer was a little too much. What would Shell Scott do? Probably bed the girl next door. The only problem was that my next-door neighbor was a Vietnamese rice merchant. He was five fee tall and seventy years old. Not my type.

"I don't work for midgets. Not even ones who are killers." I looked at Fred Chef like he just got out of the nut house.

"Vertically challenged is how I prefer to bill myself. Besides I have the evidence that you need to uncover the real criminal." I looked at all four feet plus of Chef Fred and decided that he had a story to tell.

I listened. "What evidence?"

"It seems that your employer Mr. Shonestein is up to his elbows in debt to some North Beach gamblers. You known gumbas, mafia types. He's been playing cards and dice games. He owes these sleazy mobsters over $500,000. Look at his insurance policies. They have paid off. The death of each drummer brought Shonestein a half a million dollars. He needed that money to stay out of the gumbas hands. Then he loses the money again to those Italian criminals in North Beach."

Chef Fred is not politically correct. I asked: "What did the loan sharks look like?" I remembered garlic breath 1 and 2 and could sympathize with Shonestein's need to pay the gambling debts.

"You wouldn't believe it, the head one looks like Brian Jones that dead guitarist for the Rolling Stones."

Now things were getting complicated. "The police, the insurance companies, haven't they investigated. Loan sharking is illegal." Suddenly

I didn't feel like a private eye, I should have known all this or at least uncovered it.

"Ah, Trevor, you are naïve."

"What have the police implied?" I was getting frustrated.

"The police believe that it is simply a matter of poor salami. The only problem is that I am a salami junkie. I stole some of it. I ate at least a pound of the salami after I delivered it backstage. When I hire out for special catering, I always bring a salami dish. So I am the suspect." Chef Fred continued: "So whomever killed the drummers did it in the dressing room. Elliott Shonestein is my guess."

I am always suspicious of people who used the word "whomever." Too much education. All this made sense. "But why hire me?"

"My reputation, Trevor. It has declined. A French Chef who can't even serve salami without killing someone will never get a job."

A French Chef who serves salami should be banned from cooking, " I smiled always the clever P. I. Chef Fred smiled. He knew I was joking as I dished up my third plate of lobster.

"What am I to do Trevor?" I looked at the guy and felt sorry for him.

I thought that the Doggie Diner could use a new cook. Then I remembered that the Doggie Diner had gone out of business. As I thought, Chef Fred placed $5000 on my desk. I could be bought. No doubt about it. Now I had collected over thirty thousand dollars and still had no clue about who was killing the Start Me Up drummers. I was now representing three clients looking for the same killer. One of my clients claimed to be the killer.

"Ok, Chef Fred, you have a P. I." I wrote out a contract, he signed it, we shook hands, and he packed up the food but left behind the shrimp and chicken. I sat and reflected as I ate the rest of the chicken. I still had no clue. I had to find a common thread in the case. That is as soon as I picked the chicken from between my teeth. I made some notes on napkins, and then I made some more notes. The napkins were spilling over the desk. I had research but no club what I was doing. I did have a lot of napkins.

So I rearranged my napkins. I jotted down the names and the motives of all the suspects. It was time for lunch. I wasn't hungry but a coffee would do. I walked down Haight Street to Amoeba Records and picked up the latest Rolling Stones CD. Maybe there was a hint in the music. If not, I would enjoy listening to it. I picked up a free copy of the Guardian and the SF News. I could read the porno ads if I got bored.

I walked over to the Rock N Bowl Coffee Shop and ordered a café mocha. I sat in the corner and began the process of sorting out my clues. I was after all a P. I. It was time to find a suspect. Maybe I was working for all the suspects. I wasn't sure. It was time to make sense out of this puzzle.

The napkins yielded some clues. The poisonings were all done backstage, the list of culprits was small as Chef Fred had made sure the salami didn't contain poison. If it did, he was dead. Last time I looked he was alive and plunking money down on my desk. Maybe he was the killer and hiding it. I didn't think so. The killer usually didn't hire a private eye to find him. Elliott Shonestein was not a good guess. He was making too much money. But then again there were the insurance policies. Maybe he did it to collect on the drummers to pay his gambling debts. That seemed unlikely. The police and the insurance investigators would have him busted in no time. So the search for the killer continued. I felt like I was in a locked room mystery. What would John Dickson Carr do? The English detectives all had better luck on obtuse cases. I pulled out a Michael Innes book that I carried and read about Inspector John Appleby. Maybe I should get a pipe and become a little wiser. Maybe I should concentrate upon the case. I looked up and there stood Chastain Johnson.

"Hello cutie." She smiled at me and licked her lips. Now I was really confused. Maybe she wanted a bad lay.

I never thought of myself as a cutie. But a man had to get what he could. "Chastain, as I live and breath. Following me"

"As a matter of fact we need to talk. Not here." She walked out and I followed like a puppy dog. We walked down Haight to my office. We climbed the stairs.

"Jesus, Trevor, do you cook your lunch here?"

"No, it's a long story."

"Tell me," she smiled

It was the smile that always disarmed me. So I wove the story of Chef Fred into the conversation. She smiled.

"Chef Fred is why I'm here." Now she had my attention.

"You see, Trevor, may I be so formal and call the great detective by his first name?"

I knew sarcasm when I heard it. "Go on," I said without conviction.

"It seems like you have been hired by every major suspect in the poisoning of the Start Me Up band. Not a good omen." She smiled. I hated that it showed her superiority. Not to mention great looking teeth. She also showed her legs and I appreciated looking at the long legs and the rest of her. Being politically correct was difficult.

"So!" I had no clue where this conversation was going.

"So!" she smiled again. "We have to bring you aboard on the case. Sort of."

"I guess I am not ready to enroll in rocket science school, what case?"

Chastain lit a cigarette. I was against FBI agents smoking. I made an exception for her. "Let me start from the beginning. It seems that Elliott Shonestein or some one close to him is responsible for some of the mayhem. Then again anyone including Chef Fred, Joe Irvington, the Carlos Santana look a like and even the purple Mafia boss Don Gino could be the killer. We are working the case with the DEA because the salami comes from Vietnam along with a sizeable cache of drugs. What would the mafia think."

"Salami from Vietnam?" I didn't have to look confused. I was. "What do you mean?"

"It's bootleg Salami."

"Come on, Chastain, Salami from Vietnam. Bootleg as in illegal."

"Read my lips, Trevor, we have a giant conspiracy that doesn't make sense." She threw her cigarette on my floor and snubbed it out with her shoe. Remind me to give her a breath mint. "Your buddy Emilio may be involved in salami smuggling."

"Correct me if I sound a bit lame, Chastain. Salami smuggling from Vietnam. I don't think it's possible. " I didn't smile.

"You're the key to the case, Trevor."

"What's my role?"

"I was hoping you would get around to that. We need you to do as little as possible to solve the case. It seems everyone involved wants you in the loop. We are going to follow you everywhere.

Who is we, Chastain."

"The FBI you moron."

"Sorry, but client privilege prevails." I smiled.

"Let's make a deal," she scratched her leg. I looked too long at her and she poked me.

"What kind of deal?"

"We will lead you to the two suspects and your clients must get an updated report on your progress. All the information will come from the FBI. You don't have to do a thing." This sounded like what I was doing for money. I looked pensive.

I smiled: "What's in it for me?"

"You will make no progress. So what we tell them is complete fiction with some real facts to throw them off the track. We will leak information to you. Then we will do our best to make sure that this material leads the killer to make a mistake. And above all no Guitar Jac. He is too intelligent and could solve the case."

I wasn't sure whether to laugh or cry. I believe that I had just been insulted. Big time. "I have a responsibility to my clients." I looked unhappy. "I have some thoughts on this case, would you like to hear them."

"No." Chastain raised her leg. It did distract me. She shifted in the chair and a breast bounded. It was a nice touch. Then she lit a cigarette. That was not a nice touch.

"Just read our reports and fill in your clients. I don't want you thinking or analyzing." She smiled. She licked her lips. Another means of disarming me.

"You think my job is to be an incompetent asshole." I didn't smile.

"I think you are more than qualified for that position." She smiled. I was getting to like her smile less and less. "Just continue to solve it the way that you have, Trevor. If you find anything let us know." She stuck one of her cards in my belt buckle looked at my fly, smiled and left. Now I really needed to analyze the smile.

I walked to my apartment. I was more in a fog than ever before. It was time to figure out the angles. I took the stairs up to my second story apartment. Real detectives didn't ride the elevator. Then again I remembered I didn't have an elevator. I opened the door to my apartment, I was depressed. I sat down and thought.

Chapter 11
A DETECTIVE SOLVING THE MYSTERY

I sat in my apartment and drank a couple beers, I cooked some lasagna and made a spinach salad. I poured myself a glass of Sonoma Chardonnay, I pulled out a Shell Scott book. Richard Prather was my favorite writer. His hero, Shell Scott, had never aged past thirty, he had babes and he could beat the hell out of the next man. After about an hour of reading about Shell Scott's life, I had to remind myself he was a fictional character. I was feeling like one myself. I had heard from other P. I.'s that whenever a detective really gets into a case, he discovers a lot about himself. I was coming to the conclusion that I should seek another line of work. So, to save face, it was time for some real detecting.

I walked out of the apartment and retrieved my car from the street. Pigeon do do was all over the black Ford Probe that I drove. Every other P. I. drove a Mercedes or a BMW. But they solved cases. They were paid huge fees. They led glamorous lives. I knew there was one place to solve the crime. The San Francisco Public Library. I drove down town and parked across the street from City Hall. The walk over to the library was a short one. I was deep in thought. Suddenly someone lurched into me.

"Hello, asshole. Or should I say Trevor the turd?" It was none other than Detective Sgt. Richard Sanchez of the San Francisco Police Department. I wondered what was a Detective Sgt? Maybe higher than a real Sgt. Or maybe lower. He sometimes called himself Ricardo, it was a nice touch meant for the ladies. "Where's the spade?" This was Sanchez's way of inquiring about Guitar Jac. It seems that years ago Sanchez was a budding baseball star at the University of California, Berkeley. He faced Guitar Jac in a crucial Pac 10 game with major league scouts in the stands and Jac struck him out three times. That was the end of his professional baseball aspirations. Although he was the youngest detective in the history of the SFPD, their best softball player and their most effective investigator, he had never forgotten the humiliation of not being signed to a professional baseball contract. When Guitar Jac played well at the professional game and then walked away from it, Sanchez never forgave him. Despite his surly attitude, Sanchez did me favors. We had what they call a love hate relationship.

"Richard, what's up?" I am good at small talk. I smiled. Sanchez hated it. He liked being called Detective Sanchez.

"Well, Trevor the turd." Sanchez didn't smile. He loved to make fun of my high social class standing. "I have some information for you. As I have watched you with the Start Me Up band investigation, you don't have a clue. Follow the money."

"You're going to have to stand in line, everyone else thinks the same thing." He was the second person to tell me to follow the money. Maybe I should listen.

I looked at Sanchez. He dressed like the Miami Vice cops and tried to talk like Don Johnson. He looked more like Cheech Marin.

"If I am bungling this so badly, Richard, why am I getting clues?"

"That broad, Chastain, is in our way."

"Our way," I answered with a puzzled look. "The FBI is in your way?"

"Yes, I am working this case with the California Department of Meat Purification."

"May I ask why?"

"Sure, it's simple. We have reason to believe that not only is smuggled salami being sold but that the state of California is not receiving the proper taxes." I didn't tell Sanchez that the salami was smuggled in from Vietnam.

"Ok Richard. Is this clue for me." I laughed so he could see my skepticism.

"Trevor, do I need to spell it out. Follow the money." He liked to repeat himself. The phrase sounded to me just the way Hal Holbrook uttered it in the film, All the President's Men. I always thought that I had the instincts to be a cracker jack reporter. So it was time to dissect the case.

"I need to find some clues in the archives. Solid leads." Sanchez looked bored. The library wasn't his thing. He left. I was in a fog. I walked down to the library archives. The second floor is filled with microfilm. I took the index for local newspapers and began reading the stories on the Start Me Up Band. There wasn't much. A few oblique references to the cover band concept. A couple of long articles on all the money they generated. There were half a dozen stories about replacement drummers. Nothing about the salami. No mention of Joe Irvington. Fred the Chef was nowhere in the stories. I flipped through the entertainment section and then I glanced briefly at the ads for musicians. There it was. The San Francisco Chronicle had a strange ad. "START ME UP! PICK UP PACKAGE. There was a post office box listed and a phone number 415-555-1234. Post Office Box 3083 was located in Fremont, California. It was time to detect. So I drove over the Bay Bridge, down highway 880 and turned off at Stephenson Boulevard. After inquiring at the main post office I found that P. O. Box 3083 was across from South Bay Community College. I had worked for a year at South Bay Community College and knew everyone in the history department.

I worked for Professor L. Stumpy Kohl. He was a pompous ass from Texas. He had been a preacher but ran off with a fourteen-year-old girl. Then he ran off with a twenty-year-old girl. Then he bedded every eighteen-year-old co-eds. Then he changed his name from Lester to L. He was an asshole typical of academic life.. It was a faint memory and a bad one. Fremont is the worst of suburbs. Not only was this suburban oasis totally Anglo Saxon. It is incredibly boring. There are more white people per square foot in Fremont than any city in America. I am a diversity guy. It is more fun. White girls all the time are boring.

I waited for two days in a coffee shop adjacent to the Post Office. Finally, a familiar figure opened up PO Box 3083. It was Sheldon Foreskin. My onetime colleague at South Bay Community College. I was shocked. What was he doing on the case? Had the Start Me Up Band somehow entered his life. I was more confused than ever.

I caught him in the parking lot. "Sheldon, how's it going?"

"Oh, hello," he said in a diffident voice. He had on a suit. It came complete with Professor vest and he was smoking a pipe. He was a loser without a PhD. He had never written anything in his life and so he was fired at three universities. South Bay Community College was the end of the line. He was the dean of social science and with his buddy, L. Stumpy Kohl, they fired anyone who wrote or taught well. So much for the democracy of the community college. The gossip around campus was that his 200-pound Jewish wife hadn't uncrossed her legs in thirty years. He was bitter and combative. Not abut his wife, he breathed a sigh of relief. The idea of her uncrossing her legs frightened him. After looking at his wife I thought that it was a good thing her legs stayed crossed. She had dyed her grey hair a red tone, and she looked like Paul McCartney in drag.

"This is a delicate matter, Sheldon, but I need to know what your connection is to the Start Me Up Band."

He looked confused. "The Start Me Up Band."

"Yes." I looked angry.

"It's none of your business."

"Ok Sheldon. We'll let Detective Sanchez decide that." I turned to leave.

"Wait," he said.

"Come in the coffee shop and I'll explain it." The answer wasn't what I expected. "I'm one of the songwriters for some of the original material that the Start Me Up band is recording for Warner Brothers. I work with my friend Shel Talmy. He is going blind and I do the writing as we speak. Remember Shel? He brought the Kinks to America. When the drummers died, Warner Bros. backed out of the recording contract. We still had some great songs. I wrote some original ones with only my name on the copyright. It was potential big money. Then things got messy. I was being pushed out of the picture. My songs were suddenly without credit. Someone in the Start me Up band or management was taking my money."

I was young but I remembered the Kinks

Sheldon continued: "The deaths ended the Start Me Up album contract and cost me money." I had another suspect. Maybe Sheldon Foreskin was the culprit.

"A pretty good reason the poison the drummers," I interjected.

So if you think that I'm the killer, it isn't a possibility. Just think my songs were recorded on the Warner label. I would be a millionaire."

"Warner Brothers." I stated with amazement. "They are a cover band, they don't have a recording contract." I looked at Foreskin astonished.

Sheldon continued: "We were getting ready to cut a CD of original tunes. My songs dominated the album. The only problem is that Warner Brothers based the contract on the drum sounds. It seems that Start Me Up had not one but three great drummers. They were all killed. So were my songs. So tell your Detective Sanchez to solve the crime." With that Sheldon turned and angrily walked away. I guess I wasn't going to be teaching any classes at South Bay Community College. Then he stopped and shouted: "Look up that asshole Shonestein." Foreskin stopped and thought for a moment. Then he smiled and continued: "Shonestein was destined to lose millions from the Start Me Up band going with their own songs."

It sure looked like Shonestein was my man. A good private eye knows better. It was too pat. Too simplistic.

Suddenly the case pointed directly to Elliott Shonestein. I didn't like that. Why would he hire me to investigate a series of murders he committed? Maybe he talked to Chef Fred. I pondered the evidence.

I drove back from Fremont by crossing the San Mateo Bridge and driving up the Bayshore Freeway. It gave me time to think. I was missing something. Then it dawned on me. The puzzle could be solved. I needed to go to Elliott Shonestein's office. I finally had a lead. Pam Wong had to know what was going on. I had almost forgotten about Pam.

Chapter 12
RIGHT OR WONG

It took me over an hour to reach the San Francisco downtown turnoff. The 101 wasn't crowed so I quickly pulled onto Market Street. It was time to find out what the brains behind the Start Me Up band knew. Elliott Shonestein's office was plush. He had wasted no expense. The leather couches, the large chairs, a special kitchen and a secretary who looked like a movie star. She could have been Bruce Lee's co-star. I guess that thought dated me. I walked into the office. I stopped dead in my tracks. The secretary was Pam Wong. The mysterious girl who had given me her card in the Foreign Cinema. I had lost it and forgot to call her. No bells seemed to go off with Miss Wong. Now it was time to work my real charm. I had to open with my best lines. What would Shell Scott say? Probably, "Hey babe, let's get together." I turned out to be much less original.

"Pam, I need your help." Nothing like the direct approach.

"Pam," she said. There was no smile. "Now we are on a first name basis, Trevor." I noticed there was sarcasm in her voice. There was also a hard look. Maybe my charms didn't hit the mark. Maybe I never had any charm. No sense second-guessing myself. I needed to come up with a sexy phrase.

"How about coffee?" I smiled, it was as sexy a phrase as I could muster. It didn't seem to impress her. She was thinking. "I am in a bit of a delicate position and need your help. What do you say?"

"A limp dick and no brains is more than a delicate position." She smiled.

"Will you have dinner with me?" I gave her my best smile.

"Yes," Pam agreed.

"We can have dinner, but not Chinese or Mexican. I have heard about your cheap nature, Trevor."

I said: "Busted again. I can promise you a great time in return for some conversation."

"Pick me up at six, get dressed and we'll go to dinner. You want something you pay for it."

I always liked the direct approach. "See you at six." Who knows. Maybe I can score. She looked at me and smiled.

"Don't even think about a night cap at your place, am I clear." Pam could obviously read my mind.

"Maybe a night cap at your place, Pam."

"No asshole come on,' she smiled, "at least not on this date."

"Ok," I didn't smile. I wasn't sure if this meeting meant anything.

"Do you want to see Elliot?," she asked.

"No, I am getting a handle on the case, tell him I'm making progress." I walked out on Market Street and watched a homeless guy push a cart up the street. He wore a Grateful Dead shirt and a Nixon for President, 1968 button. He looked happier than I did. Something to ponder. I walked to Fifth and Mission and paid the five-dollar parking fee. The City of San Francisco garage was supposed to be cheap.

After driving home I checked by answering machine. There were four messages from Joyce Byers. She is sort of my girl friend. We date without commitment. It is very modern. I made a note to call her. Joyce and I were fighting. It had to do with my constant requests for information from the police department. These were the little bits of information that bordered on the illegal.

She refused to continue to date me until I quit asking for information and sex. Maybe we could just end the information part of our relationship. The sex part was pretty good. That was enough for me. At this moment she was upset with me and so we had pleasant conversations. I preferred the sex.

Suddenly I felt alone. My trusty assistant Guitar Jac hadn't checked into the office for three days. We had to repossess a number of cars, there were a dozen subpoenas to deliver and a case involving a bail jumper. Maybe I could hire Stephanie Plum? So I called and left a message on Guitar Jac's answering machine.

"Guitar, it's me, we now have over $30,000 in the treasury. Come home and do some work." I didn't hold my breath. He certainly didn't need the money.

Suddenly we had a cash flow. But we were no closer to solving any of the cases. To ignore the small cases would not be acceptable. We still needed to pay the rent. Particularly since I felt like giving the almost thirty thousand dollars back to my recent clients. I could handle bail jumpers and car thieves. Really murderers were another problem. I didn't seem to have any luck with them.

I walked around my apartment thinking. It was 5 and I had almost a half hour to dress. It was time to pull out my best clothes. Pam would be impressed. Or at least she would receive a free dinner. What does a man in his early 40s wear? The answer was obvious. Go casual. Go with brand names. If all else fails, go with an expensive dinner. I got on the phone and made reservations at the Tadich Grill. It is located on California Street and was San Francisco's oldest restaurant. I stopped by Safeway and picked up a $12 bouquet of flowers and slipped the band I had saved from the Fairmont Hotel flower shop onto the bouquet. I liked to appear like an upscale guy.

I went by the car wash and had the Burger King wrappers cleaned from the floor. My 2006 BMW Z4 is a classy ride. A wash and polish made the car look human. I hoped I looked the same way. Pam's address was on Nob Hill. I was in for a shock. She lived in a three-bedroom penthouse apartment with a view of the Golden Gate bridge. I walked into the lobby and found a large doorman.

"Can I help you sir?"

"I'm here for Pam Wong."

"We'll see." He smiled. Things didn't go well for me when people smiled. A few minutes later he directed me to the elevator and pressed the penthouse button. The ride up was quick. Rich people don't stand for slow elevators. When I opened the door I was standing in an entry room. I wondered where the hallway was.

"Trevor," Pam walked over and kissed me on the cheek. Things were going better than I expected. "Would you like a drink?"

"Sure, how about a Bud." She winced. It took a few minutes and a glass of Jordan Merlot appeared. Excuse me? She smiled and went into the bathroom. I looked at the bottom of the Merlot bottle. The price tag read $65. More like my salary for a week.

"Sorry about the Jordan Merlot, normally I have real French wine available or the Cakebread Merlot."

"It's just fine, I can suffer the indignity of Jordan Merlot." I wasn't sure what to say. Wine was not my thing. That should have told me that it was going to be an expensive night. I wondered if she was embezzling money from Elliott Shonestein.

I smiled at her with a lecherous look. "You look very nice." Pam smiled.

I never took you for a charmer Trevor."

"My motto is to wear them down with charm." We talked for a few minutes and finished our drinks. It was time for dinner. I arrived in front of the Tadich Grill and used valet parking. The $15 tag caused me to wince. Once inside she ordered Pacific Oysters Rockefeller at $18 a dozen, followed by sliced tomatoes with Dungeness crab for $15 and the main course was not surprisingly the $45 dollar 12 oz filet mignon. I ordered the mixed greens for $7 and ravioli at $9. We finished off dinner by sharing triple chocolate mousse at $8. Pam ate half of each portion. She looked disinterested in her food. My pocketbook would recover.

"I hate to ask this question, Trevor."

"Ask away."

Why would you order ravioli in the best and oldest seafood restaurant in the city?" A tough question.

"It gives me more testosterone." I smiled. She didn't.

"I have been to the Tadich Grill fifty times and you are the first date to order ravioli. What do you order in an Italian restaurant?"

"Mahi Mahi," I replied.

"Ah, a smart ass. Let's get down to business."

"Let's eat and talk, Pam, I'm not easy on the first date." She smiled, I knew that I was in trouble.

After the extended battle with the chocolate mousse and four glasses of sherry, we got down to business. I needed to check my expense account.

"Elliott is concerned about the Start Me Up band. If they record a CD of original material their market value will end. He has a lot of money invested in them. So there is no reason for him to have anything to do with the three drummers dying."

"What about Sheldon Foreskin?

Pam looked quizzical. "Who?"

"The songwriter."

"What songwriter?"

"Pam, we aren't getting anyplace."

"Tell me about songwriters."

"Pete Townshend, Roger Daltry, and a couple of dead guys." She looked at me like I was nuts. "You know Pam, the Who, it's a joke." She obviously didn't know songwriters from anyone else. The Who were a band from another planet to her. Then again maybe she did know something.

"Trevor, when you grow up. Just lay out the facts to me and I will see if I can help."

I let her know my general theory. Or should I say many theories. I kept the fact from her that all the suspects and potential killers hired me to solve the crime. She might not think that I'm as astute as I appear. She also didn't learn about the FBI. Or Chastain Johnson.

I told her my main ideas. "If Elliott could sabotage the drum sound the band would not be able to record a CD of original songs. The Sheldon Foreskin material depended on a certain drum sound. I wondered if Foreskin and Shonestein were enemies. They both had an interest in the Rolling Stone cover band. The Start Me Up had the sound to make Foreskin's songs hits. It was Foreskin who told me that they were radio staples. So maybe Shonestein was trying to sabotage the Warner Brothers contract for personal reasons."

She looked at me for a long time. "I think you are on to something. I didn't know that Elliott and this Sheldon guy knew each other but there are forty to fifty phone calls a week to Fremont."

"Why would anyone call Fremont," I asked. "It's a shit hole slowly being taken over by Asian immigrants. It's not a white persons town anymore" Ups I forgot.

Pam glared. "Not exactly politically correct, Trevor."

"Pam is there any reason to suspect that Elliott and Sheldon had a parting of the ways."

"I don't know, Trevor." She lit a cigarette. "I could care less what direction their relationship is headed."

I paused to think. Now for the $64,000 questions. "Elliott made it clear that it was the drum direction which made the band different. Maybe this was a modern version of the Iron Butterfly."

"Who are the Iron Butterfly?"

I wasn't getting anywhere. "Not one of your bands, Pam."

"Tell me about them."

I hesitated. What the hell. I explained that after ten minutes of "Inna Gadda da Vida" even the hippies were crying for silence. I hummed: "In a gadda da vida, baby In the Garden of Eden, Don't you know I'm loving you." I am the only P. I. who knows the lyrics to the Iron Butterfly song. Pam looked impressed.

"What does that mean Trevor?"

"It means the music is heavy metal without Ozzy's mellifluous voice.'" I wasn't getting anywhere. Pam was vacuous to a fault. She was beautiful.

I said: "So we have an easily solved murder case, Elliott is the man." I looked confidently at Pam. Of course, I had no idea if he was the killer. She wasn't fooled.

"No, you need motive, opportunity, evidence and some reason for pointing the finger at Elliott, Sherlock." Kinky Friedman would have no trouble solving this case. I had to remember that I wasn't Kinky.

I mused on her defense of Elliott. Not an unreasonable answer. Pam was ignoring one thing. I said: " He had motive, to keep the band a cover group."

"There is something you don't know. Elliott was auditioning musicians to replace the original ones in the Start Me Up band. He copyrighted the band name. He could send any group of musicians he wanted to on the road. He doesn't appear to have a motive. It would ruin his profits."

"Chef Fred," I mumbled.

"What?" Pam looked annoyed.

"Nothing, let me do my super detecting."

"Trevor, you have no suspects, in fact you have no clue. Or for that matter clues." She smiled at her joke. I didn't "In fact, you seem to have no idea what you are doing."

"Don't you mean any clues? I think your boss is my most viable suspect. I need his personal diary. His business appointments and so on. That would help."

Pam smiled. She looked pensive. "Elliott doesn't keep records."

"Sweet." I smiled. "You must have some idea about his business affairs."

"None." She didn't smile. "Trevor, I think you need to refocus." I think she caught me looking at her breasts.

"Take your eyes off me and keep them on the case."

I think that was criticism. "I still need some idea of Elliott's business affairs.

"Good luck, I don't think he has a clue about his, as you say, affairs."

We talked for a while and I suggested that I meet her at her place. She laughed at me. I drove home alone. Striking out once again. I found a parking ticket on my windshield. Joyce Byers could fix the ticket. I got back to my Chestnut Street apartment, I couldn't sleep. So I drove up to my office. Guitar Jac was sitting at his desk. One thing is certain about Jac. If he is in the office, he is working.

"Hey, my man Jac. Homes." He looked at me like I had lost my mind. Jac hated my ghetto parlance which he pointed out was forty years behind the times.

"Trevor, do you see anyone else here? No. So cut the Negro talk."

"I haven't noticed any Negroes since the 1950s." I was still politically correct, I wondered about Guitar Jac.

"Sit down, Trevor, I have some interesting news."

"Shoot," I said. "Don't all you black guys carry a gun." As usual Guitar Jac ignored me. He scowled. Not a good sign.

"See this." Guitar Jac held up a sheet of music. It had an original song written on it. I had a band that played surf music but I was one of those musicians that couldn't read sheet music. It wasn't difficult to play "Wipe Out" or "Walk Don't Run." I had hung out with Don Wilson of the Ventures when my band opened for them and he couldn't read music. Elvis couldn't read music. Eddie Cochran couldn't read music. "Is there a point to this?" I asked Jac.

"Sit, Trevor, you are like a kid with ADD." So I sat and looked at him.

"Well!"

Guitar Jac continued: "Look at the lyrics. The song is entitled 'Stone Murder."

"Not a very catchy title." I was always a critic.

Guitar Jac continued: "Spend some time reading the lyrics. Analyze them. You do have a degree?"

Jac was right. After reading the lyrics a couple of times, it was obvious that we finally had a clue. Maybe I wasn't clueless. The song lyrics suggested that someone close to the band was killing its members. A hidden killer with no identity was a tough one to find. The food was the main clue but the Chef was not a Chef. So Chef Fred was out of the picture. Sheldon Foreskin looked like a suspect. Then again why would he sabotage his songs? The song ended with the admonition that members of the Start Me Up band knew the killer. The drummers knew the killer. At least this is what the song implied. Weird.

"This clue isn't exactly for rocket scientists, Jac, we have known about all this for a week. James Jett is the new drummer but he can't be the killer."

"Once again Trevor you are not paying attention. Read every third word backwards from the end of the song. I did. It was frightening. "Look for the Woman." That seemed to narrow the suspects. It was time to call on Don Gino Walker. He could help me with this little problem. The Purple Don knew how to solve problems. Or at least make them go away. I needed to get some things from my apartment. Mainly an expensive bottle of wine for the Don.

I got in my car and drove over to Fillmore and down to Chestnut turning right for two blocks. A miracle occurred. There was a parking spot in front of my apartment. I thought a lot about looking for the woman. Did Elliott Shonestein have a wife? Who else was involved? I was getting more confused by the hour. Then I remembered what Guitar Jac had said. The song contained a clue. Someone in the band was killing off the other members. Then why would the song be named "Look For The Woman?" The Start Me Up band was five guys. In fact, they were five rotating guys with Shonestein pulling the strings. So much for Jac's masterful clue. It was time to sit at the feet of the Purple Don. His wisdom in these matters was greater than mine.

I pondered the clue. "Look for the woman" led me to believe that Pam Wong was the killer. It couldn't be Chastain Johnson. The new clues were confusing not helping me. Maybe it was Joyce Byers. I picked up a Jordan Merlot and drove down to Don Gino's office.

Chapter 13
Don Gino: The Purple Don Leads Me Down A Path

Don Gino's office was now in the Castro. He used to have an entire building that he owned in the Mission District. The fifteen million dollar price tag persuaded him to sell it and move to the predominantly gay Castro District. He was coming out of the closet and no one seemed to care. Or for that matter notice. Maybe it was better for your health, not to notice. This was not only the part of San Francisco favored by the gay community, but since Don Gino moved in the crime rate had declined to virtually nothing. It wasn't safe for criminals in the Castro. I was a liberal so it was no problem. The walk up office that Don Gino occupied was an entire floor. There was open space and a few closed off rooms. Probably used to beat the truth out of the opposition. With Don Gino's purple suits I often wondered about his taste in clothing. No one in his right mind would question San Francisco's most notorious gangster about his sartorial bliss or anything else. Not me anyway.

"Gumba," Don Gino chortled as I entered the office. The eight Samoans lounged nearby. They grunted.

"Nice talking to you guys." I laughed. They sneered. "Gumba, I hope that is a friendly greeting."

"What is it we can do for you Trevor? Always the man of too many words." That was criticism.

"I need advice Don Gino."

"Of course, who doesn't? We all need counsel."

One of the Samoans left. Probably to beat up a gay guy nearby. After a few minutes of polite conversation, Don Gino put on his scarf, his purple hat and his purple leather coat. I wondered do purple cows exist? "We need to ride as we talk." I followed.

We walked out front and a purple limousine pulled up with a Samoan driving it. We got in.

"To North Beach," Don Gino ordered. We drove over to Broadway and Columbus. I had fond memories of seeing Carol Doda dancing topless in the old days at the Condor Club. There were still some old time Italian eateries. We went to the Golden Spike. It was an Italian institution with a five-course dinner. All you could eat. No one got in without an hour or more wait. The limo stopped on Columbus Street and we got out. Don Gino walked to the door and we were seated. So much for the hour wait. The meal was an excellent one. After a light white wine with calamari, salad, a relish try and an Italian Wedding soup we dived into cannelloni and a plate of veal scaloppini and this was followed by spumoni ice cream, assorted cakes and espresso. An after dinner wine topped off the bill. We finished and began talking.

"Did the meal suit you?" Don Gino asked.

"Yes, of course," I continue., "We need to get some things straight about the Start Me Up band."

"Trevor, come to the point."

I looked exasperated. "I have too many clues, too many loose ends and too many clients." I looked frustrated. I proceeded to explain my multiple clients, the Look For the Woman clue and the seeming guilt of Elliott Shonestein.

Don Gino drank his third cappuccino. He looked into his coffee cup. I suspected he was searching for divine guidance. "Well, Trevor, let's look at this from the beginning. If that song "Look For The Woman" is the clue, then this narrows the field of suspects. You need to run a make on Pam Wong, she looks like the culprit." He continued: "Your friend in the F. B. I. can help with that. What's her name? Chastity?"

"Very funny, Don Gino. It is Chastain Johnson. You know it, I know it. She won't run anything for me. Maybe she'll run my ass off to jail. That's it."

"You underestimate yourself, Trevor."

"I do, I know." I sounded bewildered. Maybe I was really a sex symbol or a great detective. Or both.

"There is something missing in this case, I can feel it." Don Gino took another sip of his cappuccino. He held his pinkie finger in the air. Definitely not masculine. I didn't mention it.

"I agree, let's look at the evidence." I pulled out my twenty odd napkins and put them on the desk. I counted there were more than thirty odd napkins. Clues pile up. Don Gino smiled. We looked at the napkins in earnest.

We talked about what suspects for another hour. After eight cappuccinos I thought Dino Gino might fly out of the Golden Spike. He simply smiled and looked like he might levitate.

As Don Gino left I noticed there was no bill. The entire staff lined up at the front door to thank him for his business. Nothing like having dinner with a cold-blooded killer. We shook hands. I had too much to drink, so I took a cab home. Don Gino had some business south of Market. It seems one of his cocktail lounges had changed food suppliers. Don Gino was going down to have a friendly talk with the owner. I noticed a second limousine with seven Samoans following Don Gino. I suspected that the owner of The Blue Light Lounge was about to rethink changing his supplier. The next day the San Francisco Chronicle had a page ten story on how the Blue Light Lounge not only returned to Don Gino's supply company but also added their ten other San Francisco area restaurants now purchased his line of salami. It must have been the cappuccinos. Dino Gino was a smart man and he had given me a great deal to think about.

I thought long and hard about Don Gino's analysis. He saw different sides to the mystery. The unknown, he kept talking about the hidden factor. What in the hell was this so-called unknown or hidden factor? I needed real law enforcement. I need to get laid. Enter Joyce Byers. She is not only my sometime girl friend but a detective in the San Francisco Police Department.

Joyce Byers graduated from the University of California, Berkeley with a criminology degree. Then she completed law school at McGeorge in Sacramento. She didn't practice law. She went into the San Francisco Police Department and was a detective second grade. She was five foot ten inches tall, weighed a hundred and thirty- five pounds with a 34C cup and a nineteen inch waist. Rumor has it that she had rib removed. She dressed in Armani women's suits and no one could figure out how. I knew the secret. She shopped at watchplanet.com. Her little secret was safe with me. She shopped at a deep discount.

My relationship with Joyce was on again off again. I was not the world's best boyfriend. In fact I hated monogamy. Joyce loved it. Somehow we co-existed. I always looked for a new woman. Chastain Johnson fit the bill. I didn't think it was mutual. Besides she smoked. Not my idea of love.

Chapter 14
JOYCE BYERS TO THE RESCUE

When I met Joyce Byers I was married, I was a practicing lawyer, I was successful and I had a Porsche. I am no longer any of those things. We had an affair. The only complication was that Joyce didn't know I was married. My wife did and she divorced me. She was also having an affair. So much for my detecting skills. So much for my ability to conceal sensitive information. For almost two years I dated Joyce. Sporadic dating. That means when I didn't have a hot date and she didn't have a serious date, we went out. She was a detective second class with the San Francisco Police Department Internal Affairs Department. She was working on a detail that investigated the officer's who cheated on their wives, took bribes and otherwise broke the blue code. Fortunately, she hadn't caught any of the wife cheaters. Only those who took bribes and beat up the gays. They all broke the blue code and Joyce ignored this salient fact.

Joyce had recently gotten a boob job and died her hair red. She was not only good looking, but she was a distance runner. She regularly ran marathons. Her dress was conservative but stylish. She was prone to well cut and stylish Armani Legend suits. My theory was that she was much like Detective Sanchez. All style and plenty of substance. It was hard to fool her. I had done it. It cost me my marriage. It was worth it. Now if I could divorce my former in-laws Bennie and Bertie, I would be happy. It wouldn't happen. I needed cheap rent, so divorce from their rental was not a possibility. They liked me in a sick way. I was their window in the single life. Such as it was.

It was hard to get a date with Joyce. She was looking into an incident where three off duty rookie policemen grabbed a bag of tacos from two guys closing a bar. They beat the guy to a pulp. To make matters worse, a fight broke out on Lombard Street when three-rookie policeman lost fistfights to two bar tenders. When the San Francisco Chronicle pointed out that the two bartenders were gay and had beaten up the officers, there was hell to pay in the SFPD.

A day later the police showed up at the Lombard Street bar and beat up the bar tenders. When the press pointed out that the police beat up the guys who beat up the three rookie officers the day before, there was an inquest. Joyce Byers was in the middle of it. There were now a series of nasty lawsuits. Joyce was up to her elbows in department shit. The Police Chief, Willie Clayton, had hired his son. Willie Jr. had four previous violent incident complaints in a year against his actions as an SFPD policemen. He also had a reputation for being a hot head. Willie was not Irish, so he didn't get the same protection as every other officer. It was a mess. Willie Jr. had trouble keeping his mouth shut and one day he and his father got into a fistfight during a press conference. They were trying to explain why Willie Jr. was innocent and they began beating on each other.

Willie Jr. told the San Francisco Chronicle: "Negroes needed to be beat up. It teaches them their place." With four complaints from so-called Negroes, two of whom were college graduates with engineering degrees, a third was a nuclear physicist at Stanford and the last one was a janitor. Somehow the SFPD explained away Willie Jr.'s actions. Willie Jr. was not in trouble. This amazed everyone. San Francisco was not supposed to be Mississippi. The police explained that the "Negroes resisted." They probably asked for a phone call or a lawyer. The SFPD was notorious for hiring excessive force officers.

They were all for beating up the brothers. Willie, Jr., was a white guy who hated black guys. He refused to use the term African American and was known as "the rider" to the other rookies. A rider was an officer who sought out trouble in Hunter's Point, San Francisco's African American ghetto.

Joyce was trying to find out if the Chief's son was innocent. I asked her many times to just assume his guilt. The word she used around me was "asshole." But then again she wasn't alone. There was no doubt that he was guilty as hell. She wouldn't be able to please anyone in this inquiry.

The chief called Joyce in and let her know that if he cleared her son, there was a promotion. This was a mistake. She gritted her teeth, smiled at the chief and left his office. Over the next month she was able to collect enough evidence to get the rookie fired and the dad resigned. Mayor Gavin Newsom publicly lauded Joyce at a press conference while casting glances at her ass and recent boob job. I hadn't seen her for weeks. It was time to rekindle our romance. Such as it was!

We met on Union Street at Luisa's Ristorante. Joyce always made me wait for her. It was part of our ritual. Luisa's was not only Italian but also the cook; the waiters, the bus boys and the owner were all Italians. This obviously upset the Culinary Union and Jorge Gonzalez the President of the CU, was lobbying for more Mexicans in the kitchen. Massimo, the owner, greeted me with a smile.

"Va Bene, it's Trevor."

Nothing like being a famous P. I.

Massimo inquired: "How is your father?" How is your mother?" Nothing like having parents who made some money and were well known around town.

"They're worried I'm not married. I like to hang out with my friend Don Gino. So marriage will come later."

Massimo has a way of putting things in perspective. "You are waiting for the lovely young lady?" He smiled and bowed.

Yes, Massimo, with bells on. In fact, I am waiting for any young lady."

"Ah Trevor, always the jokester. How do you always say you are waiting for the lady?"

"Bells on." He looked perplexed. It was a colloquial expression lost amongst the Italian vernacular. He looked confused.

"It's humor. Trevor humor." I smiled.

Massimo stroked his mustache: "Or lack of it," He sat me by the window. Nothing is more delightful in San Francisco than watching the beautifully dressed young ladies wander down Union Street. Not only are they spending their money, they are looking glamorous doing it. It was shopping in beautiful clothes with lots of money. Not my type of women. I couldn't afford them. As I looked out onto Union Street ogling the ladies, a hand touched my shoulder. It was a soft and feminine touch. Joyce Byers had arrived. I looked up. She had on a pair of Dolce 'n' Gabanna designer jeans with a multi colored pattern on the legs and a cashmere sweater under a leather coat. The four hundred dollar jeans were purchased at buy.com for a hundred dollars. Her secret was safe with me. She looked terrific. I had dressed up. I had the private eye Dries Van Noten blazer for seven hundred dollars, a pair of tan pants that were Hong Kong tailored for a hundred dollars. A French made Hermes stripped tie for one hundred sixty dollars completed the ensemble. My socks cost fifty dollars and my shoes from Marc Jacobs cost five hundred dollars. Not bad for $1500 plus dollars I looked like a stud.

I couldn't afford a new belt. I hope Joyce didn't notice. At forty I still have the tight buns to fit into designer pants. She looked impressed. The last time she saw me it was in my shorts in the Chestnut Street apartment with burger king wrappers on the kitchen table.

"How is my knight in shining armor?"

"Joyce, beauty and brains." I looked a little too long at her supple breasts.

"Trevor, my face, you need to look at it." She had a way of reminding me about my bad habits.

"Sorry, beauty is in many places."

"Fortunately, your penis is not one of those places."

She sat down and we ordered. I had a spinach salad followed by a meatball-laced pasta and this was followed by a tiramisu. Joyce, always watching her figure, settled for a goat chess and walnut salad with low fat dressing and a pasta in a fresh tomato sauce. Joyce ate half her meal. She took the rest home. It would probably last her a week. She passed on desert. At the end of the meal it was time to talk. I burped. Not exactly a romantic way to end a fine meal. Massimo came back with two drambuies. We drank them and reached for a café mocha.

"Trevor, that was wonderful."

"Of course, I am a lady pleaser."

"How is the case coming?"

"It's not."

"Oh!" She looked at her watch. It was time to get down to business.

"What I need is some help on my case."

She looked at her watch again. Joyce frowned: "What type of help?"

"I need a rap sheet or some info on Pan Wong. She works for Elliott Shonestein. Some type of personal secretary or assistant." Joyce looked at her watch once again. I seemed to have that effect on women.

"You know what could happen to me?"

"Sure you could come back to my apartment." I smiled. She didn't.

"I could get fired, I could get demoted and I could get charged with illegal activity."

"Hum," I admitted to myself that I hadn't thought of any of that.

"Let me think about it."

"Ok, sweetie," I said.

She frowned. "One more sweetie and I won't do a thing for you."

"Sorry." I was uneasy.

Joyce got up hastily. "Let me run downtown. I have some other things to do. I will meet you at the North Beach Café for a light dinner about eight tomorrow."

Her stomach gurgled. She hadn't eaten much. I stuffed myself. "Ok, I'll see you at eight tomorrow night. Remember Pam Wong."

"Trevor! Do I look stupid?"

"No." I didn't want to tell her I felt stupid. She left and I gazed at her derriere. It was as nice a view as the front. One day I would outgrow this fetish with women. Not soon I hoped.

I left the restaurant and walked the eight blocks over to my apartment. I would need some serious exercise. The prospect of another big meal tomorrow was not an enchanting one. Nor was the thought of what it would cost me. Maybe I would get laid. Work off the two meals. I walked over to the mailbox as I entered my apartment. There was a large manila envelope. I opened it. It contained the lyrics to the song "Look For the Woman." I studied them in great detail. There was a line that I had missed. "The woman is not what she seems." That stuck with me and gave me some ideas.

After briefly cleaning the apartment I drove up to the Haight Ashbury. I took along the lyrics to "Look For The Woman." Maybe Guitar Jac had some ideas. The song was more than just a clue. I believed that it was a road map. One I couldn't read. I parked on Stanyan Street and began the six-block walk to my office. I looked over and there was Rod McKuen's house. Not only was he the worst poet of the 1950s and 1960s but an abysmal folk singer. Naturally, I had all his books and records. I felt good, as I had never purchased a Rod McKuen CD. Were there any? Going up Haight Street used to be fun, now one has to ward off the tourists. I opened the mailbox with my key.

The mail at the Trevor Blake III Private Investigation office consisted of bills and advertisements. There was no sign of Guitar Jac. I drifted down to Emilio's for a coffee and donut. He wasn't behind the counter. There was a young girl with tattoos and a hair do worse than mine. I didn't go in and instead headed down to Amoeba to buy a King Pleasure jazz album. The sophisticated P. I. needed to expand his musical horizons. I walked back to my office and finally sat down to open up the old mail.

After cleaning up the office, I left Guitar Jac a note. I wanted him to follow Pam Wong. I drove down to Broadway and Columbus. A parking space cost $20, so I drove around until six and got a place on the street. Sheer luck. Had some time to kill so I sat at the bar in Vesuvio's and drank two Irish coffees. Jack Kerouac used to drink in Vesuvio's along with Alan Ginsberg and Lawrence Ferlenghetti. When I mentioned this to the bartender, he looked disinterested and bored. He had never heard of any of them. So much for literary recognition.

Just before eight I walked up to the North Beach Café. The Green Street location is one of my favorites. Italian restaurants are everywhere and the tourists haven't found the street. My stomach was filled with pasta and Irish coffee. The meal yesterday still filled me up. Or was I cheap? Maybe a little of both. Time to keep up appearances. I smiled when I saw Joyce. She didn't. She handed me a large manila envelope filled with sheets of paper. I was hoping it wasn't just Pam Wong's rap sheet.

We were seated at a corner table and looked out onto Green Street. I asked Joyce to wait while I looked at the papers. I asked for an antipasto plate and bottle of Ruffino Classico Chianti. The waiter obliged and I began to look over the files. Joyce looked nervous. When I saw the files I realized its sensitivity. It seemed to clear Pam Wong and Elliott Shonestein. An investigation by the SFPD turned up nothing on them. What was astounding was that it pointed to one of the lesser players. The killer was within Shonestein's circle of friends and investors. But which one? That was the unanswered question. The Chef was still the key suspect. But Chef Fred most certainly was not the killer. So I had to look for an amateur Chef. That seemed to include everyone as a potential suspect but Don Gino who never had seen the inside of a kitchen. I spent over an hour looking at the files.

"Satisfied, Trevor!" Joyce looked bored.

"Thanks. Let's eat."

"Always the romantic, Trevor."

We ordered dinner. I started with a Caesar salad. Joyce had a minestrone soup. I followed with a lasagna and she had the veal scaloppini. A second bottle of Chianti and a shared tiramisu brought us to two cappuccinos. It was a nice dinner. Maybe I would die of tiramisu poisoning. When I looked up I was dabbing at the tiramisu and she was still cutting her veal scaloppini. I guess I hadn't talked much at dinner. I had also eaten too quickly.

"Jesus, Trevor, you are not even the slightest bit romantic. You eat too fast. You lack even the casual nuances of subtlety. You want information, you want a quick dinner and you want to get laid."

I said: "Nobody's perfect. Can I have two out of three of those options? " I smiled. I was clever.

"If you weren't so damned cute, I would be mad. I will call you tomorrow." She got up, kissed me on the cheek and wandered out onto Green Street. An unmarked police car picked her up. I bet that she was working. I got up, paid the bill and drove down to Perry's on Union Street. I paid twenty bucks to park. I pay twenty bucks to park anywhere I go in the city. It was a wasted night. Not in the information sense but in the personal one. I needed a woman. Joyce went back to work. Or she went somewhere. It was Friday night and I was alone. So maybe a visit to Perry's could get me laid.

On Union Street Perry's is just across the street from the Bus Stop. This bar is owned by two retired San Francisco 49ers and is filled with young ladies looking for a millionaire athlete. I never did well at the Bust Stop. For the past nineteen years these two key bars were my home away from home. I had my first drink in the Bus Stop. Then I graduated to Perry's. I met my wife Marilyn there. I wondered why I went back. I needed to rethink my game plan. Or better yet, I needed to devise a game plan. I found a lonely bar stool. The rest were full. Guys who used to be athletes frequent the Bus Stop. Most of them look washed out. They are mostly divorced, living in nearby studio apartments and trying to act hip. Or to get laid. The patrons were a good bunch to sit in the midst of and plan the future. None of them had a future. Maybe the same was true for me.

I listened to two guys talk about whether or not Joe Montana or Steve Young was the better quarterback. I asked the boys about Alec Smith. They laughed at me. The quarterback from Utah wasn't yet an item among bar gossips.

I left the Bus Stop and darted across the street to Perry's. It was full of dot. comers, stock market types and those dressed in suits pretending to be businessmen. The ladies looked like they had just left the secretarial pool. I needed to keep that opinion to myself. Political correctness still ruled in San Francisco.

"Brother!" I looked up and Seamus the bartender placed a glass of Merlot on a napkin.

"Seamus my man." I was still filled with clichés. He left and I opened my case file.

As I nursed my drink I began taking napkins and writing on them. I added them to my case file. I think I am up to forty napkins on this case. The scenario was not a pretty one. I had too many suspects and not enough leads. The song "Look For The Woman" continued to haunt me. What type of clue was it? Who was the Chef?

"Hello," a sweet voice intoned. I looked to my right. In a John Smedley red sweater and a black cashmere Burberry skirt cut open at the front, Chastain Johnson sat with a cigarette. The no-smoking rule wasn't being enforced. Maybe Seamus thought she would shoot him. She was sitting next to me and I didn't notice. She looked beautiful. I had to remember that she was with the F. B. I. She also smoked too much. I could overlook that minor fact.

"To what do I owe this honor?" I smiled.

"Your girl friend, Joyce, when will you hear from her?" Chastain ground here cigarette out in an ashtray. Whatever happened to not smoking in bars? I would have to talk to Seamus. Maybe there were different rules for the FBI.

"I am not sure I believe this. You know about Joyce?"

"I'm the FBI remember!"

How could l forget? Maybe I'll believe you are little more than a cipher with nice tits." I smiled. Always the clever P. I.

"Believe it. Did you like your waiter?" I looked at her astonished.

"You mean at the North Beach Cafe."

"That's it, Trevor."

I said: "He was the worst that I have ever seen."

"I'll tell him in the office, tomorrow. He had a small, hidden camera and we have all the documents." She smiled. "Now 'Looking For The Woman' becomes our lead. Remember we have to solve the case. We're the FBI." I noted a smug tone of superiority in her voice. It was a false smugness.

"You mean he listened in. He was an Italian. The only one I have ever talked to who hade no idea about tiramisu. He thought it was a seasoning. No wonder the FBI can't solve a case."

"No, Trevor, he taped the whole damned conversation. He also copied the papers when you were staring at Joyce's fake tits. We are going to talk to her."

"What could she tell you, Chastain, that you can't find out?"

"Plenty, Joyce is sharp. She will run a sheet on Miss Wong and then get you the extraneous gossip. You know the good but unknown facts. She will find a way to tell you. Probably in bed. Poor girl." Chastain looked at me and continued. "Is there anybody in this investigation that you're not sleeping with Trevor?"

"Don Gino."

She laughed. "That I do believe."

"Maybe I will surprise you and jump to the other side of the sexual fence."

"Well, I can think of one person that I no longer need to bed. That is you." She smiled, I guess she wouldn't miss me.

"As soon as you hear from Joyce, call me."

"What if I don't?"

"Obstructing justice is the obvious charge. Being an asshole isn't against the law."

"I'll call." She smiled and left. Every head turned at the bar and looked at me like I was a loser. Maybe they were right. I finished my drink. After five more napkins filled with detective work, I walked back out onto Union Street. There was still time for another drink. I wandered across the street and back to the Bus Stop. I sat at the bar with a group of younger guys. They were twenty-five and arguing about whether or not Bono was too old and U 2 no longer relevant. I was attempted to suggest that without Bono there would be no world peace. But they looked like they had no sense of humor. Then again Bono wasn't known for his charming wit.

The bartender brought me a glass of house Merlot. To hell with the guys in "Sideways," Merlot always helped me get laid. I looked around, there were no women at the bar. I sipped the Merlot and thought. Not bad. At least the wine was ok; the case was out of control. I stopped smoking but yearned for a cigarette. It took me about an hour to finish the Merlot and once again I wondered into Union Street. The walk home was a quick one. All I had to do was wait for Joyce Byers to gather some more information. She couldn't fail me. Then again she could. I wonder if Chastain bugged the bedroom. I made animal sounds for a half hour and fell asleep alone.

Chapter 15
DON GINO STRAIGHTENS OUT ELLIOTT

I had help on the case that I wasn't aware of the next morning.. After attempting to find out what was going on with the Start Me Up Band, I heard the phone ring. I stumbled out of bed. The clock read 6:30.

"Hello, god damn it this better we good."

"Trevor my boy." It was Don Gino. He wanted to talk.

Don Gino was upset that his monetary gains from a silent investment in the Start Me Up band were not returning him a tidy profit. He wanted answers. I heard him holler to his bodyguards. He informed the eight Samoans that they were going for a ride. It was time to talk to Elliott Shonestein.

"Listen, Trevor, I am going to the International House of Pancakes for breakfast. Join me." Sounded like a command. Who wouldn't want an IHOP breakfast after drinking too much. I dressed and wandered the six blocks over to IHOP. It looked like a garish Muslim Church. Was there any other kind of Muslim Church?

"Trevor," I heard a voice holler from the back. Everyone looked at me with a smile. I couldn't figure out why.

"Hello, Don Gino, you seem to have charmed everyone."

He smiled. "Breakfast is on Dino Gino." I looked around and forty smiling faces were digging into steaks rather than the three-dollar breakfast special.

"I'm going to the source, Trevor," Don Gino smiled. His purple shoes glistened. Where in the hell does someone purchase purple patent leather shoes? Then I noticed the Bruno Maglis symbol. These were not shoes for the fashion novice. They are also the shoes that O. J. Simpson wore. I wasn't going to share that with Don Gino. Nothing inexpensive about the Don. We talked and he was angry. Poor Elliott Shonestein.

Later that morning Don Gino showed up at Shonestein's office. I was brought along. Why? Who knows? Pam Wong asked us to sit down. She didn't smile at me. I guess my animal magnetism didn't work well in the early hours.

A morning visit from Don Gino was not a pleasant thought. He seldom rose before eleven.. It was 10 A.M. and he looked unhappy. The eight Samoans entered the office and took seats. Pam Wong looked nervous. The midget valet was around. He wore his trademark purple suit. He was a five-foot version of Don Gino. If a comic one.

"Please Mr. Walker have a seat," Pam Wong smiled. Don Gino frowned. "Can I get you a cappuccino?" She didn't offer me anything.

"No." He snarled and pulled out a small file and began working on his nails. Pam looked at him and walked out of the room. She was nervous.

"Get Trevor a cappuccino." She left the room looking unhappy and returning with a cappuccino. She spilled some on me. I smiled. She glared.

"Elliott," she screamed into her phone, "we've got some god damned faggot in a purple suit waiting to talk to you, get your ass out here. There are also eight funny looking Chinamen, who don't look like Chinamen, with him. That other asshole is here too." Pam Wong slammed the phone down. There were no subtle nuances. She didn't know about Don Gino. She wasn't scared. Just stupid.

Pam walked over to me. Glared and walked over to the Samoans. "Excuse me, sir, would you like some coffee," she smiled. She was talking to one of the Samoans. Apparently Pam had a split personality. She got the eight funny looking Chinamen coffee.

She went back into Shonestein's private office. She quickly returned.

"Elliott will be with you in a moment."

"I will wait patently" Don Gino smiled. It wasn't a happy smile.

"Asshole, cat got your tongue," Pam Wong barked at me. I smiled. The Purple Don was seething.

"Don Gino are sure you wouldn't like a drink."

"No, unless I need to repeat myself again." She still didn't get it. The Purple Don was not used to waiting.

She spread her legs to let the slit in the skirt show everything. Don Gino wasn't interested but changed his mind. He gave her an admiring glance.

"Thank you lady, a cappuccino please." Don Gino continued to work on his nails. As he was half way through his second cappuccino, Don Gino looked up to see a smiling Elliott Shonestein.

Elliott was nervous. "To what do I owe this honor?" Don Gino continued filing his nails. He looked up and smiled.

"Come into my office, Don Gino." We all trooped in, the eight Samoans stood in a corner, the purple suited valet smiled and stood next to Don Gino. I closed the door. Eleven people in Shonestein's office was a crowd. He looked nervous.

"Elliott, you have a problem."

"I do!" Elliott looked confused. "I have paid the shall we say insurance policy that you require on my building." What he really wanted to scream was "extortion asshole." He thought better of it as he remembered the eight Samoans standing near the window. They looked like they wanted to throw him out of it. He also remembered the previous music mogul who had vanished after refusing to pay Don Gino's protection money. Or should I say catastrophe insurance.

Don Gino stood up and walked to the window. "A nice view of the city. I like San Francisco. The mayor and I often talk about the city and its beauty. Then I am reminded that I need money to donate to worthy causes. The Catholic church, Mayor Newsome's reelection campaign and the battle to end AIDS. I get upset when my finances are strained. It is then that things get messy and then I am upset." Don Gino put away the nail file. His fingernails looked perfect. He looked agitated.

"What can I do to alleviate the situation?" Elliott continued: "What does the Start Me Up band's problems have to do with you, Don Gino?"

"Ahh, Elliott, a sign of mental recognition. You may or may not recall that I own all of the small and medium sized musical venues in and around San Francisco. I also have a quiet share, in case you forgot, in the band." Don Gino paused and lit a small cigarillo. He exhaled and looked at the ceiling.

"Shall I continue?"

"Certainly," Elliott looked increasingly nervous.

"You pay heavy rent to Purple Haze Productions for staging the shows for the Start Me Up band. When they are on tour it costs about $100,000 a day."

"It's the cost of doing business," Shonestein continued. "I will cut those expenses to nothing."

"Ah, we are at the crux of the matter." Dino Gino smiled and walked over to the wall filled with pictures of Janis Joplin, Jerry Garcia and Jimi Hendrix. "See these pictures," Don Gino continued. "They all have something in common."

"They are superstars," Shonestein remarked confidently.

"No, they're all dead." Don Gino turned and glared.

"I'm not sure I understand," Shonestein remarked.

If the Start Me Up band becomes a national act, I am out a lot of money. They account for 75% of my rents. It is not just the local venues but I own about 90% of the venues they play.

"You do!" Shonestein remarked. He looked flabbergasted.

"I want the rents on the venues that the Start Me Up band plays increased. Got it."

"I do," Don Gino, consider it done."

"So you see Elliott I have a stake in your business. I am what you call a silent investor. A private partner." Don Gino lit another small cigar and continued: "I also don't like the fact that I have been made to look like a suspect."

"What do you mean?" Shonestein nervously asked.

"A Detective Sanchez came to my dog food plant to see me." Don Gino paused. "He was asking about my involvement with the Start Me Up band."

"What," Shonestein blurted. "Why?"

"It appears someone told him I was tied in with you."

Shonestein looked perplexed. "Doesn't that make you a suspect? If the Start Me Up band goes national you lose, maybe you are killing off those drummers with your salami."

Don Gino cast a cold look. "That is exactly the problem. I have nothing to do with this poisoning, I am unhappy."

"You mean you don't have a clue." Elliott said.

"Once again Elliott you are a genius." Don Gino continued: "Yes I am as confused as yourself. This time I had nothing to do with it. I will make one request. Help Trevor find out who is killing the drummers. Hold the band together and I will take care of the rest. Do you understand?"

"I hired Trevor, Don Gino, had you forgotten that?"

"Yes, you did but I have discovered that you are hindering your own investigation. You have withheld key information. Do you know how that makes me feel."

"What?" Elliott looked nervous.

"I will ask you only once, Mr. Shonestein, did you prevent your own P. I. from fully understanding the case." There was a long and uneasy silence.

Shonestein looked nervous and scared: "Yes." A threat brings the truth.

"Share it my friend with Trevor." It didn't sound like Shonestein was Don Gino's friend.

Shonestein looked nervous and he started spilling out the truth. "I forgot to mention to Trevor that Pam Wong is the chief financial officer or should we say the CEO of my little enterprise. I also forgot to mention that she is taking him to bed to find out who is killing the drummers. She is also not what she seems. She also has no idea about you Don Gino. So my apologies for her rude behavior."

Don Gino smiled. "A good answer, the truth always prevents an unnecessary beating. I abhor violence." Don Gino's valet opened the door and the eight Samoans vanished. Don Gino remained standing over Shonestein's desk.

Elliott wondered if there was such a thing as a necessary beating. "I will come clean with Trevor. What else would make you happy?"

Don Gino looked out the window. "I think the time has come set the record straight." He lit another small cigar. Lung cancer was in the air.

That was not what Shonestein wanted to hear. Shonestein ruminated about what he had not told the Purple Don. Did Don Gino know that Pam Wong and her Hong Kong connections ran his business? He was no more than a front man. She had the money. She had the control. She had the profits. Shonestein still had his life.

Was Don Gino aware that Shonestein was a front for a large drug ring? Elliott hoped not. The Don had a reputation for making drug dealers disappear. Elliott swallowed. He envisioned himself inside a can of Don Gino's gourmet dog food. His mouth was dry and he perspired. Things had not gone the way that he hoped. He had no idea about the killer. He didn't worry about Trevor The Turd. He was a moron.

"I will make all the loose ends come together, Don Gino." Shonestein looked liked he was constipated. He was sweating. That was not a good sign. "Whatever you want, Don Gino," Shonestein looked nervous. Don Gino smiled pulled out his nail file and began redoing his already perfect nails.

"Fine." Don Gino walked out the door with his purple scarf in the air. Pam Wong reentered Shonestein 's office. "There is a queer midget in a purple suit out there who wants to see you." She was obviously losing her patience.

"Send him in," Elliott remarked.

"Elliott," the little man in the purple suit shouted. "Don Gino asked me to have you report to him once a week. Any problem with that."

"No," Elliott remarked.

"Good," the midget remarked. "We all need to be kept on the same page."

Elliott Shonestein sat down in his chair. He was a wreck. Whoever was killing the Start Me Up drummers created more problems than he could handle. The meeting with Don Gino was chilling. He may have been gay but he was a stone killer. If one with a smile.

Chapter 16

TREVOR HEARS MORE THAN HE WANTS

There is nothing better than a Saturday morning in San Francisco. I woke up looked out my window. The fog partially obscured the Golden Gate Bridge. It was chilly but female joggers in tight shorts ran in the park across the street. A set of swings were filled with young kids pushed by their mothers. A group of guys were playing cricket on the baseball diamond. They all wore turbans. Everyone seemed to be under forty. I did feel old. Oh well, I could lie about my age.

Chestnut Street is one of the swinging singles places in San Francisco. Joe DiMaggio lived around the corner. I guess he wasn't really a swinging single. I watched the fog roll in from the Golden Gate bridge for about an hour as I drank a cup of coffee.

After shaving, showering and putting on my blue Dockers with a white polo shirt and some Air Jordan sneakers I walked down to Starbucks. The usual crowd was there. Divorced women over fifty trying to look thirty, dot.com yuppies, divorced guys over forty looking for women over thirty, a few constructions workers, actors and the generally underemployed. They all looked happy. I knew otherwise. I ordered a café mocha and a cheese croissant. I pulled out my napkins and began looking at the clues. It was someone close to the band. It was someone close to Shonestein. That effectively made everyone a suspect. It was time to put the clues to work.

I walked over to Lombard Street where I had miraculously found a parking place. I drove up to the Haight and parked on Ashbury. I walked over to Emilio's for donuts and coffee. Today would be a two-donut day, a chocolate French twist followed by a jelly filled twist. A workingman could afford two donuts on the weekend. As I walked down Haight Street there were signs of impending doom. The increasing number of designer companies created a yuppie domain. I wandered in through Emilio's front door as the smell of sugar wafted through my nostrils. I looked around for my blood pressure doctor, he wasn't in sight. So it was safe to enter and have two donuts and as much decaf coffee as my body could survive. After all it was Saturday and I was ready to rest.

The last seat at the end of the counter was mine. The only problem was that a Hell's Angel sat there eating a donut, drinking coffee and smoking under the "NO SMOKING" sign. No one told him. I wasn't going to say a word. I found a table in the back corner. Emilio came out of the kitchen, smiled and said: "Hellllooo, likee donut." I didn't say a word. He brought over two donuts and coffee. He knew my Saturday order. It was the same every week. Emilio smiled. I spread out my napkins. "Well bossee, you solvee crime." I wasn't sure what was up with Emilio. When we had a drink he talked like me, he figured he sold more donuts to the tourists with what he called the "fake Chinese talk." I explained to him that he was Vietnamese and politically incorrect. He wasn't Chinese. He just smiled. Everyone seems to do that with me.

"I need some time to concentrate Emilio," I continued, "this case has me perplexed." He looked at me like he wanted to help. I was glad he didn't offer. Looking at my napkins spread out on the table I kept thinking about the song "Look For The Woman." What did it mean? I was halfway through my second donut when I felt a hand on my shoulder. It was soft, feminine and reassuring. I hoped it was a woman.

"Hello sweetie," Joyce Byers smiled. She looked radiant. A tight Fiandaca black sweater and a Gucci bag highlighted a pair of Prada designer jeans. This made her a fashion plate. The brief case she carried was red full leather with room for a personal computer. It looked like it could hold a filing cabinet full of papers. The lock was 24 karat gold. How she affords her clothes on a civil servants salary is beyond me. She never failed to intrigue me. Then I remembered the Internet. She did all her shopping there. There was a lot about Joyce that I didn't know. My mind ran to the bedroom and the good times. I needed to pay attention to the more mundane details. Like my present case where I had three clients all of them seemed to be the murderer.

"Can you get me some coffee?" She smiled.

"An errant knight at your disposal miss."

"Cut the bullshit, I'm here to help, if you can shut up and listen."

"I can do that."

"Let me pull some things out of my briefcase."

I realized how insensitive I was about Joyce. I never asked her anything about herself. Except if she was on birth control pills. I never found out where she went to school, if she still had parents. Did she ever have another job? Did she have an education? Had she been married? I did know she was good in bed. At least the few times I had persuaded her to stay over. I was anything but sensitive. I had to admit my interests were carnal ones.

"Sit down, Joyce, a cappuccino and buttermilk donut is on its way."

"Trevor, do I look like a coffee and donut person?"

"What does one look like?"

"They have a pot belly sort of like you." She smiled.

"Touché."

"Ah, Trevor, I will have some orange juice and a herbal tea. Emilio came over. They talked in French. Now I knew she spoke another language. Now I knew Emilio spoke French. I am still the consummate P. I.

Joyce, may I ask where you learned to talk frog?"

"It was the summer institute at the University of Paris, the Sorbonne." She looked triumphant.

I spoke to her in flawless French. She looked perplexed.

"How in the hell did a cretin like you learn to speak French?" A fair question.

I replied: "It was two years of French and a summer at the Sorbonne." I smiled. "Our French class was on the Boulevard Raspail, in an area dominated by hookers."

"Trevor, I know you felt right at home."

"Touché." She wouldn't learn anymore from me." What I failed to mention was that I paid little attention to my Paris French lessons. I dated the teacher and only passed by one point. I wasn't sure if that was because I was good in bed or awful. Good was my hope.

"Let's get out of here Trevor, we need to talk." We discussed the case and she had some ideas. Joyce drank half a glass of her orange juice and sipped the tea. She talked at length about Shonestein, Pam Wong and Don Gino. None of whom she considered the murderer. That shot holes in my theories. Maybe the butler did it.

After we talked for an hour, Joyce remarked: "I'm hungry."

"Great, I make a great toasted cheese sandwich.?"

"Not exactly what I had in mind." Joyce put on some lipstick.

I didn't give up easily. "Where shall we go? My place!"

"How about a hamburger at Bill's. It is almost noon." She stood up.

"A nooner, I can't wait." I smiled. She didn't.

The drive to Clement Street was a short one. We headed up Stanyan and I wondered where Rod McKuen got the inspiration for all those awful poems. Maybe it was the fog and lack of hippies. It was a stark and boring street. McKuen was stark and boring. So maybe the symbiosis was the proper one. We turned on Geary and drove over one block to Clement. What used to be an old Irish neighborhood was now Chinese. All the old bars full of young Irish girls were now Sushi restaurants, Chinese bakeries or nail salons. The Chinese were complaining that there were too many signs in Vietnamese. They also complained bout the rise of nail parlors. Bigotry is an equal opportunity disease. The Chinese didn't like to spend money but they sure were keen on getting their nails done. Now the Chinese were moving out and complaining about the Vietnamese, the Cambodians and the Laotians. Some things don't change.

We parked near the 4 Star Theater and looked at a picture of Nicole Kidman as Virginia Woolf. Not even Kidman could keep Woolf from being butt ugly. I had to keep these opinions to myself, calling a woman butt ugly was no longer acceptable. Even if that woman was butt ugly. Now they were beauty challenged. I preferred butt ugly.

The patio at Bills' was empty. I ordered a Herb Caen burger and Joyce had the daily special a 49er burger. I told Bill it was a burger that didn't go to the playoffs. He didn't laugh. Joyce didn't laugh. I laughed. She loved her football. I wondered if the 49er burger was the hamburger that lost in the first round of the playoffs. Or didn't get to the playoffs. When I told her that joke, Joyce looked at me nastily. "You repeat yourself, Trevor, just past forty and you are already an old man."

Never try humor on the 49er faithful. As we ate, we had light conversation. Would Jack Nicholson win another Oscar? Was Michael Jackson a pervert? Not exactly my topics. I didn't care but I kept up appearances by listening to every word and agreeing with Joyce. She soon saw that I was bored. I am usually bored.

Joyce looked irritated. "Ok, asshole, let's talk." She didn't smile.

"Did you get some more information on Pam Wong?"

"Here," she slid an envelope across the table. It was my second secret envelope. I felt like a character in a Robert Ludlum novel. My techniques were more like the fictional detective Red Diamond. He was a mild mannered cab driver who became an ace detective once he was hit over the head. Then he had to stop his fictional girlfriend, Fiffi, from being accosted by the mobster Rocco. A fantasy. But a fun one. Maybe I should take a blow to the head. I opened the envelope and began reading. It was explosive. Pam Wong was the key to the case. She owned the business, she ran Elliott and the Start Me Up band was a cover for a drug smuggling ring. I was finally on the case. But I still had only a minimal idea of what was going on. Pam Wong seemed to be the key. It was time for me to use my charms. Or at least use my detecting skills. She had the answers to the puzzle and Elliott didn't seem to know what her role was in the scenario. Maybe I was wrong about Elliott. Maybe he knew everything.

"Isn't there enough here to arrest Pam?" I looked at Joyce hoping for the right answer.

Joyce continued at length: "Trevor, remember law school? Evidence. Motive. Opportunity. She hadn't been in law school for a long time. Joyce mixed up the sequence of events. I wouldn't tell her that she needed a law school refresher course. It is as if Pam Wong lives in a vacuum. We can't even find anyone she had slept with and that includes you. If there was enough evidence to arrest her, we would have long ago."

I gulped. My adams apple had a way of twitching when I was nervous. I think my adams apple was dancing in my throat. "Well." I started to sweat. The famous private eye in a moment of vulnerability.

"Well what, cat got your tongue!" Joyce smiled and took a bite of her 49er burger.

"I never had any real dates with Pam, it was simply investigative techniques."

"Cut the bullshit, Trevor, you need to find some evidence. You slept with her twice."

"It was in the line of duty, remember Shell Scott slept with his suspects."

"Who in the hell is Shell Scott?" She gave me a strange look.

I explained about Richard Prather and the millions of books he sold in the Shell Scott series. I even gave her his phone number in Sedona, Arizona. I also gave her the cell phone number of the lovely Tina.

"Who in the hell is 'the lovely Tina." I was crestfallen

"The lovely Tina is Prather's wife, he met her at the Mission Inn in Riverside, California where she was a cocktail waitress."

She looked perplexed. Maybe she thought I was nuts. She went on her iphone and spent some time. "Asshole," now I knew Joyce was mad. "The lovely Tina died two years ago."

"Well I guess you won't be talking to her." I looked triumphant. Why? Who knows!

"Are you on another planet Trevor? We have a case, so forget about Shell Scott. Whoever the hell he is to you."

I agreed. Silently. What could I say. "Okay."

"What in the hell do you mean okay?" She looked miffed.

"What am I supposed to say, we are having a fight not solving the case."

She said: "I don't believe what a dumb shit you are. Penis brain, think for a moment."

"What thoughts should I have? A penis brain only goes in one direction." I smiled.

Joyce looked exasperated. "For one time in your life consider how to collect the evidence and then find the motive."

"Fussy, fussy," I smiled.

A frown came over Joyce's face. She looked perplexed. "You are working for everybody in and around the case. Maybe your buddy Don Gino is behind all this. Remember 'Look For The Woman' Trevor."

Suddenly my hamburger didn't taste so good. I was ready to leave Bill's. There was no need for desert. My stomach had soured. I drove Joyce back to the Haight; she got in her car and waved to me as she headed home. I wondered where home was as she always met me at my office or come to my place. The great detective in failure mode. I couldn't understand a woman who could cut me a new asshole, then wave, smile and drive away. I was sure the wave was her middle finger.

All was not lost. I had some new leads. I parked the car and wandered up the stairs to my office. I held the manila folder that Joyce had given me like it was gold. The door was open. I couldn't wait for the surprise visitor. I would have pulled out a gun if I had one. Fortunately, I fear for my own life carrying a gun. Maybe I'll get a squirt gun.

Chastain Johnson was sitting at my desk. She looked up. A large manila folder was in front of her ample breasts. I focused on her supple breasts. To hell with the manila folder I should have focused on the envelope. Why did everyone I know have ample breasts? She looked like she was going to draw her gun. So I smiled and looked into her face.

"Well, well, Trevor, you have returned." She lit a cigarette. I thought of filing a formal FBI complaint. Breasts too big and smokes. Not exactly the mo of an FBI agent.

"To what do I owe this visit?"

"Three guesses. Maybe you want to have sex. Or perhaps you want to have a romantic dinner tonight?" Chastain looked like the cat that had eaten the mouse. I hoped that I wasn't that rodent.

"Well Trevor, that is two guesses and you missed. I will give you a free pass on the third guess."

"Do I want to know why you are here?" I looked haggard and tired.

"You look like shit, Trevor."

"Wine, women and song, now it's your guess." I continued to be clever.

She looked like she was going to laugh. "You still have one guess champ. Or is that chump?"

"One guess about what? Do I look like a mind reader?"

"Hello, Trevor, the case, the lead suspect, the culprit, maybe I should visit Shell Scott."

"Impossible Chastain. He is thirty, lives in L. A. and has been thirty for fifty years." Now she looked perplexed. I continued, "Well, you want to know what is going on with the case."

"I want to know what Joyce Byers brought you."

"Sex."

"I don't have time for this, the envelope please." Chastain had a commanding presence.

"You work fast." I pushed the manila folder across the table. She read it for almost twenty minutes. I twiddled my thumbs. Maybe I should get a nail file like Don Gino. File my nails and look tough.

I said: "What do you think?"

"I think you need to get a nail file. Look at your nails. Your eye brows need trimming." She didn't smile. Chastain looked at me for a long time. "You have a pile of nothing here."

"What do you mean?" I sounded irritated.

"This information is useless. Joyce's so called special investigative insights are missing. She fed you just enough material to keep you going. She knows much more than this file contains."

"Aren't you the FBI?" I always ask the tough questions.

"Trevor, there is a jurisdictional problem here. We can't get onto their turf."

"What turf, Chastain?" I frowned. "Do I look like a mind reader?"

"The FBI needs you to be a good citizen." She lit another cigarette. I opened a window.

"How do I become this so-called good citizen?"

"Easy, Trevor, just cooperate."

"You mean cooperate with my girl friend?"

"You got it." Chastain stuck an unlit cigarette in her mouth. The FBI agent trying to look tough. Not easy to do with big breasts. But it beats the same behavior with small breasts.

"Maybe you could spend the night with me, that might turn me into a perfect citizen." I smiled.

She didn't look happy. "I am off to work. Here is a file for you that has twice the information that Joyce Bitch gave you. The little miss goody two shoes cunt is worthless."

"Joyce Bitch is not her name. It is Joyce Sex Symbol. Sex is her middle name." I am instantly clever. I was taken back by Chastain's comment. Not to mention surprised. I couldn't resist another dig. "It's Joyce Byers and she is great in bed," I hollered as Chastain left the office.

"That makes one of you good in bed," Chastain chuckled as she bound down the stairs and across the street to have Ben and Jerry's double dip Cherry Garcia special. I think it came with LSD frosting.

I felt betrayed. I couldn't figure out where the case was going. Everyone was working against me. They seemed to be doing that by working with me. Maybe my animal sex charm would make Chastain, Pam Wong and Joyce more cooperative in the future. Then again, maybe not. I walked out to the street and she was still standing there. Chastain looked unhappy. She lit her third cigarette. There was ice cream on her lip.

"What can I do?" I looked to her for an answer.

"You need to see Elliott Shonestein and Pam Wong. They are the key." She lit her cigarette and continued: "Don't sleep on the case, work it. Don't think about sleeping with me, you got lucky once. Never again. Think! Think! Think!"

I had been doing a lot of that lately. It was getting me nowhere. "How can I interrogate the man who hired me?"

"You'll find a way." She smiled and left. I walked down Haight Street to Amoeba Records. I would buy the new CD by the Eels. There was a song by Mark Oliver Everett about his mother dying. It fit my mood and the Eels lead singer was my kind of dysfunctional. Standing on the street, I was perplexed.

The sun was beating down, as much as it ever beats down in San Francisco. With a day approaching 70 degrees, I got in my car and drove over to California Street turned right and headed for downtown. It was time for a drink. The cocktail hour was near. I could always see Elliott and Pam. They weren't going anywhere. They were prime suspects. They were also still active in the booking business.

Tonight they were presenting Rod Stewart at the Warfield. This theater on Market Street was the site of the first rock and roll concerts in San Francisco. It was 1956 and Lavern Baker sang her heart out and Fats Domino followed with a twenty-piece band. Little Richard came in with more musicians than the stage could handle. I had passes for Rod Stewart. Backstage ones. A detective legend gets special treatment. I could hardly wait to go downstairs in the cavernous Warfield green room or should I say green basement. But I needed a drink before the concert. I pulled my car into the Fairmont Hotel Court. The valet looked at my car with disdain. He parked the car. No tip for bad looks.

I walked into the Tonga Room. It was the last stand of the old style cocktail lounge. It had a dance floor in the middle of a tropical lagoon. Once an hour the lagoon burst into a mild hurricane. The water was lighted with a purple hue. The thirty-dollar pupu platter was a bargain by San Francisco standards.

Don Gino loved the place. When a special effect brought the lagoon into a frothy roll much like a hurricane, Don Gino was frequently seen dancing with a young girl. The only time this ever occurred in his life. Not surprisingly, the hurricane was the favorite drink of the Tonga Room. A long buffet table offered an all you can eat array of Asian edibles. I always had trouble with the corned beef. Not exactly Asian. They featured something called Pacific Rim Cuisine. Don Gino called it expensive chink food. I called it a mess.

I sat down at the bar. I would tip the brawny Italian bartender much less than the good-looking waitresses. Then I looked at the bartender. He could break the bar in two. He would get a large tip. I had to quite thinking that all bartenders were men. The big guy wasn't the bartender. He was stocking the bar. He sneered at me and went into the back room. The woman who approached me was gorgeous. The other bartender walked over, she was a lovely lady. Breasts to die for and she was at least forty. I wondered what happened to my favorite Italian bar tender, Luigi; he probably got a real job. The Tonga Room didn't miss a beat. One of each, a man and a woman to take care of the drinks and the politically correct San Francisco atmosphere.

"Where's Luigi?" I asked looking at the lovely lady bartender

"Learning to bartend. He got fired. Dipping his wick where it shouldn't stray."

"I'm afraid to ask." She was eager to tell me the story. It seems Luigi picked up a local male judge and they had a party in the hotel. When security busted them, the Fairmont fired Luigi and smiled at their good fortune. There was a lawsuit before the judge regarding hiring discrimination at the Fairmont. He assured everyone that he would not recuse himself. He also said he would be fair. He wasn't. The hotel won. The incident passed into history. She washed a glass as she finished the story.

The new bartender smiled. She was a Pamela Anderson look alike and took my order for a Jordan Merlot. Ouch. The glass of Jordan was a whopping $25.00 and the free buffet had a $9.50 service charge and the $8 tip set me back $42.50. I loved the spring rolls with plum sauce and the Szechwan guacamole with Irish crackers. Welcome to San Francisco. Even the food is multi-ethnic.

When the bartender collected my money, she looked at me like I was cheap. I could have gone to Woey Loey Goey's in Chinatown for five meals. Oh well, a famous private eye has to be seen amongst the people.

As I sat staring at the mirror in front of the Tonga Room bar, I had an idea how to continue to pursue the case. Then the hurricane bar began a fake storm and I watched the dance floor tilt like in a major storm. My thoughts came quickly back to the case.

What if there was a hidden suspect? Everything was too perfect. The crime pointed to Elliott and Pam. Maybe there was another angle. I finished my Merlot, dipped a coconut shrimp in some sauce, wiped the ketchup off my face and before I could head for the door a second Merlot appeared. The bartender handed me a napkin with her number on it. It read Pam at 415-555-6440. I was afraid to ask. I didn't want to complain as I saw the Pam Anderson look alike pour my merlot from a Gallo bottle. I could pretend it was Jordan. It was some time to drink and think about the case. I was refreshed and ready to fight crime. I was also full and broke.

I retrieved my car from the little shit valet. I gave him a dollar. He sneered. I got in the car and drove down Powell Street dodging a cable car. I almost hit a pedestrian when I noticed my front seat. On my seat there were twenty-five napkins. I had almost forgotten about them. Research. After looking at my notes scattered over the front seat, I had a renewed mental image of Elliott Shonestein. He had motive. He had access. He had financial gain. He had to stop the recording contract and songs for the Start Me Up band. He had every reason to kill the three Start Me Up drummers. It all seemed too perfect. I had to think some more about the case. In my car, I am able to gain a solitude that is not available to me elsewhere.

Pam Wong was another case. I had twelve napkins with her information. Why one napkin contained her body measurements was a mystery. The private eye must have all the facts. I looked at her notes and realized she had both motive and access. If the Start Me Up band folded, her little side business was history. I turned on the car radio, Van Morrison's "Brown Eyed Girl" played and I turned it off. If President George Bush listened to it, I couldn't.

Pam and Elliott were somehow the key. But how? I had to find the mysterious person poisoning the drummers. Chef Fred looked good for it. He was also too obvious. He also sounded like an honest man. He was also my client.

I drove down past another Cable Car, looked at the sumptuous St. Francis Hotel and turned right the block before Market Street. As I wound my way down to Shonestein's office, I put some of the pieces together. Whoever wrote "Look For The Woman" was a suspect. I had no luck finding out the songwriter, as the tune wasn't registered with BMI. In the midst of my thoughts I almost hit a bus and ran over a lesbian. A midget gave me the finger as he crossed in mid-street. I almost hit the little bastard. I had to be careful the quota of midgets was just at government standard. Then the lesbian hit my window with her umbrella when I stopped at the Market Street light. At least she looked like a lesbian. Maybe she was a K. D. Lang look alike. Who knows? I had to get a grip on myself.

Not an easy task. San Francisco is a nightmare for the average driver. It is also a nightmare place to solve a crime. Perhaps that greatest crime is that I am a terrible driver. As luck would have it I found a parking place in front of Shonestein's production office. After putting six quarters in the meter I was ready to attack. I had heard more than I cared about the salami drummer murders. It was time to start solving a crime. Or should I say crimes.

I took the napkins off the front seat and put them in a manila envelope. I also included Pam A's number 415-555-6440 which I would never forget. The old animal magnetism was still there.

Chapter 17
THE SHONESTEIN SHOW

When I found out that Shonestein had two offices, I began to wonder about him. The office where Don Gino and I went was a an impressive affair. I was curious to see the new digs. I took the stairs to the second floor of Shonestein Productions. The door was slightly ajar. I pushed it open. A huge logo adorned a polished wooden door and the office reeked of money. Designer furniture, all the latest gadgets like an espresso machine, a super fax ,five computers, special phones and even a small kitchen. It reeked of money and screamed out success. The wallpaper was a subdued brown and it matched the hardwood floors. The cappuccino machine was state of the art. It was not only imported from Italy but had all the bells and whistles that screamed of the right kind of cappuccino. I wondered if it also made murder easier. A cappuccino before killing. I took a deep breath and prepared to do verbal battle with Pam Wong. To my surprise she wasn't sitting at the reception desk. There was no one at the reception desk. Strange. There was an eerie silence. The room smelled of disinfectant. Shonestein's outer office was so neat and orderly it was embarrassing. Why two offices?

The door to Shonestein's private office was open. It also looked like a neat freak had just cleaned it. I walked in and Elliott wasn't sitting at his desk. There was a note. In fact, there were two notes. The first one said that Shonestein had been kidnapped. The second one warned me to stay away from the case. I took out a handkerchief and called Detective Sanchez. I was not looking forward to our conversation. It took ten minutes and three San Francisco Police Department secretaries to bring my macho friend to the phone.

As I waited for Sanchez to come to the phone, my feet stuck to the floor. I put my hand on the desk and it got sticky. I smelled it. Jesus, it reeked of salami. I took a shoe off and smelled it. Was there such a thing as salami residue? My salami adventure was cut short as Sanchez answered the phone.

"Trevor the Turd," Sanchez blared. I told him that we had a problem. He said he would be right over.

In fifteen minutes, Sanchez walked into Shonestein's office wearing his John Varvatos designer suit. The Armani's probably ran away to Italy. I didn't tell Sanchez that Varvatos hired Cheap Trick to sell his product. Maybe rock and roll people were suddenly wearing suits.

"Welcome to Shonestein productions," I smiled, "here is the evidence." I handed Sanchez the notes.

"Let me guess, Trevor, you got the killer to confess. Then you had him write two notes. You locked him in the bathroom and the case is solved." He was smiling. I took crime seriously.

"Enough of the smart remarks." I wasn't happy. I felt like the world's greatest detective twenty minutes ago, now I had to say that I was the world's worst P. I. "The Shonestein show has turned into a disappearing act." I continued. "My main suspect has vanished and a kidnapping note is on the desk. They also want me off the case."

"The mob doesn't like incompetence."

"I had a line on both Shonestein and Pam Wong. Now they have disappeared."

Sanchez laughed. "Maybe he committed suicide so you wouldn't catch him." There was silence on my end.

"Funny." I didn't look happy.

. "Don't touch anything and that includes Pam Wong." Detective Sanchez put up crime scene tape and left the building.

I walked downstairs and there was a Starbuck's. A man can't live on fear alone. I ordered a venti mocha and an oatmeal cookie. Then I remembered that tough P. I.'s didn't eat cookies and drink lattes. What would Shell Scott do? He would drink a shot of whiskey and beat up Detective Sanchez. Not my style.

The coffee smelled good and the cookie melted in my mouth. So much for the tough P. I. What the hell, I would be an exception. I drank and ate in peace and pulled out my napkins. There was something I was missing. I walked outside of Shonestein's office as two uniformed SFPD officers approached me. They wore motorcycle jackets, leather gloves and looked like they had just gotten off their Harley's. Once secured the door and the other wandered into the kidnapping scene. I followed them back upstairs.

The tall officer who looked like Brad Pitt said: "We're sorry sir, you can't come in."

"I was just here, bozo, I discovered the body," I paused and continued: "Trevor Blake III Private Eye." I saluted.

"What?" The younger policeman blurted.

"Detective Sanchez just left," I continued, "and he told me to stay at the death scene." I pulled out a card. They looked at it like it had lice on it. A small lie is better than a big one.

"Stand here and I will talk to my partner." The younger of the two officers went inside and locked the door. I waited. It was almost twenty minutes later when Sanchez ran back up the stairs to the crime scene. He walked hurriedly from the back to the front of the building. With all his energy and movements, Sanchez's suit still looked immaculate. He bought suits that didn't wrinkle. Ricardo Montalban would eat his heart out. He looked at me bewildered. Why aren't you at the crime scene? Remember I said to stay there. He wasn't smiling.

"I needed a latte. Then I helped to two motorcycle officers get to the crime scene."

"What," he screamed.

"My case too Sanchez, the detective needs energy so the coffee."

"Jesus, the boy now approaching middle age who can't get laid needs a latte."

"As I said, there are two officers in there from you department." Detective. Sanchez looked like I had hit him with a brick.

"What," he screamed. I door to the front hallway is locked. I had to come down the back steps." He continued: "Now Trevor, slowly, tell me what you found."

I went over my story. It wasn't much. No one was in the office and there were two notes. I spend ten minutes telling my side of the story. Which wasn't much. "I didn't see a thing out of place." I looked at a loss for words.

"Again why are the doors locked?"

"Read my lips, two officers who are holding down the fort. They have kept me out." He looked furious.

"I didn't send for officers."

"Oops," I blurted.

Sanchez turned the door handle. "It's locked. So let's get this straight, two of San Francisco's finest have locked themselves into the crime scene."

"There must be a problem, Detective."

"I think that's a fair assumption." Detective Sanchez reared back and broke down the door. Remind me not to anger him. I wondered why he sometimes called himself Sgt. and at other times Detective. Was he both? Perhaps he was a megalomaniac.

We walked into Shonestein Productions and found it a mess. The place was searched and files were missing. I had spent ten minutes explaining my role in the investigation to the two fake cops. That was enough for them to do their thing. The file cabinets were all over the floor; the two wastebaskets were emptied on Pam's desk. We walked into Shonestein's office and it looked like a hurricane hit it. There was no sign of the two SFPD officers. Strange. There was no body. There was no sign of blood. There was no crime scene. I was in trouble. There was no sign of the salami mess. What was going on?

"Well, Trevor the turd, what have we here?" He smiled. "A messy set of offices. No evidence of anything. Just you." He walked behind Shonestein's chair. Detective Sanchez bent down and took a magnifying glass out of his pocket. He put on a pair of gloves. I wondered if he was going to clean up the room. He looked for ten minutes around the chair. Then he took a series of small envelopes from his coat, a small brush and an even smaller spoon followed this. He was obviously collecting evidence. Either that or getting ready to have a coke party.

"Not doing coke these days are we detective?"

"Elementary police work is something you don't understand, Trevor. If you stay by the door, I'll be finished in a few minutes." I dutifully moved to the door. It took Sanchez another twenty minutes, and he filled four envelopes. With what I am not sure. He took me by the arm and ushered me out of Shonestein's office. A large yellow ribbon with "Crime Scene" emblazed on it emerged from Sanchez's pocket and he strung it across the door. He did this for the second time. The fake police had taken the original crime scene tape. Sanchez stopped and looked around the room. He pulled out his phone.

"Joyce Byers," he screamed, "get over here with the crime scene people."

We walked out into the hallway. Sanchez walked me back down to Starbucks. He smiled. I knew that things were fine. He called for a second time on his cell phone to the SFPD lab. He asked for any and all prints by tomorrow. I heard someone protest that they didn't even have the evidence. Sanchez told them he would be in at noon for the prints. That is if there were any prints. I could hear a cooing female voice telling him it would be done. I guess he did his police work with more than blunt force.

We walked back to the office. Joyce was standing at Pam Wong's desk. She ignored me. Sanchez instructed a crime scene crew.

"Someone has cleaned up the room. Look for latent prints." He told them amateurs cleaned it. "Something is missing. They cleaned up the salami stains and left everything else a mess. I suspect no prints."

"I forgot to mention that I wrote down the motorcycle license numbers." I smiled.

"For once Trevor you have done something right."

The world's greatest detective strikes again. Sorry Elvis Cole. "What did I do right?"

"You wouldn't understand, too much education and not enough real world experience.."

"A compliment no matter now ill-timed is appreciated."

Sanchez said: "It's time for another coffee, I'll buy."

"This is strange, you hate coffee, you don't like hanging out with me. What's up?"

"A good question, you have stumbled onto a crime scene."

Now I was perplexed. "Enlighten me."

"It's simple, Trevor, Elliott was drugged and kidnapped by someone. Then the two phony SFPD officers showed up and took what was left behind. We need to find what was left behind. Before the two phony cops got here, someone cleaned up the crime scene to eliminate trace evidence. The salami stains were a ruse to throw us off," Sanchez concluded.

"Now I understand why they wore gloves." I looked embarrassed. The world's greatest detective misses an elementary point. That is that there was evidence staring me in the face. I missed it."

"What did you see, Trevor?"

"Nothing but two notes."

"Have you by chance forgotten anything, Trevor?"

I swallowed nervously. "There was a warning for me to stay away from the case. That was the second note. My feet stuck to the floor and my hands smelled of salami."

Sanchez smiled. I was about to find out that my detecting ways remained primitive. "Where do we start, Trevor?" I stayed quiet. Sanchez continued: "The floor had some salami residue on it. I bet that it was the same type of salami used to kill the three drummers." Sanchez smiled.

"What else?" I looked perplexed.

Sanchez looked thoughtful. "There was a residue of chloroform on the chair. Shonestein was kidnapped."

"Ah, the smell, I thought it was bad Chinese." Sanchez didn't appreciate my humor.

I asked: "Chloroform by two SFPD police officers who vanished?"

"You got it Trevor. You interrupted the kidnapping. They went out the window after slipping Shonestein in the closet. Then they returned and carted him out to a waiting car."

"What!" I appeared to have missed everything.

"Shonestein was in the room when you entered, he was tied behind the curtain."

`Where?" I asked in bewilderment.

"Look behind the curtain, Trevor." I did and there was a door. It was slightly ajar and the wind rushed in. So much for my keen powers of observation. A hidden door.

"What now, detective?"

Sanchez smiled: "All you seem to have is questions. You are the detective; tell me, Trevor, you must have some answers."

I didn't like my answer, I said: "I don't have a clue."

"Let me help you solve the case," Sanchez lit a small cigar. He blew a smoke ring and continued: "What we have here is a turf war between music promoters, an unidentified songwriter and someone in the restaurant business."

"So carry it to the next step, detective."

"These differences tell me a lot." Sanchez blew smoke at the ceiling.

"What does that tell you?" I didn't sound like the private eye who could solve a crime.

"What is going on is not clear. Your job, Trevor, is to find the link between the various suspects, and then follow the money." He sounded like Robert Redford and Dustin Hoffman in that movie about Nixon. "Follow the money." I think Hal Holbrook said that.

He paused and took a long drag on his cigar as the female barista brought him a free latte. She sneered at me. So much for being the world's greatest bachelor. Sanchez had that effect on women. I pulled twenty-five of my napkins out of my pocket. I spread them on the table. I didn't like the direction that this case was headed.

"Tell me Trevor, what do these napkins show?" I smiled. Always the detective. I could offer some insights.

"The napkins contain all that is known about the case." I felt like I had everything down.

"They demonstrate a pattern," Sanchez said in a serious tone, "they show your disorganization and inability to solve the crime." He looked at the napkins for fifteen minutes.

"If you study the napkins long enough detective, you can see that it is a songwriter posing as a Chef."

"That is a problem Trevor. Everyone is a songwriter."

"Not Don Gino." Sanchez didn't laugh.

He lit another small cigar. "Do you see anything?" Sanchez looked at me pensively. I guess he expected a deductive answer.

"For once I can be serious, I think food is the answer. Somewhere in this mess the connection to the killings of the Start Me Up drummers is food. It is also the Rolling Stones."

"What!" Sanchez said mockingly.

I was not happy with this answer. "Maybe Mick Jagger has a sideline as a serial killer,"? I remarked with dripping irony.

"Believe it or not Trevor that is a possibility. Look for the Rolling Stone who kills." I couldn't believe it, for once he was serious. Sanchez jokingly continued: "They are on the road constantly maybe someone goes after the Start Me Up band in the Stones camp. The Stones tour is always followed by a Start Me Up gig, so a Stone employee could be our culprit."

I couldn't believe Sanchez's reasoning. "You've got to be kidding. You mean Mick and Keith work as part time hit men. Hey, maybe so. They haven't had many hits in the last twenty years." Sanchez looked at me with disdain. Obviously, he couldn't take a joke.

We walked out onto the street. Sanchez looked up and down Market Street. He paused. "Trevor, we have a problem."

"Yes." I knew that but what was the problem.

Sanchez said: "The killings point to Shonestein. If he's alive we're fine. If not, we have trouble. So find him. Let Pam Wong know I want to see her."

"I don't have a clue where Pam is," I explained. "Then do a missing persons on her."

"Sanchez need I remind you that I am not the police."

"Use Joyce Byers." I didn't like the tone in Sanchez' voice.

"Remember I am not the police." I wanted to have the last word.

"You just think you are." I couldn't disagree. We shook hands and I wandered off. Things were now very complicated. Elliott Shonestein may or may not be the killer. Pam Wong vanished. It was time to see Don Gino. I had to prepare for Don Gino. He wasn't one to waste his time on speculation. Research is the key to being a great detective. I had to find what Don Gino was up to in the business world. We always made small talk and I needed something to talk about. Small talk was not my forte.

I also needed a night of rest before going to see Don Gino. I drove down to Chestnut Street. I parked the car. Soon I was hiding behind a tree. Bennie and Bertie were standing on my doorstep. I walked around the tree and over to Fillmore street. I turned left and walked up to Union Street. Once more I turned left and poured myself into a seat at Perry's Bar. I spent the rest of the night drinking Merlot. I hoped it wasn't Gallo. When I got the tab for $60 I knew that it was at least Clos du Bos. The private eye must have good taste at all times. No one talked to me. There were no pretty girls for the famous detective. Something was wrong. Maybe it was Pam Wong.

At just after two on a cold San Francisco morning, I wandered down Chestnut Street. Bennie and Bertie were long gone. Probably at home talking about how much they loved President Bush. Or maybe they were searching out people like themselves. Why two right wing fools, who were my ex-in laws, liked me remained a mystery. Must be the private eye personality. I unlocked the door. There were no messages on the answering machine. I could sleep without interruption.

Chapter 18
HANGING OUT WITH DON GINO

I slept in the next day. After a shower and a nine o'clock breakfast of a Noah's cheese bagel, a Starbuck's decaf and a banana I headed for North Beach. I spent an hour looking at my napkins. Sanchez was right, they were a disorganized mess. There had to be a clue in there somewhere. I just hoped that Emilio forgave me for not coming into his shop for donuts and coffee. I picked up an Italian cookbook in North Beach specializing in salami. I needed to find out more about the fatal meat. After purchasing some cannelloni, I got the car out of the city garage. It was only ten dollars. Then I remembered that I had left some important notes in my office.

After leaving North Beach, I drove up to my office, double parked, and took the fifty extra napkins off my desk. A detective had to be prepared. I laid them in the front seat with my original twenty-five notes. I was disorganized but I did have evidence. Or at least napkins. Why I went to North Beach, then to my office and then back to North Beach suggests my lack of organization. Or for that matter crime solving capabilities. But I now had an idea who the Chef was.

I drove the car down Haight Street and noticed the high priced condos going up. Either the hippies were making money or the yuppies, I turned left on Fillmore and another right on California brought me to the Fairmont Hotel. One of my Stanford classmates owned the parking concession, so I left my car there with a special pass. I parked and walked back over to North Beach. I love walking through Chinatown. A small sword caught my eye. For $30 I left the Ho Hee Hing Gift Shop with a miniature replica of a samurai sword. Tom Cruise eat your heart out. It looked like a sword for midgets. As I stopped and gazed in the window I noticed a man with a brown raincoat and a broad brimmed hat covering his face about twenty feet away. It was the same guy in the brown raincoat that came out of the Fairmont Hotel as I walked down California

Street. I continued down Grant and quickly ducked down Sacramento and into the alley.

The guy in the brown raincoat followed. I stepped out from a small alcove and grabbed him. The next thing I knew I was on the ground looking at a gun. I have to remember to carry a gun or learn to fight. I wasn't good at either. Now it was too late. He smiled. I didn't. He slowly moved away and holstered the gun.

"Well, asshole," he pulled out a San Francisco Police Department detective shield. It was none other than my good friend Detective Sanchez in disguise. "You've just assaulted an officer."

I said: "Let me get this straight, you follow me and I've assaulted you." I didn't put it in the form of a question. He smiled. It seems everyone was smiling but me.

"I'll make this real clear for you P. I. Trevor the Turd, we need some answers. You have been around all the murders and evidence. We need to have coffee. I'll buy."

The thought of another coffee with the detective was not a happy one. "I'm busy, Sanchez."

"I know, it's off to see Dino Gino everyone's favorite gay mafia boss."

"Try saying that to his face." I smiled. Sanchez looked nervous.

"You've got a point, not a smart idea. I don't want eight Samoans looking for me. Not to mention a crazed midget. C'mon Trevor we are going to Woey Loey Goey's for lunch."

"I couldn't resist a free Chinese lunch. The Chinese delicacies were the best in San Francisco.

"What a spender Sanchez. I know I get any luncheon special." We walked into Woey Loey Goey's and were greeted by Alice. I admit that is a strange name for a 75-year-old Chinese waitress who has known me for twenty years. She sat us. I ordered the tomato beef chow mien, the gai war won ton soup and the pork asparagus. I could eat for a week at home with the leftovers. Sanchez settled for Gai War Won Soup. Probably trying to fit into a new wardrobe. A younger waitress showed up, maybe twenty-five, and she brought Sanchez a free beef and broccoli and slipped her phone number into his pocket. It wasn't Alice, it was her daughter. She'd recently had a boob job. It seems everybody I know is having a boob job. Not me.

"Ok detective. I am all ears," I said wiping a tomato stain off my pants.

"We need some inside information, the case is cold." Sanchez looked flustered. I started feeling sorry for him. He looked and sounded like Hal Halbrook in All The President's Men.

"What do you have in mind?" I didn't believe the answer.

"I want you to ask Don Gino to fix any problems in the case?"

"What!" I screamed. I couldn't believe my ears.

"You're asking me to have a mafia don come into the investigation and you'll look the other way."

"You got it, that is exactly what I want." Sanchez didn't smile. He was serious.

"Look at it this way, Trevor, a few grease ball musicians are killed, Don Gino can put this whole case back in order. He is, should we say, an interested party. He can operate through you."

I looked incredulously. "Ok," I said. We shook hands, Sanchez paid and bill and we left in silence. He left a twenty. The bill was eight dollars. Now for the fun part. Trying to tell Don Gino that he had just been made an unofficial policeman. I walked up Grant for two blocks crossed at Columbus and wound my way up the upper side of Grant Street. I turned left on Green Street and went into Don Gino's Restaurant, The Purple Pasta. He bought it to launder money he made in the Mission District with thirty illegal betting parlors and a loan office. The restaurant was named for an old San Francisco coffee shop. The owners were going to sue. Then they found out Don Gino owned the place and sent a letter with their blessing. No one liked to make the Purple Don cranky.

As I walked into the Purple Pasta I noticed two Samoans sitting at the bar. That meant there were six Samoans lurking somewhere in the hinterlands. Probably hidden behind the plants. The two Samoans were drinking milk. Obviously not real men. No need to tell them. I walked into the back room and there sat Don Gino eating a big plate of pasta, drinking a glass of vintage Antinori's Classico Chianti and poking at a spinach salad. Don Gino always the health nut.

"Trevor," Don Gino called out with a smile. He was obviously glad to see me. Nothing like having a Mafia Don for a friend. I sat down and another plate of food appeared. The waiter came silently, put the food down and left without a sound. I wasn't going to tell Don Gino I had just eaten. No sense upsetting the Purple Don. I began eating.

"That's Guido, he was a hit man in Sicily, makes a good waiter, huh?" I agreed. I wasn't one to tell a Sicilian hit man that he had garlic breath. Or that he was clumsy putting down the plates of food. Or that his clothes didn't fit.

I decided to eat the food. The linguine was great, the salad had goat cheese and pine nuts on it. It was also made with a special spinach dressing and it was the best I ever had. I was slurping up a huge plate of tiramisu and drinking a cappuccino as we began to talk. I was also feeling my gut expand beyond my pants. Oh well, I would work it off with sex. Or better yet running down Chestnut Street.

"Well Trevor, what is it?"

"It's a long and complicated problem, Don Gino." I paused nervously, I wasn't sure how to ask him to join the detective agency. Or for that matter how to tell him that he was about to become an unofficial member of the SFPD. I was silent for a moment.

"Yes, you are ill at ease, something is bothering you." Don Gino lit a cigar. I hated smokers. No need to tell the Don. "Let me ask it another way, Trevor. Some people are obviously squeezing you or you must do something you dislike."

"Yes." I spoke with a whisper obviously scared and nervous.

"Not only are you my friend but as we get to know each other I look upon you as family."

Great. Now a gay Mafioso is adopting me. I thought of a hundred ways to tell Don Gino that being adopted by the only gay Mafia figure in the world was not my idea of security. The more I thought about it maybe I should be quiet. "I have three problems Don Gino, Elliott Shonestein, Pam Wong and Detective Sanchez. Where do I begin?"

The Don ordered two more cappuccinos. "Try Me," he remarked.

"That was a James Brown song." I smiled. Always the wise cracking P. I.

"Get to the point, Trevor."

I explained the missing body. Where had Elliott Shonestein gone? What was Pam Wong's role? I told Don Gino that Detective Sanchez wanted his help to settle the so-called murder problem with the three Start Me Up drummers. I told him that the police treated the murders as open homicides. They didn't have a clue and Detective Sanchez was stymied. He had deputized Don Gino through me. I was surprised by Don Gino's response.

"I am, shall we say, an interested citizen. It would be my pleasure to assist Detective Sanchez. I have long admired his work. He is one of the few people that I call sir. It is my respect for him."

I exhaled and relaxed. "Thanks." That was all I could say.

Don Gino reminisced: "Sanchez and I attended Mission High School. We were on the football team and we were on the varsity wrestling team for three years. During our senior year I was number one in the state at the 160 pound division and he was number one at the 175 pound division." Don Gino smiled. Good memories obviously.

I tried not to look astonished. It was hard. I said: "Gee." Not exactly the answer of a brain surgeon.

"You are surprised, Trevor."

I lied: "No." There was an uncomfortable silence. I had to come up with a lie. "I can see you wrestling Don Gino, not Sanchez." The lie seemed to placate him. I proceeded to explain that I would like Don Gino and his associates to assist me in solving the crime. I nervously explained my plan and laid my seventy-five napkins on the table.

Don Gino looked for a long time at the napkins. He said: "they look disorganized to me." He looked at them again for almost fifteen minutes. I twitched nervously. "I do see some clues here."

"Enlighten me." I still looked nervous. There were now eight Samoans sitting at the bar drinking milk. They weren't smiling.

"What do you see?"

Don Gino responded: "Like I said follow the money." Where were Woodward and Bernstein when I really needed them? I think Detective Sanchez said the same thing.

"What money?" I was frustrated.

"Find Pam Wong and get into her books. Remember Trevor her books, not her pants."

"I know the difference Don Gino." I proceeded to explain what I did knew and the financial connections between Shonestein and the various booking agents. One of whom was Don Gino. He smiled. He knew something I didn't and looked pleased.

Don Gino listened intently. He waved for another cappuccino. It appeared miraculously. He sat smoking and looking at the wall. I knew enough to be quiet.

Finally Don Gino spoke. It is kind of like E. F Hutton, everyone listens. "What we have here Trevor is a deception. I am not sure where or how or why." He relit his cigar. He puffed out long plumes of smoke toward the ceiling and continued to think. The eight Samoans sat quietly at the bar cracking their knuckles. Something was up.

"This case is one that I will take an active interest in. You my friend have to be my eyes and ears. No one is talking to me. I am very angry about this whole situation." Not a good sign to make the Purple Don unhappy.

I looked at Don Gino confused. "How can I be your eyes and ears?"

"You are going to work for my distribution company."

"Your distribution company?" I asked with a puzzling look.

"Yes, Joe Irvington is simply the front man for my salami and restaurant supply business. He also handles the catering that I do for the rock bands that play the Oakland Coliseum, the Warfield, the Fillmore and every other venue in town. Bill Graham tried to horn in. Then he died mysteriously in al helicopter crash. Don Gino smiled. I sweated.

"After Bill Graham died," Don Gino continued, "Jerry Garcia came to me and we had a long talk, he was walking away from the Grateful Dead and he asked me to talk to Mr. Graham about his financial ways." Don Gino smiled and continued: "Unfortunately, the helicopter crash ended Mr. Graham's life. It was sad." I didn't think the Don felt that way.

Don Gino continued: "The murders of the Start Me Up drummers point to me. Someone is trying to frame me. I also control Pam Wong and Elliott Shonestein. I have a corporation that controls their business. They are stealing from me and Miss Wong is laundering drug money through my businesses. I am not happy. She has deceived me."

"What should I do?" I felt funny. The great detective with no clue.

Don Gino said: "Shonestein has been kidnapped and Miss Wong has gone into business for herself. She is smuggling in small amounts of cocaine and selling them to the bands. She is much like Yoko Ono. Not the smartest cookie alive. I didn't know about this until recently. If they are killed, I am the chief suspect. I don't like that. You must find another way to solve this delicate and complicated crime."

Perhaps I can infiltrate Irvington Brothers. Are you sure you want me to work for you," I inquired.

Don Gino looked angry. I guess I wouldn't tell him that he shouldn't call Yoko Ono a cookie. His eyes were blue pools that stared through me. "You can say no to our proposed partnership and your new job with my distribution arm," Don Gino suddenly became silent. Not a good sign.

"Oh, no, I mean oh yes I am happy to go to work for you. With you, I mean anyway you want it. Does that mean I can somehow solve the crime?" The Don looked happy.

Don Gino laughed. "You have nothing to fear from me. You are like a son." Once again I didn't look overjoyed. Don Gino continued: "I have some special juice at City Hall and an aide to the Mayor will announce on Sunday that your P.I. license has been revoked for incompetence. That same newspaper story will quote the Irvington Brothers as happy to hire you. You will be removed from the case. At least in the public eye."

"What does this do for me?" I asked quizzically.

"You will be the person responsible for delivering food and other goods to the Start Me Up band. In your new job, you will announce that you have enrolled at the culinary academy. I will see to it that you become a well-publicized chef in training. As an insider you will solve the case." Elvis Cole would never suffer this humiliation. Joe Pike was there to beat up anybody who insulted Elvis.

I was perplexed but I wasn't about to tell Don Gino that his plan was a crazy one. I suspected there was no one who would talk to him honestly. Certainly not me. At least not if I wanted to live. I agreed to go to work for him and to have the SFPD suspend my private investigators license and to have a story leaked to the San Francisco Chronicle. The Chronicle would report that my license was lifted for incompetence. That story would humiliate me. I would be called the most incompetent detective in the history of the city by the bay. I would never be compared to Dashiell Hammett. Humiliation was not easy to take. I left Don Gino's restaurant and walked on Green Street back to Grant Street. I walked by the Condor club. It was now a sports bars. Too bad all the horny guys who had watched Carol Doda dance in her topless bathing suit couldn't come back from the grave to see her. Too bad she was fifty and her tits were bouncing off the pavement. Now it was the Oakland Raiders on the Condor's television that entertained the unwashed drunks. Progress wasn't always positive. I stood at Broadway and Columbus and thought about the good old days. Then again they weren't so good. I needed a book.

I walked by the City Lights Bookstore. Pam Wong was standing at a window table and reading a book in the poetry section. Lawrence Ferlenghetti was standing at the counter ringing up a sale. I had read Ferlenghetti's epic "Coney Island of the Mind." I enjoyed it but didn't understand what he was doing. He looked alive and healthy. Kerouac and Ginsberg were dead. Ferlenghetti was alive. He was also past eighty. Wine, women, song and poetry. Obviously, ways to stay alive. The difference was that he liked poetry and women not drugs and booze. My kind of guy.

"Hello." I smiled at Pam Wong. She turned and looked at me like I had a disease.

"Trevor!" She paused lost for words. She reached into her purse. Hope it wasn't for a gun. She pulled out a pack of Marlboros.

"Any tips on the case?"

She lit a cigarette under the no smoking sign. Ferlenghetti rushed back with a Chinese guy who had lifted too many weights for too many years and they roughly escorted us to the street. I wasn't smoking.

I looked at Pam and knew I had to get some information. "How about a drink in Vesuvio's?" This was the North Beach bar that Jack Kerouac made famous by drinking Irish Coffee. She agreed. Her face told me it was with great reluctance.

The private eye sex symbol image was not working. We sat at the bar. She ordered a Cakebread Merlot from the reserve list at $25 a glass and I had a $5 beer. I wondered what in the hell is a reserve wine list? Somewhere Jack Kerouac was rolling over in his grave. Vesuvio's was one of the favored haunts of the beatniks. They had jug red wine in Kerouac's day. Progress is not always progress. I had been noticing a lot of that lately.

"Need I remind you Trevor that Elliott hired you to find the killer."

"That was before he vanished, before you held information back from me, before the police informed me that you may have a side business." I smiled. Always the deductive detective.

Pam smiled. "My business interests are none of your concern."

'Tell Detective Sanchez that."

She looked angry. "He spends too much time looking for women in the local bars and too little time figuring out the case. You have more answers, Trevor, you just don't know it."

"Sleep with me, Pam and I will give it all up." Always a wise ass.

"I will sleep with you when I grow a penis."

I guess we weren't going to have any further social contact. "I just have one question."

What!"

"I want to know who wrote "Look For The Woman."

"Sorry Trevor, that is a trade secret. If I knew I would tell you. We get the lyrics in the mail. They aren't fully copyrighted. Elliott has a copyright lawyer working on it." She opened her purse. I was hoping it wasn't to pull out a gun to shoot me. Instead she handed me an envelope.

"What's this?"

"It's an envelope, dickhead, the one that the lyrics for "Look For The Woman" arrived in at the office."

I took the envelope. It was my first real clue. It was time to test it. I wasn't sure how, but I would figure it out. I left Vesuvio's and walked down to the city garage. It was time to rethink the case.

I drove to my office. The Haight was full of the usual weekend hippies or were they yuppies? Or were they hippies who grew up got jobs and became yuppies? Who cared. Who knew. I walked down to Emilio's. Might as well ruin my day with a gigantic cup coffee and a highly sugared donut. I walked into an empty donut shop. The health Nazi's frowned on donuts but Emilio still made a nice living. He talked about having a side job. I never paid much attention to the random discussions of his other employment. It was probably an imaginary job. What I suspected was that he was a cat burglar. He always had a lot of jewelry. Then he had no jewelry. The rumor was that the fences loved him. This deduction helped to explain the expensive art pieces in his house. How many donut shop owners have an original Monet over the toilet? Plus a Van Gogh over the kitchen table. He needs some interior decorating tips.

"Trevor, would you like a low fat bagel?" Emilio always used perfect English when the donut shop was bereft of customers. He had taught me how to use words like bereft when he finished his M. A. in English literature at San Francisco State.

I looked in horror. "What?" A nasty looking bagel plopped down in front of me with a huge cup of decaf.

"So, Trevor, what is new?" Suddenly Emilio sounded like everyone else. The donut shop was empty and he could talk like himself. I went over my case with him. Surprisingly, he gave me some great advice. The clue was in the song, "Look For The Woman." He pointed to two suspects. He also suggested that I follow the money. Everyone had been talking to Woodward and Bernstein. He urged me to get close to the new drummer and the other band members. But first I had to go home and rest. The newspaper story of my license revocation would cause a stir. It was also embarrassing to look like a bumbling incompetent. So I went to bed by myself on a Saturday night. Shell Scott was probably in bed with three women all of whom were beautiful and blonde. I fell asleep thinking of my favorite Los Angeles detective Elvis Cole. He would never stand to have his license revoked. He would look at his Pinocchio doll and fight back. Joe Pike would show up to beat up the entire SFPD.

As Sunday morning came with the bright San Francisco sunshine, I felt good. The Golden Gate bridge was shrouded in a light fog and the sun broke through on the Marina Green. It was unseasonably warm and I took a cup of coffee to the roof of my apartment building. I felt like I was in heaven. It was a false omen. I wandered back into my apartment. The phone rang. The first call was from Guitar Jac. He had heard the story of our license revocation. I was sure he was worried about having to go to work. Maybe he couldn't buy brie to go with his Dom Perignon. I convinced Guitar Jac that everything was fine. He reluctantly bought the story. He didn't like the idea of someone making fun of us. Jac told me that he was driving to some afternoon blues jams and he would see what he could pick up about Elliott Shonestein. No sooner had he hung up, the phone rang again.

It was time Joyce Byers. She wanted to go to city hall to help me get my license back. I was not as forthcoming with her. I told her I didn't want my license back. That didn't work. She knew I was a lying sack of shit. I had only one option, to tell her the truth. Finally, I got her to understand. There was more to the story. I even convinced her she didn't need to know. She hung up with a parting sentence.

"If you are lying to me, Trevor, I will cut your balls off."

"You'll have to stand in line." I hung up uneasy about our future relationship.

Then my ex-brother in law, Bennie, called and he told me Bertie was distressed. She was worried people would make fun of her because I was once related to them by marriage. Not exactly the concern of a loving person. Bennie was worried that I couldn't pay the rent. I assured him otherwise. He told me that he was doing magic shows for the people who loved him. I listened in horror. He was about to do a magic show for my birthday. I told him I couldn't wait. What else could I do, I needed cheap rent.

They arrived at my apartment and told me about their travel plans. I wasn't interested but I listened. Bennie and Bertie were about to spend two months in Puerto Rico. Not in France, England, Italy, Spain or some place civilized or exotic. They elected to camp on a small island where after two months they could say that they gave directions to the natives. Strange people. They could feel superior to the Puerto Ricans. No wonder America was hated abroad. Bennie wore a Reelect Nixon button on one sport coat lapel and Reelect George W. Bush on the other lapel. He was the ugly American reincarnate. Also one who didn't listen to the news, read a paper, read a book or analyze any political issue. He was fun at happy hour. It was because he paid.

Bennie went on about the Puerto Ricans being foreigners that didn't understand the good old United States. I said nothing. Last time I looked Puerto Rico was part of America. That made a lot of Puerto Ricans unhappy. My brother in law pointed them toward revolution. After two months of Bennie and Bertie, the Puerto Ricans would be crazy. Realizing that Bennie and Bertie needed some extra money, I gave a three-month rent check and they left happy. The main thing was that they left. I could now bed single girls. That is if I could find one who would talk to me.

I spent the rest of Sunday pampering myself. I drover down to the Cannery, found a parking place and wandered over to the Buena Vista for an Irish coffee. Sitting in the window looking at the Golden Gate Bridge reminded me how lucky I was to live in San Francisco. That luck soon ran out. Detective Sanchez wandered into the Buena Vista with a concerned look. In fact, he looked downright unhappy. Another Irish coffee was delivered to the table. Detective Sanchez sat down.

"Have a seat," I smiled. He didn't.

"We need to talk, Trevor."

"Gee, I thought you came in for an Irish coffee.

He lit a cigar, always a good sign. The waitress brought him an Irish coffee on the house. He wore a pair of blue Dockers with a white yachting shirt and a blue cap. Always the fashion plate. He paused and looked out at the sailboats engulfing the Golden Gate Bridge. He took another drag on his cigar. The waitress came over to see if he needed anything else. He had finished his Irish coffee in two gulps. She ignored me. She quickly brought him an Irish Coffee. You guessed it, a complimentary drink. Her phone number was on the napkin. I picked up the napkin. Sanchez was thinking. The silence was devastating.

Sanchez was still thinking. Finally the awkward silence ended when he spoke. "Your little plan to go to work for the Irvington Brothers is crazy. If it was Don Gino's idea, I have some words for him. You won't get anywhere at the Irvington's."

"I don't know why Don Gino wants me to work for the Irvington brothers, I will do it, and no one says no to the Purple Don."

Sanchez didn't look happy. "What does Don Gino have in mind?"

"I don't know." I don't think I sounded convincing.

"Come clean, Trevor."

I was silent. No sense pissing off the Purple Don and Detective Sanchez on the same day. I lied: "It was my idea and it is a good one. I will take Woodward and Bernstein with me to follow the money. Don Gino had nothing to do with the plan."

Sanchez looked at me like I was crazy. Probably a good deduction. "Who in the hell are Woodward and Bernstein?" I didn't respond, so much for police literacy.

"They are the press." He looked at me with disdain.

Sanchez got up: "I will talk to you later." He took another napkin from the waitress. She glared at me. Obviously, it was her phone number. She saw me take the first napkin.

"Anything else Sanchez?" I was immediately sorry I added that little dig. He turned around and looked at me and he continued to think. He held up his hand. I knew that was his way of telling me to sit. It was like training a dog. You hold up your hand. The private eye listens. Elemental. He also lit a cigarette. So it was to be a long epilogue to his exit.

"By the way, Trevor, the new Start Me Up drummer will be announced in a few days at a press conference in the Warfield Theater. The threat to kill him on the spot is real. You need to be there and take care of the situation. We will have officers, undercover detectives and a set of poison sniffing dogs. We need to stop the bastard." I was the key and I couldn't believe it.

"My new job, Sanchez, puts me on the spot. I will take care of him."

"That's exactly my worry." Sanchez put a ten-dollar tip on the table and left. The Dow Jones must be paying off this week. I thought about stealing the tip. Too late the buxom waitress put it down the front of her uniform.

"I walked out of the Buena Vista, put a dollar in a bum's cup and handed him the waitresses napkin. I said: "Call her, she's been eying you from the BV." If you are hip in San Francisco you say BV not Buena Vista. I am hip.

I still had the weekend or a part of it to think about the case. I went home to my Chestnut Street apartment and spread the now eighty plus napkins I had made on my desk. The case was starting to make some sense.

Chapter 19
OFF TO THE IRVINGTON BROTHERS

On Monday morning I showed up at eight am sharp to begin my new job with the Irvington Brothers. Third Street was bustling with yuppies, reinvented dot. Com business types and young women who were now more often the boss. I dropped into Starbuck's for a café mocha. I ordered a venti with an extra shot. I needed the sugar rush. I didn't need the six-dollar price tag. I could hardly wait to begin my undercover job with the Irvington Brothers.

I stood on the curb at Third Street and admired the San Francisco Giants baseball stadium. They called it A.T. and T. Stadium and for thirty million dollars I could have it named the Trevor Blake III Stadium. I will pass. The stadium is gorgeous. It gives the area class. I noticed a newspaper vending machine. I looked at the front page of the San Francisco Chronicle. There was a picture of me and a story that continued on page eight. I lost my P.I. License for incompetence. How could I have made the front page. I smelled the hand of Don Gino in this escapade. It must have been a slow day with the Iraqi war. The San Francisco Chronicle story was not a pleasant one. Now I had a cover. Everyone believed that I was incompetent, a fool and off the case. I hoped the SF Chronicle was wrong. At least about the part of being incompetent and a fool. I noticed a few people staring at me as I walked up Third Street. Not what a famous private eye has in mind.

The Irvington Brothers office is like a time warp. There is an old wooden desk from the 1950s, and a picture of Joe, Dom and Vince DiMaggio playing in a San Francisco sandlot. The only good thing about the office is the good-looking secretary with the great boobs. She sat reading a Betty Freidan book. She looked at me with a sneer. Some things don't change. I expected to be called asshole. She smiled. "Hello Trevor, can I get you some coffee.?"

I was speechless: "Sure." It didn't sound like an emphatic sure but a perplexed one. She didn't seem to notice. Rocket science was not her major.

"Follow me your office is down the hall, Joe won't be in for two hours, he is bonking the mistress." More surprises. Maybe Betty Freidan had a clue to what was going on?

I walked into my new office. There was even a brass nameplate with my name on the door. A freshly minted one. Obviously Don Gino had a hand in the machinations. The office was a modern one with all the toys. I sat down and went on the computer. I dialed up AOL and went onto the Start Me Up website. The band would announce a new drummer tomorrow. There was a press party complete with hors d'ouvres. A memo on my desk said the Irvington Brothers would cater the party. I had taken a two-day course at the San Francisco culinary academy some years back to impress the ladies. So I could help cater the party. The phone rang. It was Don Gino. No doubt checking up on his minion .

"Trevor, the party announcing the new drummer is tomorrow." Don Gino paused. "I have set up the party, you are catering it."

"I know about the party. I just got off the internet," I continued. "I don't know a lot about catering a party."

"I will take care of it," Don Gino reminded me.

"Don Gino, not only have I not handled the catering I didn't know how to go about it."

"Get on it," he went silent. Not a good sign.

. "Now I have some problems. I need to find some waiters, a clean up crew and a series of Chefs."

"Handle it, Trevor."

"Will do." I hung up. My skills in the cooking department were minimal ones. I had forgotten most of my culinary lessons. Maybe someone would think I was the Chef killing the drummers. I was in deep thought.

The phone rang again. It was Don Gino. My thoughts were interrupted by Don Gino's call. He coughed. "I have taken care of it. That is I have the chefs, the clean up crew, the waiters and some of my people to work the room." I could imagine eight Samoans quietly working the room. No problem. They would wear tuxedos and blend into the woodwork. No sense sharing my thoughts with Don Gino.

"Good, I will put together a tray of goodies that are killer, come of think of it they will just be tasty." Always the humorous P. I. I spent the rest of the morning while the secretary and myself put together salami, cheese, fruit and vegetable trays. It was a culinary sight. I needed a break.

I drove down to the Ferry Building, parked my car and wandered into the Slanted Door's kitchen. Chef Alan Kirschbaum specialized in a mix of Asian and California styles with a kosher touch. Kirschbaum called it "Jews meet California and the Far East." His reputation as an innovative Chef was international and he quickly set me up with a series of trays that made me look like a Chef. I swore him to secrecy. I would take credit for the food. When I told him that I was working for Don Gino, the food was on the house. Kirschbaum was worried. He gave me some advice.

"Trevor, remember not to overheat the items. Whatever you do make minimal use of the microwave. Otherwise the food will taste like rubber. Also, keep the chilled items chilled." He smiled. "I know your inattention to detail, Trevor." He wrote out an elaborate list of instructions for preparing and serving the food. I was trying to pay attention. There were no guarantees. My concentration left a great deal to be desired. The only thing that saved me was that I was after all a famous private eye.

I drove back to the Third Street warehouse. An even bigger sign that read Border's dwarfed the big sign that read Irvington Brothers Produce. I stopped in Border's bought a John Sanford mystery, sat down with a cup of coffee and a croissant. No one was in the bookstore, I smelled bankruptcy.

I missed Emilio's donuts. Then I read the first two chapters. Maybe my life could be featured in a Lucas Davenport novel, I would call it Inept Prey. I took eighty plus napkins out of my pocket and laid them on the table. The Border's crowd was a motley crew of businessmen, unemployed college graduates, young girls and a mixture of truckers and teamsters. I was enjoying the calm and the quiet. Suddenly a hand touched my shoulder. It was soft. It was feminine. It smelled of expensive perfume. Why not, after all I am a detective and a sex symbol. I turned and looked.

"Hello asshole," Chastain Johnson smiled. "We need to talk."

"Why am I not surprised. Coffee?"

"What am I holding in my hand?"

I looked. "Coffee."

"Very good." She didn't smile. "I am going to have six undercover waiters at the press conference that you will cater to announce the new Start Me Up drummer. Nothing better go wrong."

"Does this mean I won't get laid if someone is killed?"

"Enough of the jokes. Just do your job. No extra detective work." She walked out the door. She did look good from the back. But she looked equally as good from the front. I didn't discriminate when it came to good-looking young ladies.

I closed the John Sanford book. Lucas Davenport inspired me. It was time to solve the case. I looked up and everyone was staring at me. As she departed, I heard Chastain mutter a loud "asshole." I bet Elvis Cole got more respect. I walked over to the Irvington Brothers warehouse and back up to my office. The truck from the Slanted Door showed up with the food. I sent down two Teamsters to load the food into a truck that had refrigeration and a controlled area for food. The Irvington Brothers are good union men. No one wants Harvey Schwartz showing up to cause trouble. The ILWU rep was a nasty Irishman with a Jewish name.

Science and technology made it inevitable that I would present a wonderful smorgasbord. I looked at my work. I had to remember I was the front man. I would take credit for it. My lack of experience made me nervous. I was about to become a famous Chef with no idea of what I was doing. I did the same thing as a P. I. so things could still go well.

Chapter 20
THE CHEF RETURNS

The Chef parked his car at the Fifth and Mission garage. It was a short walk to the Warfield Theater. The Chef carried his small suitcase. He had his customary Chef's coat and hat neatly folded in his case. He walked casually up Mission Street. He turned up one block and saw the Market Street sign for the Warfield Theater. He decided to stop for a cup of coffee. There was a Starbuck's a block from the press conference. He went in for a cappuccino. He was so nondescript, no one paid him any attention. It was not easy to go unnoticed when you were a six foot seven former basketball star. Inconspicuous dress. Good manners. A shy demeanor. A boring personal countenance. Was there another kind? All of these were practiced character traits. These were the personality elements that caused the Chef to blend in with the crowd. To go unnoticed and kill at will.

He finished his coffee and walked to the side entrance. It was where the artists arrived at the Warfield Theater. He was on the pass list. Huey Lewis was in front of him. The stage door was open. No one was around. Huey was to be a witness to murder. The Chef calmly walked downstairs. He began setting up his equipment. About a half an hour later security showed up and checked with him. They figured that he was in charge. The Chef moved to one corner of the hospitality room. He set up the salami trays. The mortadella salami was his favorite. He also liked the gypsy salami made in Canada. It would kill on the spot. Maybe the Canadians were getting their revenge for the decline of the dollar.

The chef looked at himself in the mirror. He was pleased. He wore his Chef's jacket that read, the Slanted Door, and no one paid him an ounce of attention. He had worked for Chef Kirschbaum and was fired for insubordination. He told Kirschbaum he was too short and muscular. He was also an asshole. The Chef kept the hat and a monogrammed apron.

Security was everywhere. The Start Me Up band was aware of the potential poisoning. The Chef needed a new spot for the poison. He couldn't kill everyone. Just the new drummer. He looked in vain for a spot to plant his mixture. There was none. So the Chef set up a special table. It was labeled "The Press Luncheon." If he killed Joel Selvin or Greil Marcus no one would care. In fact, Marcus couldn't bore people with his theories. Marcus was looking stuffed from so many free backstage parties. He had a doggie bag to take things home to the wife.

Then eight Samoans showed up. He could tell that they weren't fools. They were dressed in style and they were quiet and unobtrusive. That is if eight three hundred pound Samoans could blend into the crowd. They still looked menacing. Just high fashion menacing. The Chef wasn't fooled, he knew that Don Gino sent them. Fortunately, the Chef knew the Samoans. He exchanged pleasantries with them and left quickly. When he reached the street, the Chef was nervous. The new drummer would live. A journalist might die but not a drummer. There had to be another way to end the new drummer's life. The Chef lit a cigarette and stood on Market Street. He sneered at the losers who walked by. Then he saw his nemesis.

Trevor Blake III entered the backstage area and supervised the unloading of the truck. He was obviously working with Don Gino and the eight Samoans. Sure enough the Samoans unloaded the truck and remained backstage. Trevor ignored the chef. He set up his kitchen.

The Chef walked over to Trevor. "Hello." His muted tone and friendly smile prompted Trevor to shake his hand.

"Kirschbaum sent you?"

"Yes, he did." The Chef put his hat back on and took out some lip balm. He rubbed it on as Trevor set up the food.

The Chef also noticed FBI agents coming backstage. Not hard to tell them apart from everyone else. The only exception was a young blonde who looked more like Marilyn Monroe or Pamela Anderson than anyone else. She also had Jane Mansfield's breasts. Jane was dead and didn't need her breasts. She also smoked too much. The Chef smiled. My how the FBI had changed.

"Excuse me, Trevor," the Chef remarked, "I need to take a break."

"Go right ahead, we have almost four hours until the press conference. I am setting up the refrigeration."

"Good, thank you," the chef politely bowed and smiled.

The Chef walked across the street to Wendy's. He ordered a Jr. Bacon Cheeseburger and coffee. He looked at the cheeseburger and knew that he couldn't' eat it. He drank the coffee. He had to devise another plan. He smiled. It was all too apparent. He would come back on the scene and surprise them. They were looking for poison. He had to take the one tray and get rid of it. They could have their little victory. The new Start Me Up drummer would be introduced, survive the press conference and meet his end at a later time. How the chef wasn't certain. Then he had an idea.

The clouds were hovering over Market Street as the Chef walked toward the Ferry Building. He went to Giovanni's Cheese Shop and purchased some imported brie and a cranberry mozzarella. He bought a bottle of Frog's Leap sauvignon blanc and some imported French crackers. The non-eaten Wendy's cheeseburger made the Chef feel guilty. He needed to have a proper snack. He walked the two blocks back to his car and was unaware that he was being followed. The cheese was placed in the trunk. The Chef drove to his nine million dollar home at St. John's Wood. No one knew about this house. He kept his non-descript suburban home for his business front. His visitor looked as the Chef walked into his sumptuous home. The visitor was Guitar Jac.

No one realized that he was one of San Francisco's major cocaine importers and he was in partnership with Pam Wong. In fact, she didn't realize the depth of his evil. She would be terminated soon and the Chef would be the last suspect anyone would look to.

He thought of a plan to implicate Trevor. To meet young ladies, the master detective had attended over twenty cooking classes. He was known as something of a gourmet and a wonderful cook. As a ladies man he wasn't known. He struck out at every opportunity. His visitor took some pictures of the Chef at his home and left in a new Lexus.

The Chef didn't see any harm in trying to make the police suspicious of the Blake Agency. He stood at his window and dialed his cell phone. After three rings his importer, Harvey Isaacs, answered the phone. They talked about a new shipment. Suddenly the Chef noticed something.

"Harvey, what are the chances of a well dressed, forty year old Negro standing on my street?"

Harvey sighed: "Get off it, he probably owns a home nearby. They are not all athletes and in the entertainment business."

"I guess you're right." The Chef looked back out the window. The Negro was gone. Guitar Jac was getting in his car. He pointed his camera at the Chef's window as he talked on the phone. He also recorded the phone call. Guitar Jac had bugged the Chef's home phone.

The Chef's house was not only the most expensive on the block, but had the most custom work. He had closets that were eight feet high and filled with rows of suits purchased on London's Saville Row. He favored the conservative pinstripe that made the English so boring. He even had bowler hats. He was a man of tradition. He was also a serial killer. The three Start Me Up drummers were poisoned easily. The evidence pointed to Don Gino Walker and Elliott Shonestein. The Chef orchestrated Shonestein's kidnapping and made it look like the eight Samoans and Don Gino were the culprits. The police were too stupid to see the obvious clues. Shonestein would return. He would once again become a suspect. There was nothing they could do, the Chef had it all planned.

There were only three people he worried about Don Gino Landry, Detective Sanchez and Private Investigator Trevor Blake III. He should have worried about Guitar Jac. They were all capable of uncovering his criminal past.

The Negro who worked for Trevor was also a concern. The Chef could never remember his name, he was dangerous. The Chef had to be careful. The stakes were too high. Obviously, Don Gino and Trevor were working together. The sight of the eight Samoans bothered the Chef. He had to remember to cover his tracks. He was such an obvious suspect that no one considered him.

The Chef went about his business. He had to change his plan of attack. It was time to switch from poison to a makeshift explosive device. He went into his secret kitchen workshop and took the cheese, the wine, the crackers and a chemistry book. A quick death through a college chemistry book. That is what the Chef planned with a smile. He began to experiment with a set of chemicals. It took some time to develop a delayed toxin. The Chef called it death by stomach pain. He took almost three hours and found a series of chemicals that would react about five hours after the cheese was ingested. Everyone was looking for salami and the next death would be by cheese. The only problem was to make sure that the new drummer took the cheese home. That would not be a problem. Pam Wong would deliver the cheese and he would never realize it. She would be the culprit and again everything would point to her and Elliott Shonestein. Partners in crime.

The Chef's only concern was Pam Wong's lack of morality. She liked to sleep with everyone. That is everyone but the Chef and Trevor Blake. She would have to be contained. There was something about Pam that made the Chef nervous. She wasn't what she appeared to be and there was a mysterious air to her.

Everything was in order for the press conference. I was ready.

"Trevor," I turned and Detective Sanchez stood nearby looking like something out of GQ. "We need to cancel the press conference for a day."

"Fine, can I ask why?"

"No," Sanchez smiled and walked away. I put away the food in the refrigerator and realized I needed some more to feed the throng. I headed back to the Irvington Brothers for more food.

Pam Wong ended her surveillance of the Warfield. It was time for dinner and a plan. The three and a half hours before the press conference would give her time to help end some of her problems. Pam was concerned that Trevor The Turd was getting close to her side business. Guitar Jac was seen following her around town. He was not exactly inconspicuous. She needed a foolproof plan.

Chapter 21
Pam Wong Returns To The Office

Pam Wong stood on Van Ness Avenue smoking a cigarette. A dinner at the House of Prime Rib hadn't given her the inspiration to return to the office. The cars on Van Ness Avenue sped by as she threw her cigarette into the street. Pam knew she was in trouble. Not only with the police but Elliott Shonestein, the drug lords in Hong Kong, her silent partner in the suburbs, and also with Chastain Johnson and the FBI. Trevor the Turd didn't fit into the fear equation. He didn't get it. But his FBI companion did. She didn't trust Chastain. Who could she turn to? Pam thought about it as she lit another French cigarette. She loved French cigarettes. She hated the French. They could do only a few things right, one of them was cigarettes. Another was wine. Another was art. Another was music. Pam was in love with Johnny Hallyday. She continued smoking and thinking about sleeping with Johnny Hallyday. Finally, a cab pulled up.

The Sikh behind the wheel smiled at her. His Turban had a jewel in the middle. She got in and smelled his oily headdress. He smelled like he hadn't had a bath in the month. He turned to her and smiled. His teeth were yellow. Ugh?

"Where to pretty Chinese lady?" He smiled and a tooth was missing. The rest of his front teeth were filled with gold. The dashboard was fully of little religious statues. Maybe he was part time Mexican.

"Take me to 620 Chestnut." He no longer smiled. It was a five- dollar cab ride. Hardly worth stopping for and he didn't see a big tip. He did see big tits. The ride was short and silent. She got out and didn't tip.

"Nice ass, Chinese lady, is your husband good to you."

"Fuck you, raghead." Pam pulled out a cigarette. She lit it and blew a plume of smoke his way. "Asshole." She needed to relax. That creepy bastard looked like he wanted to get laid. She thought even Trevor had a better chance. She sat down on his doorstep and waited for him. The cigarette smoke wafted to the top of the enclosed entrance. She watched it curl around the stucco.

Pam looked at the park across the street. Young girls jogging, young guys playing baseball. Little kids on the swings. Trevor's apartment was in an area filled with swinging singles. All of whom were ten years younger than Trevor. He just didn't get it.

Suddenly two middle-aged people showed up who look like they might have voted for George Bush. They introduced themselves as Bennie and Bertie. They were dressed in clothes from Sears. Bennie had on plaids and stripes and seemed proud of his ill matched clothing. Bertie had short-cropped grey hair and a pantsuit that took away any feminine qualities. That is, Pam thought, is she ever had any feminine qualities.

"You are?" Bennie asked. He smiled at Pam. He had perfect white teeth. "You have noticed my teeth," he remarked, "a quick trip to Tijuana for implants." He smiled again.

Pam responded: "I'm a friend of Trevor's"

Bertie looked at her figure with envy. "And young lady what kind of friend is that?"

Pam smiled: "One who wants to jump his bones." Pam knew that their pricklish middle class sensibilities would be offended and she laughed. "That is if he has any bones left after the divorce." Pam took a drag on her cigarette.

"She picked him clean," Bertie remarked. "We are proud of our daughter, she got what was coming to her."

"You mean every dick in her law office, I know your daughter and she is a disgusting right wing, Republican with little mental agility." Pam smiled. She liked her use of language.

"Disgusting." Bertie commented and walked back to the car. Pam noticed that Bennie was staring at Pam's breasts. "They're real," Pam countered.

"Well, nice to have met you Pamela." Bennie tripped on the curve walking to the car. Bennie couldn't help noticing her nice ass. It had been awhile since he viewed such a young tush.

Pam sat back down on the doorstep. Bennie looked back and couldn't take his eyes off Pam's breasts. So much for middle class morality. She would wait for the son of a bitch, Trevor had to show.

I left the Irvington Brothers warehouse. Finally, I had enough food. I walked over to SBC Park. The San Francisco Giants were playing that night and the sidewalks were crowded. I stopped at Border's for a coffee and bought Alafair Burke's new novel Close Case. I loved the first two. She could write like her dad. Only she was clearer. She was also cuter. She was also out of my league. I walked up to Fifth and Mission and drove my car up to California street, in the midst of heavy traffic I turned left on Chestnut and was just about to park in the street. I saw a sight that made me damn near crash my decrepit auto. There was Pam Wong standing in front of my apartment. She was smoking. Nasty habit. If she slept with me, I wouldn't mention it.

After parking around the corner on Lombard Street, I stopped in Arab Al's Liquor Store for a bottle of Fat Bastard Merlot. The label would make for conversation if all else failed.

"Trevor, big score tonight?" Arab Al was not subtle.

"Just a quiet dinner party."

"Buy a Jordan or something with class."

"No thanks." I waved to Arab Al as he was waiting on a single woman. She had his attention. "I can come out and clean your windshield," Arab Al remarked. Nothing like a full service liquor store.

I walked around the corner whistling my favorite Disney tune "Zip A Dee Do Dah." I spotted Pam. She wasn't smiling.

"Jesus, Trevor first an Indian cab driver and now you whistling an Uncle Remus song. No wonder your country is so far between. At least culturally," she concluded. She snubbed out her cigarette.

"How's the cancer coming, Pam." Pam appeared to have a serious case of PMS. I looked stunned. I had seen her. I had thought about what she was doing in front of my apartment. I had no answers. Finally I spoke. "Want a glass of wine?"

"Unlock the god damned front door, Trevor, I am cold, angry, frustrated and in need of some answers. Besides I have no desire to get to bed with you."

"That would be bad for our relationship," I smiled. She didn't.

"We need to talk. Forget the god damned wine."

Not exactly what I hoped for. But I couldn't afford to be picky. She was being prickly, so I tried to soothe her. "Come on Pam, we can talk, I just got the new Van Morrison CD "Magic Time." It will put you in a romantic mood."

Pam lit a cigarette. It looked like lung cancer was on the horizon. "I have some confessions." She continued, "I am not what you think I am"

I thought about the lyrics to "Look For The Woman." "Finally, Pam, I get some clues."

"You are clueless, you stupid bastard." I had to agree.

Ah, I was now Trevor Blake III, confidante, psychiatrist, amateur lothario and crowned stupid bastard. We took the elevator to the second floor. I opened the door. She walked in my apartment and looked around with disapproving eyes.

"Well, Trevor, we a little short on the housekeeping." She noticed the dust balls in the corner.

I did have a comeback. "No, the CDs are all well organized."

"Cut the crap and listen."

I did. She sat down in my favorite chair. She shifted around in the lounge chair. She had great legs. The second best boob job I had ever seen. Chastain was still number one. I had to get my mind on the case. "Shoot!" I said. Private eye's know how to get to the crux of a matter.

"Elliott has been kidnapped. He has gone into a silent partnership with a criminal known as the Chef. I think they have taken him to throw the suspicion off the Chef. He is my partner."

"It's not rocket science, Pam, tell me who the Chef is and we arrest him. It is real simple."

She frowned and looked embarrassed. "I don't know him."

"Let me get this straight. He is your partner and you don't have a clue as to his identity."

"He has me go to a post office box in the Castro. It is there I receive my orders."

"Your orders." I laughed. It was a mistake.

"Listen asshole, I take orders from no one. He paid me one million up front wired to a Hong Kong bank. I am rich and smart, unlike you." Touché.

I had a comeback." Maybe I'll send you a thousand to be my concubine."

"Make it two million and I will think about it." Pam smiled. I was getting a lot of that lately.

"Touché. Let's get back on track. I need some help in finding the Chef, he will led me to Elliott."

"You have to find an amateur Chef, not a real one. He is a gourmet cook but has another job in and about the music industry or maybe the business end."

I couldn't believe it. That didn't eliminate anyone as a potential suspect. It simply added a new suspect. A Mysterious Chef no one could identify. Not even Elvis Cole could solve this crime. Then again he had Joe Pike. They could beat a confession out of the perpetrators. Things were getting more complicated. "Since when is a criminal a Chef," I laughed. "Is he cooking at Clown Alley?" I shouldn't make fun of Clown Alley, I had many a meal there.

Pam looked deep in thought. She continued: "There are ten high end restaurants that Elliott has invested in. They all turned a nice profit until about six months ago. There is a down side to the restaurant business. He needed a million dollars plus to keep them open. He didn't have it. His partner met with him and made it clear that they had another set of partners. Those partners were loan sharks or the mob. They were former drug dealers gone straight. They now invested in restaurants." Pam nervously lit another cigarette. Chain smoking to death.

She continued: "The people that Don Gino put out of business in the Mission District formed a restaurant group which also smuggles drugs in from the Far East. I was part of that business deal. There is just one problem."

I couldn't wait to ask: "What?"

"I have no idea who the Chef is, what he is doing or where to find him. I also don't know any members of the investment group. All I know is that they have names like Dominic, Tony and Rocky."

"Let me guess, Pam, they aren't Asians."

"You're a racist asshole, Trevor." I just had an addition to my asshole identification.

I said: "So you came to the world's greatest detective." Sorry Elvis Cole.

She smiled. "Yes. We need to collaborate. A partnership brains and beauty. I have both attributes." Humility wasn't one of her attributes.

I thought it was impossible to get another collaborator. I had too many already. But I couldn't be choosy. "How can we work together?"

"You have pieces of the puzzle, trust me."

I didn't want to trust anyone. I also didn't know what pieces she meant. "Ok, try me." I had no idea what this meant but it sounded good.

"The Chef is so well known that no one suspects him. He had another name a long time ago. It was "creampuff."

"What!" I looked perplexed. "Creampuff. What is going on?"

"Listen Trevor find out what creampuff means and we solve the crime."

I loved the emphasis on the term we. The world's greatest detective with an international partner. I looked at Pam Wong. Things were getting stranger by the minute. "I will look into it." She got up and walked out. I had no idea what creampuff meant. I took a drink of the wine. She hadn't touched her glass. So much for Casanova the private investigator. I spread my napkins out on the table. As Pam Wong left and took the elevator down to the first floor, I watched her hail a cab. It pulled off with the smiling Sikh cab driver talking rapidly. He was talking a mile a minute. Probably practicing his English. Or is it sikhilish?

I rethought what Pam had said. She had given me some new clues. They still didn't make a lot of sense. I knew that the answer to the crime was in the napkins. I was tired and laid down on the couch. I got up with the glow from the small alarm clock reading 6:00 A. M. I struggled to the kitchen and made a cup of decaf, it was the hazelnut decaf kind. Maybe I was cream puff and didn't know it. I turned on the radio. It was 680 KNBR and they were talking about Felipe Alou and the San Francisco Giants. I was bored and turned on KYA as Van Morrison sang "Magic Time." I could use some magic time. He cold use some magic time. Van was starting to look and sound like a grumpy Irish dwarf.

It was time to head back to the Irvington Brothers and get my catered food ready for another press conference. I forgot to ask about who the new Start Me Up drummer was or if he had credentials. It didn't matter, he would fear for his life. A promise of millions of dollars caused one to ignore things like death. I pulled into the parking lot on Third Street and saw Detective Sanchez' undercover car. If a 1966 purple Mustang was undercover. Maybe it was a loaner from Don Gino. I walked slowly to my office. Sanchez was sitting at my desk with his feet on my desk. "Making yourself at home." I smiled. He didn't. I never used my little office at the Irvington Brothers so it didn't matter.

"Trevor, we need to talk about Pam Wong."

"What's to talk about, she finds me irresistible."

"Cut the crap, who is creampuff?"

"Let me guess, my apartment is bugged."

He smiled. "We haven't heard any heavy breathing lately." Then Sanchez looked serious. "Trevor, even the FBI has a bug in your house."

"I take it something is wrong!" I couldn't figure out where this conversation was going. I also didn't like multiple bugs. I needed a private life. Then I remembered I didn't have one.

"Always the brain surgeon, Trevor, we still don't have any real leads. So I have asked my good friend Don Gino to send you on the road with the Start Me Up band."

"What! Am I some sort of a target for the Chef?"

"The who?" Now Detective Sanchez looked interested.

"Pam Wong explained that her partner was a Chef and she was instructed to do certain things. She has never met him and only has contact through a post office box." I paused and wanted to lit a cigarette. Then I remembered I hadn't smoked since college.

"Now we are getting somewhere Trevor. Going on the road with the Start Me Up band is the last ingredient in solving this case."

I looked unhappy. Sanchez didn't seem to care. Going out on the road with a band who looked like the Rolling Stones and played like Gary Lewis and the Playboys was not high on my priority list. "I need to organize the hors d'ouvres for the press conference for the new Start Me Up drummer. So I will call you when and if I find out about creampuff."

Sanchez walked out of the office and the temporary office computer specialist slipped him a napkin. Probably wanted to ride in the 1966 Mustang. Or take a ride with Sanchez in his apartment. A San Francisco detective with a big penis, not a bad calling card. I walked down the hall to my special kitchen and started putting together some of the trays of food for the press conference. Others would arrive from the Slanted Door. They had probably already started setting up the tables.

I called Don Gino and asked for some help. He let me know that he had eight helpers in tuxedos that would be by in an hour to pick up the food. I shuttered. Eight Samoans in Tuxedos. Not exactly your basic undercover squad. It was time for the postponed press conference.

Chapter 22
EIGHT SAMOANS IN TUXEDOS

A large purple van pulled in front of the Irvington Brothers Warehouse. I looked out the window as eight Samoans in tuxedos got out of the van. People on the sidewalk parted as the Samoans walked into the building. They rode the elevator to my office. I was under whelmed. They walked silently into the office. No one smiled.

The receptionist looked at the Samoans with a sense of urgency. She not only looked frightened but also was bewildered by their appearance. I ran out into the hallway.

"Don't worry Maria, they are with me." She glared at me.

"Trevor, they scared the hell out of me."

"Sorry." What else could I say. They scared the hell out of everybody. The eight Samoans glared at me. Fortunately, I had Don Gino's protection.

The biggest Samoan held an ornately wrapped box. "Don Gino spent this along." I opened a purple box and looked at a purple tuxedo. No sense pissing off the Purple Don. I put on the tuxedo. I hoped that the Warfield Theater didn't have a prize for bad dress. I was sure to win it. Then again I might have eight competitors.

We drove to the Warfield. It didn't take long to set up the food. Everything was ready for the press conference. Then I saw her in a black evening dress. Pam Wong stood in the corner, smoking a cigarette. She looked radiant. I directed the Samoans to take the food trays over to the serving table. There was already an entire table set up by the Slanted Door for the press. It had an assortment of salami's that Chef Kirschbaum had put together with little umbrellas that give a short history of the nine types of salami on the table. Gourmet overkill in action. The Samoans looked at the table suspiciously. Then they looked at Pam Wong with lust.

They didn't look happy. I walked over to the luscious Pam.

"Well, sweetheart, what's up." I always use my best Humphrey Bogart speech at parties.

She took a long drag on her cigarette. "What a line, is that Humphrey Bogart or Michael Jackson? You look and sound more like Michael. Hey, a gay white man who can sing and dance."

"Always the smartass, Pam."

"We need to find Don Gino." She looked serious.

"Take a look at the refreshment table, see the eight Samoans in tuxedos?"

"Yes," she looked quizzically.

"They are Dino Gino's bodyguards."

"Are they gay?"

An Asian with homophobia, I wasn't sure I was hearing right. "Call one over and see for yourself." She did. A long conversation took place. Pam Wong turned around and walked out of the building. I asked the Samoan what was going on. He looked at me and said nothing. I didn't think I could strong arm him. So I went over to the hors d'ouvres table and rearranged the trays. I tried to look busy. I noticed two packets of cheese and took them into a room where the press waited for the introduction to the new Start Me Up drummer. It was cheese from the Slanted Door. Chef Kirschbaum out did himself.

After bringing in another table for drinks, I began to set up the bar. I also brushed off the purple tuxedo that Dino Gino kindly donated. The tuxedo had to look good. I thought I glowed. I didn't complain. No sense making the Don angry. The catering work was done. So I poured myself a glass of Clos du Bos Merlot and settled into a chair. It was an hour before show time. The press started to arrive and the corporate types came into the room. I hoped that no one asked me for a solution to the crime. I didn't have one.

Elliott Shonestein was still missing, Pam Wong was looking for Don Gino and I was wondering who would run the press conference? My amazement continued as two female waiters showed up and one had gorgeous breasts. New breasts. Surgically implanted breasts. She had a face-lift to look like Chastain Johnson. She was Chastain. Ever the diligent detective. I smiled at her. She gave me the finger.

"Well, well, the lovely Chastain." I smiled.

"Quiet asshole." She continued: "I'm disguised as a Playboy bunny." Obviously, an outdated remark. I ignored it.

"Let me guess you are both FBI. You got it, meet Barbara Lawrence. If it was possible Barbara was even more beautiful than Chastain. She also looked meaner. The FBI obviously was breaking the law. I had to comment and turned to Chastain. "No ugly people were hired. Fat girls deserve jobs." Chastain seemed perplexed and angry.

"No sexist comments, penis head." She smiled.

"I couldn't compete with the FBI." We talked about strategy. The eight Samoans would serve the food and Chastain and her partner the drinks. There were also video cameras throughout the room. The Chef would be caught.

The press conference began at exactly seven thirty in the evening. A flourish of psychedelic lights hit the floor and the Rolling Stones' signature tune "Satisfaction," blared as Elliott Shonestein's lowest level assistant, Bill Gramaski, strode to center stage. He was from New York and had made his fame promoting a group of San Francisco singers and dancers known as the Cockettes. It was an all male performing troupe that dressed up like women. Ugly women. They made the Village People look like amateurs. They also made the Village People look like George Clooney. When the Cockettes' lead singer, Sylvester, died of AIDS, Gramaski became a booking agent and hooked up with Shonestein.

"Ladies, gentlemen, the press, welcome," Gramaski smiled and lifted his glass. "Let us all toast our new Start Me Up Drummer, let's have a drum roll for "Oblivion."

I couldn't believe it a drummer named Oblivion. It got worse. A good-looking young girl came out from backstage. She didn't look like Charlie Watts. Not only was the Stones drummer old as hell, he was weathered. Oblivion looked like she dropped in from a beauty pageant. She was also a woman. Was I missing something? Gramaski explained her credentials. She missed out getting the job as the drummer in the Donnas, the Ravonettes and Lavay Smith and Her Red Hot Skillet Lickers. I didn't know how to tell Gramaski that this was not earthshaking news. She stood up to the microphone.

Oblivion spoke. "Cool." She smiled. Not exactly a rocket scientist. I stood there frozen. I noticed "oblivion" was tattooed on here arms. She wandered from the stage and loaded a plate full of food. No one had tasted the food. With two of the Samoans guarding my innovative plates, there was no chance of poisoning. Everyone seemed to have a good time. Oblivion downed the food and didn't appear sick. No one paid any attention to the food. There was buzzing about a woman drummer. The Stones might consider replacing Charlie Watts. This was impossible. Geritol was going to sponsor their next tour. My musings came to an end when a scream came from the pressroom.

I ran to the pressroom and the San Francisco Chronicle rock music critic John Wasser lay dead on the floor. He had a smile on his face and a piece of salami on one side with a toothpick and cheese on the other side. It was stuck in his hand. Maybe Pam Wong had been around, no one died looking that happy. Then again maybe Chastain Johnson had her top fall off. I needed to think serious thoughts. I called for the police. The room was locked up. Then I forgot I had the FBI on the premises.

Chastain Johnson was inside the room in a minute. She looked at Wasser. "Well I guess he has written his last nasty review." She lit a cigarette and looked around the room. She called over one of the Samoans. "Lock the doors." The eight Samoans suddenly covered the four exits.

She called for the crime lab. It would be ten minutes and every butt hair in the place would undergo DNA analysis. Chastain walked back into the interview room.

There were at least sixty media types attacking what was left of the shrimp. "Ladies and gentleman. We have a corpse. John Wasser has died under unfortunate circumstances." She looked around the room. Note pads were poised. The Chef obviously needed publicity.

I wondered if there were fortunate circumstances to death. I said: "Chastain, we need to get Detective Sanchez down here." She looked at me like I had asked for a date. "You know jurisdiction, local authorities." I smiled smugly

"Later, Trevor, he'll just screw it up. Sanchez can's solve what's in his pants, let alone a crime." No sooner had she uttered her words than Sanchez came through the door with Don Gino and Pam Wong trailing behind. All the usual suspects were on the scene. A medical examiner showed up. Chastain pulled her pager out and told him the FBI forensics team was on the case. A few minutes later a Federal toxicologist showed up. I had never heard of a federal medical examiner. But there she was. Another great looking blonde. Maybe the federal government shouldn't revise their hiring policies. Old sexists like myself liked what he saw. I guess I was really a confirmed early middle-aged sexist. My only complaint was that the medical examiner didn't appear to have had a breast job. She was five ten, a hundred pounds and looked like a super model. Oh well, breasts were overrated. Probably had a lower paying position.

Everybody was milling about and there was a great deal of confusion. Don Gino walked up to the stage. "We are reviewing the film," Don Gino remarked. "The surveillance cameras have everything." The Don smiled. Maybe he was the world's greatest detective. It took half an hour and Detective Sanchez announced that he was arresting Pam Wong for the murder of John Wasser. I had made the mistake of asking who wanted Wasser dead. Detective Sanchez showed me his list. It included Huey Lewis, Bono, the Edge, Tom Waits, Van Morrison, Keith Richards, Jimmy McCracklin and Joel Selvin.

"Why would Joel Selvin want him dead," I asked quizzically, "Wasser trained Selvin."

Detective Sanchez smiled: "You dumb shit, figure it out."

"Oh!" I guess Selvin didn't like his job. "Do they have alibis?"

"They all have alibis, Trevor." Sanchez lit a small cigarillo. "Everything points to Pam Wong."

I guess "Look For The Woman" cinched it. To my mind she looked like a good suspect. That was enough to convince me that she was innocent.

Sanchez led her off in handcuffs with Chastain Johnson looking mad as hell. I had seen a lot of that lately.

"Chastain, what's up?" I looked at her and continued: "Has Detective Sanchez solved the case?"

"You're a dunce, Trevor," she turned and left the room. I preferred to be a dunce rather than an asshole. So I was making progress.

I wandered out onto Market Street. The press was three deep on the curb hollering questions at me. A guy holding a sign "Jesus is coming," shouted as the press shouted. It was a confusing situation. Maybe Jesus was opening at the Warfield. The private eye who is famous and mute walked back to the Irvington Brothers office. It took me half an hour as I headed over the Mission and then turned right for the warehouse. Third street was filled with yuppies on their way to bars, baseball and boring activities. I walked up to my office and sat down. Pam was charged with providing poisoned cheese. I had no idea what was going on. The phone rang.

"Hello," I droned.

"Cut the cheese," a low voice bellowed.

"What! Is this some kind of bad joke."

"Call Sanchez and tell him to cut the cheese up." The voice hung up. I dialed the SFPD and asked for Sanchez. He answered quickly,

"Trevor the Turd."

"Cut the cheese, detective."

"What!" He sounded confused. He also sounded angry. He went into a tirade about what an immature asshole I was. "I have to check something Trevor, hang on."

Sanchez put the phone down. I couldn't hear anything. No one seemed to be being beaten with a rubber hose at the SFPD. Maybe it was a silent rubber hose. I waited for more twenty-five minutes. He returned to the phone. "What is going on Trevor?"

I explained to him about the mysterious phone call. I had no idea what cut the cheese meant. Then it dawned on me. Pam told me that someone had given her some cheese and a note from the Chef at the Slanted Door. She was directed to take the cheese from the Slanted Door to the press conference. The Chef who gave it to her had a signed note from me. A good forgery. Pam Wong had the note in her purse. It proved the Chef gave the cheese to her in the Slanted Door. He had an ulterior motive She was supposed to eat a piece of it. She was to be the next victim. I explained to Sanchez that the note was from the Chef.

"I'll get right back to you Trevor." Sanchez sounded interested. Pam was in a nearby holding cell and he had her purse. The Chef was playing with us. He had not only outsmarted us, he was making fun of the bumbling investigation. I was nervous, since I was the head bumbler.

In an hour Sanchez called back. "We checked everything out and she had no connection to the murder." Sanchez paused and I could hear him lighting a small cigar. Or maybe he was arranging the napkins with the phone numbers on them. He continued:" We're still going to hold her for the murder. Protect her so to speak."

"What is my job?" I could hardly wait for the answer.

"You are to continue the fictional tale that Pam is the murderer."

"What if the Chef doesn't buy it? You can't tell anyone about this. Who knows maybe Joyce Byers is the killer." I couldn't believe my ears. My sometimes girl friend suspected of murder. Then it dawned on me, he was kidding. I'm a P. I. without a sense of humor.

"I'm not sure I can pull this off Sanchez. You may be on the wrong track." Try to show him as little respect as possible. It might rattle him. "I need something to tell my clients." I pleaded with Sanchez. "Give me something to report to Don Gino, he is not happy."

"That's strictly your problem. Didn't you go to college, figure it out." He hung up.

I went back to my office at the Irvington Brothers warehouse. I spent some time making a list of clues, suspects and facts. It didn't help. I was still in the dark. The world's greatest detective with ten pages of notes and no ideas. I shout off the light in my Irvington Bros. office and walked out onto Third Street. The San Francisco Chronicle had an extra edition out with Pam Wong on the front page. Myself I liked Bono for the killing. He could have done it by crooning the latest U 2 hit. I retrieved my car and drove back to my Chestnut Street apartment. I expected a beautiful girl to be at my doorstep. Instead I found Guitar Jac. He had a guitar case in tow.

"Trevor, my man, we need to talk." I could hardly wait. "I'm going to open for the Rolling Stones in Los Angeles. I need you to come along as my valet."

I couldn't believe my ears. "Me as your valet."

He smiled: "You got it."

"That means Mick and Keith get to see me as a servant."

"Right."

"I don't know Jac."

"Trevor, it's all part of the plan." I suddenly saw my role. Private eye infiltrates rock concert and finds killer. I could see the newspaper headlines. There might even be a movie in it. I would be front-page news. I might even get laid.

"How does touring with the Rolling Stones protect the Start Me Up band?" I was after all still a private eye.

"The Start Me Up band plays the Whiskey A Go Go on Sunset Boulevard and you will also be there to guard Oblivion. Sleep with her if you have to."

"Right, Jac, a good P. I. does anything to protect a client. I don't know if I can get by the tattoos." We talked about strategy and before he left I was presented with a "Guitar Jac On Tour" coat. It was black leather with red letters. Things weren't looking up sartorially but the case was beginning to make sense. As Jac pointed out someone in the Rolling Stones camp was trying to end the Start Me Up band's success. I couldn't wait for the headline in the New York Times, "Trevor Blake III Arrests Mick Jagger for Murder." I could get laid with a headline like that. I could also get sued.

I went up to my apartment and packed. It was time to join the Rolling Stones on tour. I would take my guitar and sang a few of my surf originals for Mick and Keith. "Santa Cruz Surfer" and "Woodside Wahini" were two of my sure hits. I had written them twenty years ago and no one had discovered my songwriting genius. I went to sleep that night with blissful dreams of groupies, the Rolling Stones music and free range chicken, diet salad and yuppie water. That was what the Stones were eating backstage. My how times had changed. Sex, drugs and rock and roll were an anachronism. I may be one too.

Chapter 23
ON TOUR WITH MICK AND KEITH: SORT OF

The next morning I convinced Joyce Byers to drive me to the airport. She was still sort of my girl friend. I wasn't sure why. I didn't have much time. I also liked to play the field. Maybe she was an associate girl friend. A part time girl friend. On the way to the airport I talked about the new Trevor Blake III. She laughed.

"You're the same old asshole, Trevor."

As least she looked happy. "I'll make it up to you when I return."

She looked at me incredulously. "Make what up?" I couldn't think of a good answer so I turned the radio up. "Satisfaction" played and Mick's vocals replaced our stilted conversation. His voice sounded stilted. Millionaire stilted.

I spent a lot of time talking to Joyce about Mick and Keith. She looked bored. We would be hanging out, the only problem is that I knew very little about the Stones.

"I'll give you a Stones 101 course in the next twenty minutes. She did. Joyce was a fan. I wasn't. When she talked about their business interests my ears perked up. I did get a clue. She had a business that made the Stones or someone close to them a suspect. Just what I needed another suspect.

She did her best to fill me in on their career. I wouldn't tell them that Joyce thought they peaked with "Satisfaction" in 1967 and spent the last forty plus years redoing the same old material. I kissed Joyce and got out of the car. I looked for the charter gate. It was next to gate 12. Did that mean it was gate 13? I wandered through the metal detector after holding out my tour pass. A guy named Abdul patted me down and lectured me on security. Only in San Francisco could a Muslim work for TSA and lecture an Irish Catholic on terrorism Then a golf cart took me to a private gate and a beautiful young stewardess walked me to the plane. I could get used to this. Once I entered the plane, I was depressed.

The Rolling Stone tour plane was filled with old, ugly, fat white people. They all looked like they had made too much money. They also looked like they had eaten too much. Where were the beautiful people? One fat, bald guy was holding a Marianne Faithfull CD and listening through his IPOD. I had seen a recent picture of Marianne Faithfull. She was a walking advertisement for rehab. She looked like my grandmother. Wait, I take that back, she looked worse. My grandmother was still pretty good looking. I wondered if anyone on the plane looked good.

The exceptions were the ten stewardesses. They looked like they had stepped out of Vogue magazine after breast enhancement, liposuction and every other form of plastic surgery known to mankind. They had low cut blouses showing plenty of cleavage. United could adopt this program to avoid bankruptcy. I wasn't complaining. They looked great. I found out that they were models moonlighting as stewardesses. The Los Angeles concert was scheduled for the Pasadena Rose Bowl. With 100,000 plus tickets sold the event was the largest and top grossing concert in rock history. I soon found out that a note from the Chef indicated that someone would die in Los Angeles. If it was Mick or Keith, we would all be in trouble. If it was Oblivion at the Whiskey A Go Go, I was at the end of my wits. The Chef stated in a cryptic note that he would either be in the Rose Bowl or the Whiskey a Go Go or both. Nothing like being a fun guy.

I looked for Mick, Keith, Ron Wood and Charlie Watts on the plane. I was told they took a private charter. So much for corporate rock and roll. I did have a plan. The backstage amenities were part of the contract. So I needed to find out who was catering the Stones' food. Also, who was catering the Start Me Up band's gig. What in the hell was a cover band doing with catered food?

When I got off the plane I was told to take a cab to an undisclosed address. I got into a cab and the driver spoke English and didn't wear a turban. I was shocked. He handed me a card "Warren: The only White Cab Driver in L. A." Not exactly an advertisement for good taste. He did have a point. I was dropped off at the recording studio. I walked inside. Obviously, Mick and Keith wanted to talk to me. I walked into a large studio. The Stones' new producer, Bob Denham , sat in the corner listening to playbacks. The original bad boy band sounded young and fresh. I listened to three cuts and knew that they had a hit CD. They were playing with fire in the studio.

After wandering around the mixing facilities, I saw a familiar face. It was Sheldon Foreskin. What was he doing in the Stones' studio? Time for the serious detective to go to work. I looked at the Stones CD cover, "A Bigger Bang" was a great title. It described the problems in my case. Foreskin walked over and introduced himself. He didn't remember me. He was a college professor. They have tenure. They fear only God. Foreskin let me know he was Jewish. He also let me know he was a songwriter. He didn't remember anything about our meeting in Fremont, I guess I don't make a lasting impression.

As a college professor, Foreskin reminded me that he didn't need to remember anything. He was tenured and worked on other business interests. A strained conversation began.

"Well." Foreskin smiled. "The detective is on the case." He did know something.

"Hello." I could see this conversation was going nowhere. "Well Professor Foreskin what's the occasion? An article on the Stones for the Journal of American History."

He looked at me like I was insane. "No, I am also in the music business. I am also a very private person. So fuck off." That was too much also in two sentences. College professors are redundant. Foreskin looked a me angrily. I guess we weren't going to be best friends. "Nice to see you too." He stalked out of the room. In his three-piece suit, with his well-trimmed mustache, his watch fob and a book on The Puritan Ethic in his hand, he was the prototype of the asshole professor. I walked over to the mixing board. For an hour I talked to the assistant mixing director. His name was Adolph Brimstone and he lived about an hour out of London. He told me about his tranquil suburban home in Guildford and talked about his neighbor Eric Clapton. He had known Mick since the late 1950s. Brimstone played me two songs left off the album. The first one "Murder By The Rolling Stones" was put back in the can because of songwriting copyright problems. The second song "Stone Murder" was a sure hit. The Stones wouldn't release it until the songwriter gave the Jagger-Richards credit that would give the two Rolling Stones fifty per cent of the writer's credit. The Stones could not identify E. Baylor, the songwriter, or make a deal for full rights to the song. So they cut the song and left it in the can. It would be released at a future date. That is when the songwriter agreed to give up fifty per cent of his royalties. Or maybe it was her royalties. What did I know? The other tune "Looking For The Woman" was considered too dangerous for feminist America. The mysterious songwriter, E. Baylor, also wrote it and not even Dan Bannerman at Bug Music could identify him. Times had changed. When did the Rolling Stones think of being politically correct? Then I realized it was all about money. They wanted a portion of the songwriting to release the songs and the majority of the publishing rights. That's were the money was in rock, and roll and the Stones were business savvy.

After an hour of listening to the Stones' outtakes I left. I pulled my portable digital dat machine out of my pocket. I caught everything on tape. I would make some bootleg CDs. Nothing illegal. It was just for evidence. The CDs would also make nice gifts to friends. I had three different takes of "Murder By The Rolling Stones" and six cuts of "Looking for the Woman." Adolph Brimstone told me that there was a clue or two in each song. He had this very precise and intelligent English way of analyzing things and I knew he had given me to a clue to solving the crime. He said that he knew Dave Williams. I wondered who in the hell is Dave Williams? So far I hadn't gotten very deeply into the mystery. I did have some new notes for my napkins.

I headed for the band's hotel. It was time to do some serious detecting. I brought out a small new brief case. I took out the 80 plus napkins that I thought were the key to the case and placed them on the bed. It was time to figure out the murderer. As I was in deep concentration, the phone rang. It was Guitar Jac. He wondered if he should include some Ritchie Havens' covers in his set. I couldn't believe he was opening for the Stones. How this happened, I didn't want to know. Maybe a version of "Handsome Johnny" to show opposition to the Iraqi war. Then Guitar Jac reminded me that he supported the Iraqi war. He had been a Republican since Ronald Regan was elected president. Guitar Jack was an 80s guy in a 60s body. That is in everything but politics. I urged him to stay with his set list. He reluctantly agreed. It was time for something to eat. I wandered down to the hotel coffee shop.

A great looking blonde sat me down. In Los Angeles, there was a great looking blonde every two feet. The waitress came over and I started to read from the menu.

"What'll it be asshole?" I looked up it was Chastain Johnson.

"Let me guess, undercover." She smiled.

"Trevor you are a genius."

"Isn't the FBI going outside its jurisdiction? Isn't this an LA case? The LAPD think that it's their crime to solve."

"Hello, Trevor, get with federal law, we have drugs which are federal as well as international murder connections. Remember the three drummers were killed in three separate states and there are also international money laundering problems. Is that enough for you?"

"I'm aware of everything." Of course, I wasn't aware of any of this. I didn't like her attitude. "You are making this case one that has too large a scope." I was on a roll now. "You are taking federal law and expanding it."

"Fuck off, asshole." I got the point.

I wondered if Elvis Cole got this level of disrespect. Probably not. I put on my best tough guy voice. "Well Chastain, I think I have some new leads, believe me I will not share them with you." Laughing she saw it as an empty threat. She was a terrible waitress. She walked away without taking my order. A real waitress came over and I had the deluxe cheeseburger with fries and coleslaw. I ordered a cherry coke. A real private eye needed his nutrition to fight the bad guys. A little sugar always helped the adrenalin. As I finished my feast I noticed that one of Don Gino's Samoan's was seated in a corner booth reading the paper. I knew the Samoan couldn't read. I looked at him. He stared daggers at me. I looked away. No sense pissing off a gorilla. Something was going on but, as usual, I was the last to know. I got up left a five-dollar tip, paid the bill and wandered into the hotel lobby. That was a mistake. In the center of three luxurious couches Don Gino sat with his nail file. Redoing his nails was not a good sign. This was when Don Gino was angry.

He smiled. "Hello Trevor."

I walked over. "Greetings." I was becoming a monosyllabic communicator.

"Ah, Trevor, we have some things to discuss."

I sat down. No sense making the Don unhappy. "What can I do for you?"

He stopped filing his nails. "No Trevor, it is what I can do for you."

Verbal sparring is not my thing. "Make it clear, what are you talking about?"

"Is someone about to be killed tonight?"

We didn't seem to be getting anywhere. All we are doing was asking each other questions. "Enough, Don Gino, what do you have in mind?" Sorry another question.

The Don looked serious. I tried to pay rapt attention to his next comment. No sense making him mad. There was a moment of silence. Don Gino lit a small cigar. "The problem we have is one of logistics. There are two concert venues, thus two possible sources of poisoning. My proposal is that you go to the Whiskey A Go Go. There you can watch over everything. My feeling is that this next murder by the Chef will implicate me. That makes me very unhappy." He paused. It wasn't a good sign when Don Gino took time to think. He was angry.

I tried to lighten the mood. "Things could be worse." He looked at me like I was an idiot. Apparently I didn't lighten the mood.

"I will send along Terrence and Tommy. They will watch your back. They will also make sure Miss Oblivion stays healthy."

"I don't think we have to worry about Miss Oblivion, she almost castrated her former husband. They had an argument over what's for breakfast."

"Not a problem Trevor, the Samoans will handle Miss Oblivion with discretion." I liked a crime boss who spoke perfect English. It made me feel safe when he was laundering money through the Catholic church, his dog food factory, his food wholesale business or his grocery store. Don Gino's betting and loan sharking combined with legitimate business put him just below Bill Gates in net worth. He made his money the old fashion way, legitimate business tied in with protection, gambling and loan sharking. Drugs and prostitution were stamped out. He was the only crime boss who had the approval of the Mayor and the SFPD. His eight Samoans were also known for their charity work. Everyone loved the Samoans around him. I wasn't eager to have them around. How could I tell the Don that three hundred pound Samoans at a disco weren't exactly the undercover help I needed. I failed to mention that to the Don. I bid him farewell and went to my room. It was time to look at my napkins. I now had eighty plus clues. They were beginning to make sense. There were also beginning to be too many napkins.

I slept for an hour and got up to put on my disco clothes. Well not exactly disco clothes but my nighttime duds. I looked in the mirror. A pair of Perry Ellis slacks went well with my Ted Baker shirt and my Aldo shoes. Always the fashion plate.

I walked outside the hotel. It was show time. After jumping into the cab I smelled the pungent odor of curry. The cab driver was called Alex but he wore a turban and was a Sikh. But obviously one who was more American than Indian. "Where to?"

"Drop me a block from the Whiskey a Go Go, down where Gazarri's used to be."

"I loved Gazarri's," the Cabbie remarked, "I always took my turban off, and they thought I was a hippie. I love American girls. You tell them you are for peace and you get laid." I got out and tipped him well. Maybe I would take his advice. Who knows when you need a literate Indian cabbie.

As I walked down Sunset Boulevard memories of some good times came to mind. The best one was when I took one of the girls in the cage home. There is a huge cage outside the Whiskey and each night six different girls dance in the cage. The one I met made it a lovely one-night stand. I guess all one-night stands were lovely. It was ten years ago. I will never forget it. Tracy Fremont was her name and she had a set of breasts like I had never seen. I didn't think that she was an FBI agent. That was the one and only time I saw her. A pleasant memory. I hadn't had too many of those recently.

I was on the guest list and bypassed the line waiting to get past the velvet rope. There were at least twenty people with Start Me Up t-shirts. Others held CDs. A few had pictures of Oblivion seated on the drums. Oblivion's t-shirt was now the best selling Start Me Up item, even though she had been in the band for only a week. Ah, the joys of merchandising.

The club was dark. It took awhile for my eyes to focus. I heard a harsh voice. "Can I get you a drink, sir," the Samoan waiter asked. Was it possible for Don Gino to be an unseen eye. "I'll have a brandy Alexander."

The Samoan sneered: "Sir, wouldn't you like something more masculine."

"No." I screamed. After all I was the masculine P. I. The Samoan left. He came back with a 12 year old malt Scotch in a snifter. So much for my assertive nature. I walked to the backstage area. I flashed my pass and walked into the refreshment room. On the table was the usual smorgasbord of edible teats. No one was eating it. Not even a nibble of food was gone. A Samoan in the purple tuxedo was at each end. I didn't think I could trust Don Gino. There were now three Samoans on the case. The Start Me Up band drifted in and began to take small plates of food. Finally, some one broke the food taboo. They ate sparingly. Oblivion loaded up her plate and ate half of it. The rest she put in baggies to take home. Maybe she wasn't getting a full salary. You wouldn't want a fat rock star. I was bored but I had a job to do.

I looked backstage for signs of foul play. I saw none. It was weird. The police dog brought in to test the food was still alive. I couldn't believe the Samoans. The dog had been feed every piece of food. He survived. He would have to wait to become a part of Don Gino's dog food empire. I looked at the band set up. Then I noticed it. The drum set was off kilter. I wondered onto the stage. I looked inside the drums and there were two sticks of dynamite. A timer was attached. I ran to the microphone.

"Check, check," I hollered. The microphone was on and I flooded the Whiskey with my voice. "There's dynamite in the drums." The crowd didn't move. They probably thought it was a punk rock trick. They started to cheer. Who said rock and roll crowds had brains.

"No, man," somewhere hollered. "There's oblivion on the drums. She is dynamite" Laughter went up. I thought to hell with these people and ran through the crowd to the door. Suddenly two Samoans were on stage hollering to exit the club. The Samoans commanded a respect that I failed to possess. There was a rush to the door. It was a miracle. No one was caught in the crowd. The Whiskey a Go Go emptied. The last time this happened was when Sonny and Cher played the place in the 1960s. The Start Me Up band was on the street with their fans. Maybe there was no scare. Then a mammoth explosion took place. The front of the Whiskey A Go Go was blown to pieces and the crowd was hit with flying glass. The owner had talked renovation. Now he had no choice. Police sirens wailed and an ambulances rushed to the scene. No one was dead. But there were plenty of cuts from flying glass. I walked over to the Start Me Up Band. They were shaking. Something was wrong. Oblivion was nowhere in sight. The fourth Start Me Up drummer was dead or missing. I was perplexed.

"Trevor the Turd," I heard the voice and knew the drill. Detective Sanchez stood behind me smoking a small cigar. Don Gino was to his right.

I said: "Gentlemen." What else could I say?

"We need to go inside Trevor." We did just that. The Whiskey A Go Go would need to be rebuilt. It was not a pleasant sight. It smelled of cordite, whiskey and marijuana. Maybe Saddam Hussein could make this into a new bomb, the entertainment explosive.

Don Gino smiled: "Well, you did save the band. Where is Oblivion?"

"That is the $64,000 question." We searched for her for an hour. No sign of Oblivion. Neither a corpse nor a living personage was evident. Oblivion was missing. We walked back outside. There were at least a dozen radio and television people asking questions.

"Trevor," Annabel Fong of Channel 4 shouted, "have you solved the case?"

"Yes," I smiled "Bob Dylan did it." Then I vanished behind the police line. Don Gino stood next to me looking unhappy. He was a big Bob Dylan fan. After two hours of investigation, no one had a clue. It was time to go home.

I wonder if Mick and Keith had as much fun playing the Rose Bowl. I got back to the hotel tired and depressed. "Excuse me sir, what's you're a name?"

I smiled. "I'm Donovan." I broke into a chorus of "Sunshine Superman." The young girl looked at me horrified and ran away. I wondered could Donovan get a gig. I went up to my room. The day was an exhausting one. I had every intention of going right to bed. I opened the door. Chastain Johnson was sitting on the bed. She wasn't smiling. I wasn't smiling. She was smoking. My room smelled like an ashtray. She also a flimsy clothes on, so I didn't complain.

"Hello dickhead!"

Some things never change. "Let me guess? You don't want to get laid! "

"Bingo, Trevor. We need to talk."

"I'm getting a lot of that lately. I opened a bottle of Perrier. I loved yuppie water when someone else was paying. I sat on the bed. I looked at the television. There was no sound but the screen showed the front of the Whiskey A Go Go exploding. I turned on three more TV channels as the Whiskey was exploding on all of them. A talking head came on and explained it. Who knows what he said. Chastain simply sat and the bed quietly. I wasn't sure if she was thinking or perhaps figuring out a way to castrate me. I was hoping it was the former. She looked at me.

"Speak Trevor." It sounded like an order, so I obeyed.

"I have some ideas. I need to get out my napkins." I proceeded to arrange my 80 plus napkins as Chastain looked on in horror. Always the careful private eye.

"What could these napkins tell us?" She did look interested. The case finally interested her. The world's greatest detective was about to strike.

"Here is the clue, Chastain." She looked at the napkins like I was nuts. Not necessarily the wrong deduction. I pointed out the lack of recent food poisonings. "The pattern is changing. The Chef is also a demolitions expert. He has a knowledge of explosives. The next stop is Seattle. The Rolling Stones will play at Safeco Field. It's a baseball park. The Start Me Up band is booked into the Key Arena. That is a basketball arena and the Start Me Up band will draw 20,000 and the Stones will have an 80,000-seat house. It is on this tour that the final attempt will be made on the Start Me Up drummer."

"I hate to interrupt you Trevor, but there is no Start Me Up drummer, she is missing. Dead. Kidnapped. Scared. Who knows." She smiled.

"Ah, now for my master plan, I have the new drummer for the Start Me Up band."

"Let me guess Trevor, Don Gino, one of the eight Samoans, Pam Wong or am I missing something?

"Yes, you are." I thought for a moment. Had to keep them guessing. "The new drummer will be Guitar Jac." She started laughing uncontrollably.

"I don't believe you Trevor. Charlie Watts is white. Charlie Watts is a drummer. Charlie Watts is old. Guitar Jac is an African American, he is a guitar player and he is young. Have I missed something?" I wanted to tell her my plan. But now wasn't the time.

"Yes, you are ignoring the obvious. Guitar Jac is a multi-instrumentalist. He is a trained detective. He has a black belt in judo. He can also play the drums. He can sing."

"Have you forgotten that Charlie Watts can't sing?" She smiled

"Just a minor point, Chastain, no one will notice. Don't you see the beauty of my plan, Guitar Jac is on stage to catch the killer, brilliant, yes. I went to Stanford, Jac went to Stanford. Understand!" The detective putting the minion in their place.

"Yes," Chastain interrupted, "and like you he went to Stanford. What is it about you Stanford people, five minutes into a conversation about the weather and you are telling me that you and Guitar Jac went to Stanford. Maybe I should cheer. Personally, I Don't give a fuck where you went to school."

"Chastain, doesn't the FBI have a code of conduct. No swearing and no recreational sex. Not to mention a limit on daily cigarettes."

"Maybe you can solve this thing." She looked at me and smiled. "Then again maybe you can kiss my ass." Touchy, touchy.

"Sounds good to me, the best and the brightest are from Stanford."

"Need I remind you solving this caper is not exactly something that you have accomplished. Remember Trevor you have yet to solve a crime."

"Picky, picky." I didn't smile..

"Let's stop arguing. Maybe you have a point Trevor." We sought out Detective Sanchez and Don Gino. We explained the idea of putting Guitar Jac undercover. There was only one problem, Guitar Jac. He wouldn't like the idea of playing a white man, he wouldn't like the idea of becoming a drummer. He wouldn't like the idea of being a target for murder. He hated the Rolling Stones. The Start Me Up band ranked even lower. I had to pull out my ultimate weapon. Persuasion. I only hoped that the groupies, the money, the temporary fame and the adventure would appeal to him. If not, we were back to square one.

He had already opened solo for the Rolling Stones. He had song copyrights that were making him money. He certainly didn't need any more money. He had an inheritance. My theory is that you never have enough hair, you are never too thin and you never have enough money. Try telling that to Guitar Jac. He was in a dressing room where he was resting after having opened for the Stones in the cavernous Los Angeles arena. Now it was time to try to convince him to go undercover. An African American pretending to be Charlie Watts wasn't exactly undercover but we had no other choices. It was time to talk turkey to Guitar Jac. The case had to be solved my reputation was on the line. That is what was left of it.

Chapter 24
GUITAR JAC AS CHARLIE WATTS

We went up to Guitar Jac's room. Media types surrounded him. A CD mogul from Starbucks Coffee was talking to Jac. They wanted to sign him to their label. Coffee today, conquer the world with rock and roll tomorrow. That was the Starbucks motto. I wondered if I had that right Starbucks Coffee! I heard it with my own ears. Jac negotiated a deal to have eighty of his songs and eight unreleased Rolling Stone b-sides on a CD that sold only with coffee at Starbucks. The Starbuck's record man, brought out a contract and Jac signed it. I moved in and saw the signatures of Keith Richards, Mick Jagger, Ron Wood and Charlie Watts. Too bad Brian Jones couldn't sign it. A sum at the bottom of the contract specified a guarantee of One million dollars for each signatory. I didn't know that Mick and Keith worked that cheaply. I knew Guitar Jac did. Charlie Watts probably couldn't speak.

During his opening for the Stones, Guitar Jac had performed four original tunes. The loudest applause was for "Rustler's Blues." This was the tune that Starbuck's wanted as the signature title for the CD. Guitar Jac beamed. He had written this song, while taking History of the West at Stanford and it remained one of his concert staples. His Professor, W. Turpentine Turner, replete in cowboy hat sang a version of Jac's song one day in class. It remained a Stanford legend. A number of media types looked in awe at Jac. Professor w. Turpentine Turner even had a you tube version on line. He charged a dollar to watch the video and Stanford's football team got the money. No wonder they went to the Rose Bowl.

The young reporter from **Rolling Stone** asked fawning questions. He wore a Guitar Jac button. I had to interrupt this love fest. Then Greil Marcus showed up. He fired questions as Jac. My friend ignored him. He muttered: "I am the world's greatest rock critics." I muttered: "I am the world's greatest detective." It was a standoff.

Everyone looked at me like I was from Mars. A famous detective isn't always recognized. "Hello folks, we need to talk to Guitar Jac." I smiled and continued. "Come back tomorrow, he will be parting the Red Sea and helping Steve Spurrier install a running game at the University of South Carolina." They looked at me like I was nuts and left the room. Guitar Jac looked at me like I was nuts. Don Gino sat in the corner looking like I was nuts, to his right stood Chastain Johnson and Detective Sanchez who agreed. There was an uncomfortable silence. The room was too full for me. I wondered was there something like a comfortable silence. I had to take the bull by the balls, so to speak. Or is it the bull by the horns.

I decided to use my baritone Trevor Blake III voice. "Guitar Jac, we need you." He looked perplexed. I continued "Think resolve or resonance Jac."

"What is your resolve or resonance, whatever that means, Trevor? Remember you did get a C in Freshman English." Guitar Jac had a smug smile on his face. He had earned an A.

"I need you to come with us, Jac, we need to get you going in the Start Me Up band or maybe in the Stones." I appealed to his ego. It would help.

"What!" He looked perplexed.

"You need to come with us, Jac." We weren't getting anywhere. I wasn't making sense to Jac or anyone else. How could I explain our dilemma?

Guitar Jac spoke with a panic." No, keep me right here. I will go with the Stones to Seattle tomorrow and open in a baseball park. This is my one big time career shot."

"Sorry Jac we need you as the new drummer in the Start Me Up band." He looked aghast. I couldn't blame him.

"Trevor, I'm African American, a guitarist, a vocalist and young. Last time I looked I was not a Charlie Watts look alike. He is old, half dead and has no personality. Not to mention he is white."

"Minor details, Jac." I smiled. I always smiled when I had trouble explaining myself. I smiled a lot lately.

"Ok, Trevor, explain."

"We won't hold those minor obstacles against you." I proceeded to detail our plan. He listened intently. He liked it. He knew that I finally had a plan to trap the killer.

"Alright, Trevor, against my better judgment, I will do it."

We called a press conference for the next morning. Everyone believed that it had something to do with the Stones tour. The next morning we set up the Whiskey A Go Go for a press conference. Guitar Jac would join the Start Me Up band. Half of the journalists present had never heard of Guitar Jac. A minor detail, it wouldn't derail my master plan.

I went back to the hotel and went to bed. Guitar Jac was seen walking down Sunset Boulevard late in the night with Keith Richards. There was a story in the Los Angeles Times that a Keith Richards look alike was on the strip. He was recognized. Everyone ignored him. The real Richards wouldn't walk down Sunset Strip. So it was some lunatic who looked like him. That is how Keith gets out at night.

I awoke early the next morning and caught a cab. The Indian took his turban off and I rolling down the window. He had on a Bollywood movie on his portable DVD player and when I got out of the cab I was shaking from the ride. I tipped him and walked into the Whiskey A Go Go.

I met Joe Meek, the advance man for the Stones, and we set up the press conference. The Rolling Stones announced that there would be a new opening act. They called Vancouver British Columbia and convinced British blues legend, Long John Baldry, to fly into Seattle. He actually drove the 150 miles. He needed the money. His small condominium north of Vancouver needed a paint job. So the readily agreed to the $20,000 concert fee. The stage was set to catch the Chef. He wasn't aware that I was onto him. Trevor Blake III had narrowed the clues. There were five new napkins that contained the key clues. I knew who the killer was and I would catch him in Seattle.

There was preparation for catching the killer. I needed a week in San Francisco to lay the groundwork. Fortunately, the Stones were off for a week shooting a Monday night football video. What next? A spot for Metamucil? A Geritol promo? Who knows?

Guitar Jac spent the week practicing with the Start Me Up band. The inevitable press conference was met with skepticism. But Jac loved doing Stones covers. He convinced the Start Me Up band to let him end the show with "Satisfaction." His vocal range was extraordinary Things were going well as long as you weren't a historically accurate Stones fan. Everyone was excited about going to Seattle but first there was a need to get ready for the Seattle trip. I was looking forward to being back in San Francisco and getting laid. I would go to Seattle later. Maybe I would skip Seattle. Don Gino, Guitar Jac and Detective Sanchez could solve the crime. Maybe Joyce Byers would help. I didn't seem to be doing too well.

Chapter 25
BACK IN SAN FRANCISCO AND SOLVING THE CRIME: 85 NAPKINS

I flew home to San Francisco on Southwest Airlines. The flight was short and so was my patience. I was ready for my Chestnut Street apartment. I hailed a cab and pulled up as Bennie and Bertie were leaving. I got out of the cab. But it was too late. They saw me.

"Trevor," Bennie hollered. "I left an invitation to my show at the Magic Castle." I shuttered. There was no avoiding them. If he was doing a magic show, he had to have an audience. Whether it was a willing group of people or his kids.

"Bennie and the lovely Bertie." They smiled. I didn't.

Bennie was ecstatic. "I have a ticket for you to fly to Los Angeles. My Magic Castle show is my first professional engagement." Bennie continued. "Bennie Jr. and his sister, Bernice, are coming to the show. We have a family table. You have to do more family things Trevor." Bennie smiled before delivering his final salvo. "We never see much of your family."

"Does this include my ex-wife?"

Bennie winched. "Of course, divorce doesn't stop you from being family. You will always be special to me, Trevor." I couldn't believe it. Bennie and Bertie still considered me family. "Remember Trevor to light a candle for President Bush. It shows a sign of support for your troops. He is a great man. Texas produces them."

"My troops, Bennie. Where might they be located?"

"Look at the Iraqi war, you will understand it and support it. I don't think you are patriotic, Trevor." Bennie beamed. He acted like he had just found the Holy Grail. "George the second is what I call him. He is a great leader." Bennie looked like he had just won the lottery. "I love our country." I guess that meant I didn't.

I couldn't resist asking the question. "Which book is the best on the Iraqi war?"

Bennie looked perplexed. "Book! Why read a book. Is there something wrong with you Trevor, those Communist professors write the books. None of what they say is the truth."

"You know, Bennie, ideas, knowledge. Reading materials."

"Knock it off Trevor. When I finished my MBA at the University of Phoenix I vowed never to read another book. Be a man. Think it out for yourself. You don't even use Viagra yet, how can you call yourself a man?" He smiled. I didn't. Where is Joe Pike when you really need him.

I made some small talk and watched as Bertie wandered off with her husband looking like an old hobbit. If they ever made a movie entitled "Valley of the Midgets" Bertie would have a starring role. But she was a jewel compared to Bennie who had a love-hate relationship with me. Divorce doesn't always mean you get rid of the relatives. They were getting ready for a six-week camping trip to Arizona. They were going to spend time in the caverns in southern Arizona. Where in the hell do people camp in Arizona? Bertie knitted a shawl and she wore it proudly She had labels made: "A Bertie Creation." She was sowing one of the labels on the outside of her shawl. A store in Bisbee Arizona featured them. A few months ago MSNBC did a special on Bertie Shawls. I couldn't figure out their success. They were mindless. Maybe that was the reason for their wealth. Bennie sold a dozen copyrighted magic tricks and the Bertie Shawls were big in Europe. Cheap rent prompted me to be nice. They shook my hand and left. Hallelujah. I had other things on my mind. I went upstairs and prepared my first at home meal in some time. I also ripped up the plane ticket to Los Angeles. I would be conspicuously absent as Bennie did his magic show. It was time to relax. Bennie and Bertie exhaust me.

I took out a steak and thawed it. I chopped some spinach, boiled an egg, cut some mushrooms and made a balsamic and olive oil dressing. A little fresh pepper and some grated Parmesan made my spinach salad perfect. I cut the egg in small pieces and made sure that there were some bacon bits to round out my salad. I found a bottle of Stag's Leap Merlot and opened it. I needed a $50 bottle of wine to do my final deducing. A real P. I. needs good wine. I baked a potato and cut some fresh beans. There was one frozen English desert left in the refrigerator.

I took out the sticky toffee pudding, read the instructions and put it in the microwave. The steak was a sixteen-ounce porterhouse. I put it in for my usual long baking that led to a well-done steak. When it came out of the oven it looked like I had damn near killed it. The feast de Trevor Blake, III was almost ready. The doorbell rang. I shouted in the intercom box.

"Who is it?"

"Hello, sweetie." I blanched. Who was calling me sweetie?

"Yes," I said redundantly. "Give me a clue, who is it." I didn't have a clue. It was a semi familiar voice.

"It's me, Joyce Byers, your sometimes girl friend. Remember we had a date."

I forgot. I quickly recovered. "Come in Joyce, I've prepared a special dinner." I thought to myself that I had forgotten. Thank God I cooked enough for three people. We now had two people and I corked the Stag Leap's Merlot and opened a $5 bottle of Gallo red. I ran into the bathroom and sprayed some Paul Sebastian cologne on and raced to the door. I opened it to see a radiant and happy Joyce. I felt relieved. Once again the masterful detective fools her. I had a date I didn't want. Not the best way to spend a quiet evening.

Joyce looked radiant. She shopped online at Ralph Lauren and she wore the blue Big Pony Polo with a pair of tight fitting pair of Diesel jeans. A heavenly vision. She walked into my front room smiling. A kiss and a smile followed. Eat your heart out Elvis Cole.

"Let's have a drink," I smiled. Nothing like the suave host.

She opened the refrigerator. "Look, Trevor, there's a special bottle of Stag's Leap Merlot." I wanted to cry. She could care less about wine. She took a glass, poured herself a drink to the brim, smiled and drank it down. That had to be a ten-dollar glass of wine. I needed to raise my P. I. rates to cover the entertainment costs. Maybe I would get laid.

"I am glad you like it." I hoped that I sounded convincing.

She looked at the Gallo red. "What is that?" She said it like I was about to offer her something poisonous.

"The Gallo is for cooking."

"Yuk, what did you cook?"

"Steak, Joyce just for you."

"With Gallo Red!"

"No I changed my mind, no red wine. Steak al la Trevor doesn't require it." That seemed to satisfy her.

Joyce is an extremely beautiful woman. She is also intelligent and well read. I try to overlook those traits. My mind was compartmentalized. I had my thoughts on the case. I didn't want to cook for her, I didn't want to talk to her. I was too much of a wimp to let her know my true feelings. So it didn't make for a loving evening. We talked about missing each other and all sorts of other meaningless parts of our life. I almost longed for Bennie and Bertie. They were asses but fun ones. Maybe if Bennie did a magic trick Joyce would run home. It always made me feel like running away. Joyce was not exciting. Maybe this is why she was my girl friend but I was still dating.

The dinner was ready. I hurriedly set the table. I pulled her chair away. She sat down. "It looks like a dinner for one, Trevor, a large and hungry person." She smiled. There was no fooling Joyce.

"I'm staying in shape, no more big meals. My sex life is better with less food."

"What sex life," she laughed.

Always the smart ass. I put the salad, the beans, the French bread on the table and then the coup de grace. The steak came out looking like it had been ambushed by a herd of Indians. It was almost black. Just the way I liked it. Steak al la Trevor, burnt.

"Dig in, Joyce." She looked askance at the dry and rubbery piece of meat in front of her. She was a warrior and began cutting it. She smiled. Sex symbols who are cooks have women falling all over them. We ate for a time in silence.

I broke the silence. "This is a special diet, Joyce."

"One designed to appeal to the poor, wayward girl who wants to get back in your good graces." I was afraid to ask what that meant.

She seemed to enjoy the food. My lame excuse about keeping my waistline in shape seemed to satisfy her. When the sticky toffee pudding came on the table, she was putty in my hands. We had a cappuccino and relaxed. My Italian cappuccino machine came via the Internet from Venice.

"How is the case coming Trevor?"

Best not to tip one's hand. "Fine." I smiled. "Nothing to report, really."

"Would you like some help?" She pulled out a small notebook.

Best to find out everything the police know. What have you got? I couldn't believe that the police know less than I did. Impossible. Maybe Joyce was being nice. Maybe she wanted to get laid. I needed to think of other things. I had to find out what she knew.

"Joyce, I need your help. Tell me what you have in the SFPD file." I gave her a sexy smile. The world's greatest detective at work.

"The Chef is someone very close to the scene," Joyce continued, "he has not only a financial interest in the Start Me Up band but an artistic attachment. We can't find out what it is. We are stymied. We don't know who he is. Whoops, it could be a woman. There are some clues pointing to a female."

What a revelation. Welcome to the party. I smiled at her. She didn't know much about the case. It was my turn to enlighten her. "I have some theories. Give me a minute." I wandered into the bedroom. Always keep them guessing. I came out with my 85 napkins. She looked in horror at the pile of small napkins with writing all over them. She sighed. Not a good sign. I sensed my disorganization frustrated her.

"I have a list and careful analysis of all the main characters, the clues, the major ideas, the weapons or poisons and so on." Actually I still hadn't put it all together. I did have some ideas. "From these 85, I have put together a special list of 25 napkins that point the finger to two people." I wasn't about to tell her which two and she noticed my reticent nature.

"Follow the money, Trevor."

"Let me guess, you have been talking to Woodward and Bernstein!" This was a recurring theme in the investigation. I had heard it from everyone. She continued: "The Irvington Brothers are still the key." I blanched. I didn't make the connection. It was best to look informed.

"As we speak I am about to go down to the Irvington Brothers tomorrow morning and make some inquires." I continued: "Remember Joyce I work undercover there."

"Inquires, Trevor, about what?"

"That's the question, the answer is the salami at the Irvington Brothers is the key."

Joyce spent another hour talking about her job. Where was Chastain Johnson when I needed her? I asked her to stay the night. She told me she was too tired. She also had a headache. Then she remembered she hadn't slept well last night. When she couldn't think of any more excuses, she put on her coat. She kissed me on the cheek. It had no impact.

I was ready for bed. Alone. Once again abandoned. The world's greatest detective sleeping alone.

I awoke as the sun burst into my front room window. I had fallen asleep on the couch. Nothing beats a San Francisco morning when the sun highlights the Golden Gate Bridge, dogs run by the park with good-looking girls at the end of the leash and the most important thing was that I didn't have a hangover. The Saturday morning crowd on Chestnut Street was one of young singles, yuppies and old timers like the late Joe DiMaggio who haunted the local coffee shops. There were no Donut shops. Yuppies watch cholesterol. I dressed in a pair of tan Dockers, threw on my Van Morrison tour shirt and the Air Jordans sans socks completed the cool forty year old bachelor look. The women would die for me. Or at least look at me.

I walked down to Starbuck's at Fillmore and Chestnut and ordered a café mocha. I walked up to Union Street turned left and wandered past Perry's. I crossed the street and looked in the Bus Stop. There were six people at the bar and it was nine thirty in the morning. Everyone had on Norte Dame t-shirts. They were getting ready for a football meeting. They needed to get ready to get a life. The morning crowd was on its way to weekend happiness. I spent most of the morning thinking about solving the crime. I stopped in Perry's and ordered a cappuccino. I continued to mull over the case as the drunks swilled down bloody Mary's. I should have brought my work along. I missed my napkins. It was time to collect them. There were now eighty-five. All with solid leads. Maybe I could arrange them into a book. "The Napkin Murder's: Solved By The World's Greatest Detective." Not a bad book title. I loved redundancy.

I walked back to my apartment. It was time for some serious detecting. I started my car on the third try. I needed a new car. There weren't many private eyes who drove a 1985 Volkswagen Fox with 285,000 miles on it. I arrived in the Haight just before noon and found a parking meter across from my office. The gods were smiling. I plugged in three dollars for two hours and wandered down to Emilio's. It was time for a jelly Donut and some real coffee. At least as real as Emilio made it.

Emilio's was hopping. It was prime time tourist season. There was only one seat at the counter and every table was filled. Tourists, locals and a few merchants crowded the place. I took a seat on a stool at the end of the counter. A jelly Donut and coffee appeared with Emilio smiling. He was also silent. I wondered what was wrong. I pulled out the San Francisco Chronicle and read about Jimmy McCracklin's latest blues concert. It seems McCracklin fired his band on stage and he finished the concert with solo piano tunes. "I be legend," McCracklin remarked. His bandleader, Gino Johnson, commented: "He be asshole." The opening act, Guitar Jac, had no comment. This was all the Chronicle had to report. It was too much information.

I looked at the movie reviews and scanned the news. George Bush was defending our right to be in Iraq. Vice President Dick Cheney was defending the right to dump on those who criticized the war in Iraq. The Chronicle had a picture of a portly and obnoxious assistant to President Bush who was about to be indicted. My thought was that it was due to bad hair, worse clothing and sloppy thinking. The little twerp had two chins and he looked at me from the CNN screen in Emilio's as I read the Chronicle. He announced that he was going to work for Fox TV News. He looked a lot like Karl Rove. It wasn't Rove, it was a clone of the Republican trickster. They all looked alike to me.

It was not a good time to be an American. Emilio wandered down to the end of the counter. He looked happy. Why not? He was a successful businessman and a cat burglar. Most of his money came from the burglaries. He lives in St. John Woods and his kids attend an exclusive private school. I was enjoying the calm and serenity. That ended quickly. Emilio stood in front of me smiling.

"Hello, Trevor."

I knew something was wrong. He was talking like a normal person. "What's wrong, Emilio?"

"We need to talk."

Now I was worried. Two complete sentences without his Vietnamese English. "Come by the office, I'll be there all day."

"Let me check the office." I folded up my newspaper.

"See you in an hour, Trevor." I got up, left a five-dollar bill and wondered into the bright Haight Street sunshine. A Jerry Garcia look a like smiled at me. I wanted to tell him he was dead. I climbed the stairs to my office, unlocked the door and looked at the mail. There were the usual bills, a list of restaurants offering two for one dinners and a Stanford University Alumni Directory. Thank you Leland Stanford. One of the perks of having a Stanford degree is having an alumni network that rivals the CIA for efficiency. They could find you in a snowstorm in Alaska. I looked in the directory and found a listing for two Seattle lawyers. I was going to need representation as I had a plan of action. I was expected in Seattle to find the killer. Something I had failed to do in Los Angeles.

I wandered around my office thinking. I had a lead in Seattle that would allow me to solve the crime. Or conversely a lead that might land me in jail. My lead was so tenuous that it might cause me to be a suspect. I would need a free get out of jail card. A Stanford alumnus always has connections with judges and I would need a friendly person on the bench. I found a listing for John Stixwitt. He was a Dutch-German son of immigrants who was Seattle's best defense attorney. Guitar Jac knew him as an undergraduate at Stanford. He was blonde, charming, well dressed and a shrewd orator. Not to mention number one at Harvard Law School. It was always the first thing he said when he met someone. He was also on half a dozen charity boards and helped to set up the Bob Dylan exhibit at the EMT. Bill Gates had spent so much money on the Experience Music Project that it brought Jimi Hendrix back from the grave. He was everywhere. There was no sign of Van Morrison. I made a note to call Stixwitt. I went online and found the Start Me Up band. I went on their website. Guitar Jac was announced as the drummer. Charlie Watts was turning over in his grave. Well not exactly his grave, that was still two or three years away. I fired up my computer. I fired up the coffee pot. I fired up my imagination. Then I went on the fan sites. Maybe the Chef was out there. After forty-five minutes I still had no clues. No sign of him. I needed help. I did have two suspects.

Help came in the form of a five foot six inch former Vietcong military police officer recently turned sixty who owned a Donut shop. Emilio also had a twenty-five year old wife and a first and second grader. He was my quasi, unpaid assistant. Not exactly what Sam Spade had in mind. Emilio came through the door with a smile. He sat down. He put an ashtray in front of the no smoking sign and lit a cigarette. I felt like telling him only Chastain Johnson could smoke in the office. What the hell. We could break a rule.

"I have some thoughts Trevor."

I looked disinterested. "Lay them on me Emilio."

Emilio frowned: "The English language is a beautiful and dutiful experience, please use it correctly, you can't lay anything on someone. The semantics are incorrect." Emilio smiled. He always gave the perfect English lesson. Coming from a former Vietnamese military figure it was a strange sight. One that I didn't need in the midst of a major investigation that was going nowhere. Something told me to listen to my friend. His wisdom in these matters was greater than mine.

Then again maybe I was wasting my time. All I needed was a lecture from the former Vietcong policeman. Then again he was a smart policeman and an even brighter crook. There was no harm in listening. I needed to jog his memory.

"Emilio, clues, help, deduction, you know all the things that a proper detective needs to solve a case."

He smiled. I was getting a lot of that lately. "Ah, Trevor, always the wit. You need to follow the money. You have been told my everyone this very simple idea."

"So, give me a little more of a clue."

"As teenagers would say, you are clueless."

I wanted to scream. The dangers of educating a former Vietnamese military hero was obvious. "If I hear that one more time, I am leaving for Canada."

"Well, you'll be close in Seattle." Emilio smiled and continued: "You need to look deeper into the Irvington Brothers, Pam Wong and Elliott Shonestein. They are connected to someone."

I pulled out a napkin, and began writing number 86. It would be the final clue to the killer. He was right, there was one person I was overlooking. I thought about the case and there were still some problems. Mainly, the missing folks.

I looked at Emilio and tried to couch my words in a low and serious voice. "In case you have ignored things, Elliott Shonestein has vanished from the face of the earth, Pam Wong surfaces only to smoke and the Irvington Brothers are so busy selling salami that they can't trace the source. I am stymied."

"There is a connection there, Trevor." Emilio continued. "I have booked a flight to Seattle, I have my sources in the Vietnamese community, and I will help you solve this little mystery."

I couldn't wait. I had 300-pound Samoans following me around, a gay Mafia boss, affectionately called Don Gino who in turn was helping a sixty-year-old ex-Vietcong military policeman. Detective Sanchez turned a blind eye to a gay mobster helping the investigation. I felt like I had a private eye with an entourage of crazy's. I don't think I will be voted detective of the year. Emilio left. I noticed a bag of Donuts. French crullers My favorites. I ate three and thought. The sugar rush perked up my brain. Picking up the bag I wandered outside on Haight Street and gave the rest to a guy dressed up to look like Jerry Garcia. Personally, I liked the first Jerry better.

"Asshole, I don't eat sugar, it will rot your body." He took a drag on a joint that looked like it was from a Cheech and Chong movie and threw the bag in the gutter. It was good to see that the health Nazis were still well and alive.

I walked down to Amoeba. This was my favorite CD store. It was here that I met my wife. It had been a bowling alley and I bought her a drink. We were married three weeks later. It was the second happiest day of my life. The first was when we got divorced. I went back to the Oldies section and bought the re-released Donovan CDs. With three versions of "Sunshine Superman" and twenty-six songs I was in folk rock heaven. I walked outside and headed for Golden Gate Park. I needed to walk and think. I took five napkins form McDonald's. I needed to expand my 86 clue napkins. They were wrinkled but still served the purpose.

The radiant sunshine burst through the trees and made a path of light that looked like Jesus might come through it. Or maybe Charles Manson. If you had dropped acid Jesus or Jerry Garcia showed up on the lawn. Or maybe Janis Joplin or Jimi Hendrix. The foliage was in a radiant full-blown beauty with colors everywhere. The smell of various flowers made me feel like a kid. I decided to go over to the Japanese Tea Garden. I would sit with a pot of tea and some cookies and be a private eye. Thinking was the key to solving this mystery.

The entrance fee was now five dollars. I sat down and paid another five dollars for the tea. I left a five-dollar tip. This did earn me a smile from my Japanese hostess. A nametag read: "Brenda." Probably intermarriage.

"Hello dumbshit.'" I looked up at the lovely Chastain Johnson. "Ten bucks for tea and cookies. A five-dollar tip! You can't pay the rent. You can't solve the case." She continued: "Am I missing something?"

"You are missing how to get a date, how to get laid and how to solve a case." I loved telling the FBI off.

"Always the wise ass, Trevor." She lit a cigarette.

"I have something for you Chastain." I raised my eyebrows in a sexy manner. I pulled out my five blank napkins. This was going to take me into the low 90s. More napkins would only confuse me. "Sit down, Chastain." She sat. Nothing like the masculine approach. We looked at each other.

"Now that I'm seated. Is there a point to this?" She ground out her cigarette with her shoe. Yuck! "Trevor, the point to this?" I hated redundancy.

That was a good a question. I hoped that I had an answer. No thoughts were floating around in my mind. I couldn't take my eyes off her breasts. Not exactly the behavior of a mature detective. I looked at the blank napkins. She looked at the blank napkins. There was a lull. She drank some of my tea. I wrote furtively for half an hour. She looked at the foliage. We sat silently. It was not a pleasant interlude. I ordered some more tea. She lit another cigarette. She looked bored. I looked thoughtful. I also wrote a series of notes on my five blank napkins.

"There," I said, "I have outlined my solution." She looked pensively at the napkins. She read over them quickly. Trevor you do have some points. Damned if you don't have it figured out. Maybe." She stopped and ground out her cigarette in the teacup. Yuck.

She was thinking. She spoke: "The problem is everything is hypothetical, theoretical, we can't prove a thing." She thought for a long time. I ordered some more tea. I had to go to the bathroom. I excused myself and as I walked into the men's room a Samoan with a park uniform was picking up trash. He smiled. I felt safe.

I returned. "Let's meet again Chastain. I will share some more of my clues with you." That seemed to placate her. She was out of words. Chastain got up to leave. The waitress came flying out of the serving booth. She shouted.

"Miss don't forget the cookies." The waitress looked at me with disgust. Brenda didn't like to be told how to do her job. "Who is that awful woman?" Brenda asked.

Chastain lit another cigarette. I hoped the FBI had lung cancer coverage. She looked at the waitress, 'Trevor tell the female Chinaman to fuck off."

"The female Chinaman is Japanese," I smiled.

Chastain continued: "I'm booking a flight to Seattle, Trevor, where are you staying?"

"I'll be at the Warwick Hotel. It's close to the Pike Place Market."

"I can't believe it, you are staying in a pricey hotel. Thanks John Stixwitt. He booked it. I couldn't believe it. I had eight Samoans, a 60 year old Vietcong policeman who owned a Donut shop, an FBI agent who looked like she belonged in Playboy magazine, a gangster in a purple suit and a police detective who got more phone numbers from young girls than Warren Beatty to help me solve the case. Or at least phone numbers that Beatty got thirty years ago and three face lifts ago.

It was time to go home to pack for the flight to Seattle. But I needed to talk to Guitar Jac. The nice thing about visiting my partner is that his townhouse has valet parking. He lives two blocks from the Fairmont Hotel. Nob Hill is as good as it gets in residential San Francisco living. The neighborhood is a pricey one but only a few blocks from downtown. The tenderloin, sometimes known as Nob Valley, at least that's what the transvestites call it, is only six or eight blocks away depending on how far down the social ladder you would like to fall. Guitar Jac has as much money as anyone. He tries to hide it. Ever more important, he is a Stanford graduate. Something he tells you five seconds after meeting him. He has invested his money wisely over the years. He also earned it the old fashioned way. He inherited it. He keeps it in low yielding municipal bonds and some pricey real estate. Rumor has it that he flies back to Omaha to lunch with Warren Buffett twice a year.

I found Guitar Jac practicing the drums. He was sitting on the outdoor sun area of his penthouse. A drum kit, some yuppie water and a tape of the Rolling Stones greatest hits occupied his attention. He didn't see me for some time. I sat down and watched him play. He didn't look like Charlie Watts but with our eyes closed he sounded like him. The drums at least. The real Charlie was getting over throat cancer, so no one knew what he sounded like. Finally, Guitar Jac noticed me. He smiled. I'd been getting a lot of that lately.

"Trevor, my man."

"Jac,, we need to have some sort of plan to prevent your untimely demise."

"You talk like someone from another era or another planet." He continued: "I forget you were too young to experience the 60s but you dress, look, talk and act like it. Badly I might add." He smiled, happy with his conclusion.

I couldn't disagree. This case made me feel like I was from another planet. "I'll be at the Warwick Hotel, call me when you get in."

Guitar Jac wrinkled his nose in disapproval. "I'll be at the Fairmont. The penthouse suite. Let's meet tomorrow night and go over our plan. How can you stay at the Warwick? It has such a pedestrian location. Not to mention a three-course dinner special for thirty dollars. Please! Show some class, Trevor." Guitar Jac's nose wrinkled as he said Warwick Hotel. It was like he had a case of hotel pox.

"As Don Imus might say: 'Don't educate the Negro."

Jac laughed. "All you white guys are alike. You think alike and look alike. Don Imus is a jerk." He was also my favorite talk show host.

"I have a plan, Jac, just call me." I wasn't sure what my plan entailed. But I had the clue to the killer. We chatted for a while and listened to a John Coltrane box set. There were six CDs of everything he had recorded in the 1960s. I wondered if Charlie Watts had heard any of these songs. Guitar Jac was never musically predictable. We had some Brie and imported French crackers and washed it down with a Cakebread Chardonnay. I remembered that Imus was wrong, it was good to educate the Negro.

"You hospitality is appreciated Jac." He smiled.

Guitar Jac not only had money but good taste. Jac complained that the Cakebread Reserve was too fruity and sweet. He would pay a hundred and fifty dollars for a fine wine and then complain about its lack of unique taste. I thought about the Gallo in my refrigerator. It was midnight when the last Coltrane disc ended. I was in saxophone heaven. It was time to go home and pack for Seattle.

The next morning I was up early. At six o'clock I did fifty push-ups, went through a routine with my five-pound weights. I ate two French crullers, thanks to Emilio, downed with a cup of decaf. I sat down and spent some time rearranging my ninety plus napkins. A private eye can never have too many clues.

I arranged them on the desk. I went into the bottom drawer of my dresser and pulled out a small handgun. Something told me I would need it. I turned off Van Morrison's Enlightenment CD. I looked over my apartment. It was neat and clean. I had time on my hands. I packed my suitcase and called a cab for the San Francisco airport. I needed Enlightenment and only Van Morrison could provide it. Or maybe some young girl. Or may a good seafood dinner in Seattle.

The turban headed cab driver nodded as I got into the car. I began to wonder if wearing a turban was a requirement to drive a San Francisco cab.

"Hello mate," Turban head said in perfect London style English. "I got a movie script, you're not a producer are you? When I go to England, I show it to my friends in the pubs. It's a sure hit."

"No, I'm a serial killer." He didn't react.

He lit a cigarette, drank his coffee and never said another word. The raghead populace was diverse in San Francisco. When we arrived at the airport, I gave him a $5 tip.

"Cheap asshole," he hollered. Ah, San Francisco and the joys of a multicultural life.

Chapter 26
OFF TO SEATTLE

I was ready to fly out to Seattle. But I wasn't eager to see our airport. The San Francisco Airport is in a state of perpetual remodeling. Everything is freshly painted. It reeks of chemicals. Finding a gate is not an easy task. Miraculously, there was a large sign with an arrow. That was the good news. The bad news was the TSA crew and they looked like they were at least high school graduates. I think I had studied too long at Stanford because I couldn't quit analyzing people. Maybe this is why I am a great detective. Two security guards who looked like they had flunked out of junior high school manned the Gate 3 entrance. Next to them were two more TSA inspectors. They had buzz cuts, smiles and looked like they wanted to beat me up. They looked like they wanted to beat everyone up. Abdul would be in danger. The security check was a simple one and we were in the airport departure lounges. I had a lot of time to think. The picture was coming together. I now had a handle on the Chef. The flight to Seattle was quick and I slept most of the way.

When I landed the Seattle-Tacoma Airport, I discovered like SFO it recently underwent a remodeling. Unlike, San Francisco it was complete. There was a restaurant and shopping concourse featuring, Ivar's seafood, Anthony's Home Pier and other assorted restaurants. A huge Border's bookstore in the middle of the shops added to its ambiance. This meant that you didn't have to leave the airport for the Seattle dining experience. I bought a cup of Ivar's clam chowder and ate it as I ran outside to catch a cab. It was raining. Welcome to Seattle. It's always raining. I climbed into the cab. I was astonished the driver was white and Swedish. This might take some psychiatric adjustment.

"Hi, I'm Warren," the cabbie smiled. "Where to?" There was a Warren in Los Angeles. Maybe all white guys had the same name. I had to control my bigotry.

"To the Warwick Hotel." On the ride downtown the cabbie told me his life story. He had a PhD. in Latin. It was from Harvard. He did this because he didn't want to work. At age forty he finished his doctorate. No one hired him. He had a trust fund. So cab driving got him close to the masses. He was writing a book on the reasons for the decline of Latin in the pubic schools. Not exactly your best selling topic. I think that I drew these people to me. At least he didn't have a turban. I noticed a picture of an Indian guy on the driver's board.

Warren smiled. "That was me when I lived in India." He had a sense of humor. Warren continued: "The cab is owned by a Sikh. His name is Suecheng Smith. I think there is intermarriage in the family." I tipped him ten dollars and went into the Warwick Hotel. He didn't call me an asshole. I guess that the tip sufficed. I was given the key to room 808. It had a nice view of the garage. It also had double beds. Maybe Chastain Johnson would show up. I shouldn't make jokes. A knock on the door revealed Chastain. She didn't say a word. She lit a cigarette, as she walked into the room. Chastain looked around with disgust and coughed. Obviously, she hadn't been talking to the Surgeon General.

"We need to talk."

"Really!" Always the cool private eye.

"The attempt on Guitar Jac's life will come backstage at Seattle's Key Arena. We have it on good authority that there will be something different. It won't be food poisoning. The Chef has other skills."

I spread out my ninety plus napkins. "The key to the crime is right here."

Chastain looked at me horrified. "What key? On the pieces of paper in front of you that have no organization and no direction. Jesus."

"No, it's still Trevor." I smiled. Always the witty and chatty P. I.

"Who booked this room?" Chastain put a mint in her mouth.

"You'll see. I have an extra bed, care to stay?"

She laughed. Not a good sign. "Thanks but no thanks." She smiled and left. Well it wasn't a bad idea. I had a day to kill, so it was time to see some real music. I walked down to the Pike Place Market and sat at a table in the Athenian with a beer. I watched the ferries come in for three hours and had another three beers. I was thirsty.

Then it was time for dinner. I took a cab to the Flying Fish for a Pan Asian dinner of coconut shrimp and an assortment of fresh vegetables. I felt like the veritable tourist. That night I went down to Pioneer Square and heard Little Bill and the Bluenotes at the New Orleans House. Little Bill's hit "I Love An Angel" established him as the penultimate bluesman. We remained friends. It was a great night punctuated with a bowl of gumbo. It was my desert. Or was the good music my desert. It was one in the morning when eight Samoans marched into the New Orleans

House. Every head in the room turned. Through the door in a purple cape, a purple hat, a purple walking stick, purple shoes and a white tie, Don Gino strode. A small man in a purple cape followed him. I will have to talk to him about the white tie. The small man has to go. Definitely out of character.

"Ah, Trevor." I wasn't sure if that was approval or disapproval. He continued: "We are ready to catch our killer." I thought we. Eight Samoans, a gay Don, an FBI agent and who knows who else came along. Everyone was looking at Don Gino. The Samoans walked around the room. Then everyone noticed the Samoans. No one looked Don Gino's way. Fear was the ultimate weapon.

"To what do I owe this honor?" Don Gino lit a cigarette. It was a habit that was catching on.

"Well, my San Francisco private eye, I have it on good authority that the Chef plans a different attack. He is still upset that you stopped the bombing of the Whiskey a Go Go. After the insurance claims, the owner made money. Crazy huh!"

I pulled out ten of my key napkins. I showed them to Don Gino. He saw what everyone else had missed.

"Ah Trevor, you have a better grasp than I thought." We talked at length about our plan. It wasn't fool proof. It could smoke out the killer. There were four possibilities. We walked outside at 3 in the morning. We drank for more than an hour after the bar closed. No one wanted to tell Don Gino that there was a two o'clock drinking curfew in the state of Washington. There was also no bill. Everything was on the house. The New Orleans House knew Don Gino's reputation. So there was no closing time. Always good to be with the Don.

Don Gino dropped me off at the Warwick Hotel. The 5 Blind Boys of Alabama were staying there. Although it was 3:30 in the morning the Blind Boys were going through a rehearsal. It was amazing to see Clarence Fountain, the spokesman for the band, talk about their version of "Atomic Bomb." Then Jimmy Carter began singing some lead vocals. No, not the president! I am listening to them in the special rehearsal room set up for the bands. It was a nice touch. Lately, Japanese tourists flooded the hotel and they were appreciative of the American music. Most of them wanted an Ichiro autograph, but then so did I. I went up to bed. Tomorrow would be a telling day. It was essentially a day off but I had to set up my plan to ensnare the Chef.

Entering the room I saw a green light on the phone. Ah, messages. I punched the message center button and was informed of two new messages. The first was from Pam Wong. She asked me to meet her tomorrow at Noon at the Dahlia Lounge. Lunch was on her. The second message was more disturbing.

"I know your stupid plan, Trevor, so don't look for the obvious." The Chef continued: "it will be something different. This time your witty plan and that of your Negro accomplice will be for naught." I imagined he was smiling over the phone. Then again I imagined everyone was smiling. Without realizing it the Chef had made a mistake. He left a valuable clue. The phrase "will be for naught" pinned the killer's identity down. I went to bed with a smile. The phone call was a stupid mistake. I was hot on the Chef's trail. It was only a matter of time.

The next morning I walked once again down to the Pike Street Market. I loved that place. A few years ago someone tried to turn it into condos. The good people of Seattle stopped that. Thank God. I settled in at Tully's with a large decaf and a cherry scone. Eight dollars and twenty-one cents. Not a cheap energy boost. Private eyes need sugar. It helps the thinking process. I took out my key napkins and looked at them. I had a plan. I walked through the market and bought some smoked salmon, a large loaf of sourdough and a pint of home made blueberry jam. Private eyes need nutrition. Walking back to the hotel, it was time to get dressed for lunch with Pam Wong. I put on my blue Hawaiian Tommy Bahama shirt and my Ben Sherman jeans. Always the fashion plate. Pam had good taste in restaurants.

The Dahlia Lounge is one of Seattle's premier restaurants. The owner, Tom Douglas, remains a Seattle legend. The fusion of California cuisine with Asian influences made the Dahlia Lounge the place to be seen. It was also the place to eat, and the food was delicious. I was dressed to be seen. I arrived at five minutes to twelve. I asked for a window table. Why? Who knows? The street was murky and old. I ordered a decaf coffee and it arrived on a fancy plate with four kinds of sugar. I sat and looked at the street. A half hour later there was no sign of Pam Wong. I ordered.

My first course was a duck salad, followed by a noodle soup with mussels and an Alaskan salmon stuffed with shrimp. A cream Brule finished the meal. Pam Wong never showed. The food almost made me forget her. That is until I got the bill. Maybe she would show up late and pay the bill. I had my cell phone. It never rang. I paid the bill. It was a bargain, only $78 and I left a $22 tip. Even Elvis Cole didn't tip like this. Now what to do about Pam.

As I walked back to the hotel, I had two thoughts. She didn't give a damn or perhaps she was the victim of foul play. I called around. No signs of Pam. Not a good sign. There was a shock when I entered the hotel lobby. There stood McKenzie Dee. He was an old musical friend who performed a Monday night tribute to Ersel Hickey at the Tractor Tavern in the Ballard section of Seattle. He had the clothes, the look and the sneer of this obscure rockabilly singer. Ersel Hickey had one hit "Bluebirds Over the Mountain" and retained a strong cult following. The cult now extended to McKenzie who drew capacity crowds. He also performed at bar mitzvahs and for Aryan Brotherhood celebrations. He was reported to be the Hell's Angels favorite singer. Sonny Barger had a picture of McKenzie over his toilet. In other words he would perform anywhere.

McKenzie Dee was a weird guy. His diet included iodine, usually taken in a seafood salad, and he loved to say that the iodine kept his hair black. He also ate only meat and drank strong black coffee. He walked toward me. I could hardly wait.

"Trevor, good to see you. I have an hour off." McKenzie drove a city bus. We talked for some time and I assured him that I would come see his show.

"Any luck with the Ersel Hickey tribute CD?" I was trying to be polite.

"Not yet, no demand." He lit a cigarette. The same kind, Lucky's, that Ersel Hickey smoked. The late Ersel Hickey who died of lung cancer.

"Well, I'll be the first to buy one."

"Trevor, I have a feeling about the Start Me Up band. There is someone connected to the group that is doing the crime. It's not an outsider."

I looked at McKenzie. How the hell could he know anything? No sense ignoring him. "Tell me what you think McKenzie."

"Follow the money, Trevor." Not only had I heard this before, I was tired of this notion.

"Sure thing, McKenzie." We talked for some time and I told him that I would see him shortly. I took the elevator to 808. My green light was blinking. Another message. I played it. The elusive Pam Wong apologized for standing me up for lunch. She wanted to meet me at 3 that afternoon at the Pike Street Market. She told me to be at the Athenian with a pitcher of Mac and Jac beer. Not a bad request. I could do it. I changed my clothes. Something very casual. A Van Morrison tour t-shirt, a pair of Docker shorts and my blue Air Jordan's with the white stripes made for the cool tourist look. Why I wanted that look I wasn't sure. The Athenian was full of drunken Indians, longshoremen and tourists. It had a beautiful view of Puget Sound and waitresses with bee hive hair dos, cigarette breath and a surly attitude. The young waitresses were in their fifties. It was my kind of place. Tom Hanks picture hung on the wall. The movie Sleepless in Seattle was shot there. It was alleged that Hanks ate every meal at the counter. He loved the Filipino food. In my mind, it was second to the fresh seafood. I left the Warwick Hotel with the sun shining and a faint breeze. Was this really rainy Seattle?

I walked over to Pike Street turned right and in four blocks I marched into the Pike Place Market. There were guys in the market throwing fish to each other as the tourists watched and they even sold some. There was a scrawny guitarist singing the blues and selling CDs. The Greek sign for the Athenian emerged. Two drunken Indians were sleeping in the doorway. Welcome to Seattle.

It was easy to find a booth. The lunch rush was over and the dinner crowd was still shopping. I settled into a booth and ordered a pitcher of Mac and Jac. I loved smooth beer and this was the best. I quickly killed the pitcher. I ordered a second one; after all I was walking. A minute after it arrived, so did Pam Wong. She looked gorgeous. What else was new! She sat down, smiled and lit a cigarette.

"Tonight's the night," she remarked.

"A Rod Stewart song, Pam, you are hip." I needed to impress her. I wondered if that meant I was going to get laid. Probably not.

"We need to find something," Pam remarked sitting down.

"You mean we find the killer."

"No, I mean you finally get a handle on the Chef," She smiled. "Maybe you even get laid."

I think she said this already. Obviously a tease. "Tell me something new, Pam."

"Trevor, the key is in the Start Me Up band's Key Arena concert in Seattle. It comes just a day after the Stones perform at Safeco Field."

I was running out of patience. I knew all this. She said she was going home. "I'll see you in San Francisco, Pam."

"Remember things are not what they always seem."

"Pam I have memorized the lyrics to 'Looking For The Woman."

"Do you really understand them Trevor?"

"No!" Not only did I feel stupid, I was perplexed. I added five more clue napkins. Things were exactly as my 90 plus napkins indicated. Suddenly, I saw what I missed. Oblivion was the answer. But to find Oblivion would be a problem. She had vanished. No one had seen her. She had her fifteen minutes of fame with the Start Me Up band and walked off into the sunset. Or perhaps was kidnapped into the sunset. Or maybe she walked up Sunset Boulevard and was still at a party. It was time to call in the cavalry. That would be Joyce Byers. I pulled out my cell phone and started to dial. I watched Pam Wong walk out of the Athenian and dialed the wrong number. What an ass. Legs that never seemed to end. Long and sexy. I was distracted. I had to remember that Joyce was my sometimes girl friend. At least when I couldn't find another date.

I got Joyce on the phone. It took some sweet-talking to get her to run a background check on Oblivion. I didn't know a thing about Oblivion, including her real name. I wasn't sure the FBI database contained a file for Oblivion. Joyce assured me that she was on it.

The next call was to Chastain Johnson. She wasn't answering her phone. I felt a hand on my shoulder. She was standing next to me.

"Hello to the lovely Chastain." I smiled. It melted women. Chastain didn't look like she was going to melt. She looked agitated.

"No dickhead, no smart remarks." I smiled. The same old Chastain.

"You called?"

"I did." The joys of modern technology. I continued: "We need to find some background on Oblivion."

"An insignificant female drummer." She lit a cigarette.

I was irritated. "She could be the key. Thank about it, Chastain, she comes into the band under strange circumstances and vanishes. We Don't know a thing about her. Maybe she's the Chef."

"Ok, give me a day." She walks away. I had more phone calls to make. I called Don Gino. He was staying in the Penthouse of the Fairmont Hotel. The eight Samoans had their own apartment. No answer. I got up, left a five-dollar tip and wandered through the Pike Street Market. I bought some smoked salmon and blueberries. I started eating the blueberries as I walked out of the market. Suddenly there were four Samoans walking with me. Hardly a coincidence.

"Don Gino wants to see you."

"Really guys, I thought maybe we were going to see Akibono." They walked me out to First and Pike and there sat the longest purple Cadillac I had ever seen in my life. The door opened. The stale smell of cigarettes and Paul Sebastian cologne escaped into the fresh Seattle air.

"Trevor, my brother, come in for a talk." I got into the Cadillac with a Delbert McClinton CD playing and Don Gino handed me a tall frosty glass of Mac and Jac. With everyone watching the P. I., I wondered how we would solve this case. Don Gino sipped his champagne.

"I hear by the grapevine that you need some information on Oblivion."

Maybe there was a universal bug on my phone. "You got it." Don Gino handed me an envelope. It contained three pages on Oblivion. It was not promising. She was a person who almost didn't exist. I wondered how you could not have a background and become the drummer in the biggest Rolling Stones cover band. It was time to do some detecting.

We drove down to Seattle's Pioneer Square to once again see Little Bill and the Bluenotes in a rare afternoon gig at Larry's First Avenue Bar. Without the winos and Indians, Pioneer Square loses some of its ambiance. But when Little Bill tore into "I Love An Angel" all was forgiven. I mentioned to Don Gino that Little Bill never did afternoon gigs. Don Gino smiled.

"I have my ways, Trevor. I am Little Bill's biggest fan." He lit a small and long cigar.

I hoped that involved a hefty booking fee and not the threat of extermination. Little Bill joined us after the set and it was obvious that he and Don Gino were good friends.

"Trevor," Little Bill continued, "Don Gino was my best man when I got married. It has all worked due to him."

I wondered if Don Gino had threatened to kill Little Bill or the wife if he got divorced. We talked and Little Bill left by saying he had never heard of Oblivion. Little Bill knew every drummer. I was puzzled, either had anyone else. We now had a real mystery. Where was Elvis Cole when you really needed him? Or Joe Pike to beat information out of the key suspects. Joe would have his hands full. There were too many key suspects.

I stood up and spoke authoritatively. "I hate to interrupt the mutual admiration society guys, we need to solve the crime." Don Gino and Little Bill looked at me in an agitated manner. My detective helpers appeared to be on vacation.

Don Gino went into his pocket. I hoped it wasn't for a gun . It wasn't. He wanted to cut the end off a Cuban cigar. Don Gino lit up. He looked like a gay version of Kinky Freidman. He inhaled and blew smoke rings in the air. At least Kinky didn't wear a purple suit. It would be fun to watch him sing "Asshole From El Paso" in a purple suit.

"Trevor, we need to find out a bit more about Oblivion." My sentiments exactly.

My cell phone rang. It was Joyce Byers.

"Hi Trevor, we've had some word of mouth information." Sounded like a San Francisco phrase to me. I wasn't sure what that meant. It appeared that Oblivion didn't exist. She came out of the thin air. Joyce told me that she had checked with the FBI, the state resources for criminals and non-criminals and finally found a bookie that knew Oblivion. Her real name was Judy Schaeffer. She was an aspiring drummer and had joined the Joan Jett band in the 1980s. She finished second in a contest to see who would be the Bangles new drummer. That meant she was old as dirt. She was hired by someone to come into the Start Me Up band. They found Schaeffer with her fingers cut off, dead in a San Francisco landfill in the last few days. She called herself Oblivion and she had auditioned for the Start Me Up band. They laughed at her. The new Oblivion came in with Elliott Shonestein's approval. Something was fishy.

Every indication was that someone placed Oblivion in the band with a plan for financial sabotage. She was never destined for death. It appeared she worked with the Chef. The bad news was that she wasn't a she. Then again maybe that was the good news. She was a female impersonator. Joyce Byers' file even had her medical records. There are some things even a private eye doesn't need to know. San Francisco couldn't have more than 50,000 drag queens. Things were not getting easier.

"Don Gino, I need the purple Cadillac and two of the Samoans." Don Gino looked at me like I had lost my mind.

"There must be a reason."

"Trust me, would I take advantage of the Purple Don?"

He looked thoughtful. He smiled. "Take it my son, I will be having dinner at the Axis." This was one of Seattle's finest 1st Avenue bistros located in the heart of Belltown. It was the place where Seattle's overly heterosexual gathered. I decided not to inform Don Gino of that little fact.

As Don Gino left in a cab, I looked at the two remaining Samoans. They did not look happy. I piled into the back of the Purple Cadillac and they got in the front. Power has its rewards. I told them to drive out to

Ballard. I looked behind me and saw six Samoans in a SUV. It was time to check out McKenzie Dee's tribute to Ersel Hickey.

The purple Cadillac rolled up to the front of the Tractor. Buckle Bob Boliver was taking $5 at the door. He did a Hank Williams night on Tuesday and at times he and McKenzie did an Everly Brothers show. They were a little too weird. I needed a drink. So I went next door to Hattie's Hat. This quaint little restaurant served food but no one was eating it. I ordered a decaf coffee and a Bailey's Irish crème. Then I ordered two more Bailey's. No sense letting the coffee ruin the mood. It was a little warm up before the main event.

I walked into the Tractor. Standing near the door McKenzie Dee's twin brother, McArthur Dee, regaled people with tales of rock and roll. McArthur was a talented singer who drove a bus, abused his wife verbally so she smoked marijuana daily, and he laughed at people who invested in property or the stock market. "I invest my money in 45s," McArthur commented. He was a lawyer who hated practicing law. He had an online law degree and he was terrible in court. The judges loved him because he was entertaining. He didn't know a thing about the law. At the bar after a long court day, he was the life of the party. He had driven a bus before spending fifteen years completing law school, and he lectured everyone on subjects that he knew little about. I loved him like a brother. I even liked his underpants collection. He had collected fifty pairs of Carol Doda's underpants. The former topless dancer, now old and sagging, signed ten of his pants. McArthur was a true collector.

"Hey Trevor," McArthur hollered. "Ready for a real estate wedgie." This was a reference a recent land purchase that I had made in Arizona. He loved to act like he was a member of Mensa. He said that he was Nostradamus Jr. He knew all.

"Hello, McArthur, still the truth."

"The whole truth and nothing but it." He smiled. Not only was he a stupid man, he was a self righteous one. He had once been a Jehovah's Witness and it showed in his dogmatic thinking. We talked and I walked over to the corner. The lights went out and a spotlight shone on the stage. McKenzie Dee walked out with a startling resemblance to Ersel Hickey. He began singing "Bluebirds Over the Mountain" and Mike Love of the Beach Boys stood in the front row cheering. At almost every show a celebrity showed up. It made for a large audience. After the show I went backstage.

"Great show," McKenzie. I turned to see his twin McArthur.

"If you like second rate impersonators," McArthur smiled, "myself I prefer the real thing."

"Enough guys." I kicked McArthur out of the room. "He is a real shit." I turned to McKenzie to apologize.

McKenzie laughed. "Hey man I have put up with this for years. He is still in high school at forty." We talked about how McArthur's binge drinking and failure to be honest with himself or his friends created a euphoric bubble that protected him from reality. He had every Pacific Northwest record and a wife he verbally berated. His kids had moved out. One was a drug counselor and the other a high tone lawyer. They seldom saw their father as they lived in New York.

He was shrewd. He used humor to hide his ugly side and a sick personality. It was time to get rid of him. I told him we had private business.

"You are going to get a real estate wedgie, Trevor." He smiled and left. McArthur never liked a phrase he couldn't abuse. I breathed easily. McKenzie took off his Ersel Hickey clothes and took a shower. We drank a beer and talked about Oblivion. She was the key. But how? Then I began to see the picture. Basketball, female impersonators and the Rolling Stones were the key to solving this crime. How all that went together was beyond me.

"How does McArthur know about my property?" I was puzzled.

"McArthur is a computer hacker and a whiz at getting into other people's business." McKenzie paused and thought for a moment. "McArthur is passive-aggressive and a huge Rolling Stones fan. There is something going on. I think McArthur is in the mix."

I took out a napkin and added McArthur's name to my list of suspects. It was my 96th napkin. Suddenly, it looked like everyone was a suspect. He was a strange duck. He hollered at his wife hourly, bought strangers beers and talked about his musical expertise. He had written a book on Del Shannon. No one knew that his brother, McKenzie, ghosted the book for him. It took me about an hour to find out that McArthur was a potentially violent sociopath. Maybe I could introduce him to Bennie and Bertie. They were intellectual sociopaths so everyone would get along. They could tell stories about me. That would not only make them feel better but provide the needed abuse they thrived on.

I talked for a time to McKenzie. I told him that a basketball clue, a tie to female impersonators and the music of the Rolling Stones were the keys to solving the crime. He looked at me like I was nuts. Maybe he was right.

Chapter 27
BASKETBALL, FEMALE IMPERSONATORS AND THE ROLLING STONES

I left the Tractor and had a game plan. I stood out in front of the Ballard music club. It took an hour for a guy in a turban to pick me up. He didn't talk all the way to the Warwick Hotel. When I didn't tip him, he let me know he knew one English word: "Asshole." Stand in line everyone is calling me that.

The next night the Rolling Stones concert would offer one important clue to help me solve the case. The Chef was a prime Stones fan and would be lurking backstage. He would stand out.

An even better clue would happen the next night when the Start Me Up band played the Key Arena. This was the Start Me Up band's first concert at a major arena that seated 20,000 that sold out in minutes. It would go a long way toward legitimizing their appeal. It would also go a long way toward satisfying the Chef's manic money desires.

I needed some special consideration, so a pass was arranged for the Stones' show at Safeco Field. It was one that gave me total access. If the Chef was in the area reserved for the band and close friends, he would show up the next night at the Key Arena.

There was too much to think about, I had to get ready. So I went back to the Warwick Hotel and put on my rock and roll clothes. A Cream t-shirt, circa 1969, combined with a pair of Ben Sherman jeans, a tight pair of pointed toe Beatle boots that I had bought on e bay were offset with a scarf. If Mick wore a scarf, so could I. I looked in the mirror. Perfection. The private eye in disguise. I picked up a bag from Nordstrom's. Just in case I bought along a Rolling Stones t-shirt. Never can tell when you might meet Mick or Keith.

I took the elevator downstairs. As I entered the lobby, I heard a female voice.

"Going to a masquerade ball dickhead." The lovely Chastain Johnson stood staring at me like I was from Mars. I smiled. She had on a white cashmere sweater with black pants. There was nothing left to the imagination. She looked like a Ford model with breasts.

It was time I had the last word. "Basketball, female impersonators and the Rolling Stones." My words made no sense to her. I continued: "You see Chastain, logic is the key to solving this little caper," I liked to talk like a P. I. Maybe Robert Mitchum said that in a movie. I continued: "You see I have tied up all the loose ends, the villains well come under my scrutiny.

"Villains!" For once the lovely Chastain was dumbfounded. She was at a loss for words. But I had a clue to the crime. One that would solve it. I didn't feel like sharing it with her. She smiled. What the hell I could share it.

"Hello sweetie," I smiled. She frowned.

"Trevor, no one calls anyone sweetie. Particularly an FBI agent."

"Old school." I said.

"Let's talk." She lit a cigarette. I wasn't surprised.

"Well where do I start?" I paused. "This case depends upon basketball, female impersonators and the Rolling Stones." I held up napkin number 96 it provided the final clue. She looked skeptical.

"I hate to say it but you may have the final clue," Chastain smiled. She got up and rubbed against me. She left for the Rolling Stones' concert.

I caught a cab a few minutes later. In a half an hour I would be backstage and would finally get to meet Mick and Keith. A lifetime dream come true. I realized that maybe I had on the wrong clothes. So I went into my Nordstrom's bag and put on my vintage Rolling Stones t-shirt. The one with big lips. All the better to be the hidden detective.

Safeco Field was a mess. It was impossible to get near it. Everyone had on Rolling Stones t-shirts. I wasn't alone. It took an hour to get backstage. Then I met Zandra Filippi. I didn't ask for it but I got her life history. She was from Mira Loma, California and wrote the Stones a letter when she was twenty-five. They offered her a job. She was great looking with a thirty-six Double D bust, a face that was unlined and an erotic personal style. These things qualified her for the right job. I suspected she was more than her job description suggested. She was the Stones personal assistant. Whatever that meant. She had held the job for twenty years She was now in her mid-forties and looked like she was twenty-five. She had a habit of licking her lips as she talked to you. Mick and Keith obviously hired her for her professional skills. At least I hoped that was the case.

"If you follow me," Zandra remarked. "I will take you to the second backstage room."

"Thanks." I smiled. She licked her lips.

"Your name again."

"Still Trevor." I licked my lips for effect. Maybe I was going to a special room. Then I saw the dungeon she described as special. I was sure it was the one for losers. I walked into the room and found Stephen Tyler and the rest of Aerosmith warming up. They were eating free-range chicken, organic rice and sautéed spinach. Large bottles of mineral water open with crystal glasses filled to the brim put the finishing touches on the meal. There was a drug tray. It was full of vitamins.

"Hey, guys, where are the drugs and groupies?" They looked at me like I was nuts.

"You're about twenty years too late, man," Stephen Tyler remarked.

He had Liv's lips. But then again so did Mick. So did Angelina Jolie. I was secretly in love with Liv Tyler despite the twenty-year difference. I decided not to inform her father. Aerosmith were great guys and they spent the better part of an hour talking about of all things Guitar Jac. I was floored. They loved his music. Called him the new Taj Mahal or Ritchie Havens. I could hardly wait to see Jac's new ego. They left for the stage.

Zandra Filippi came back in and escorted me to a private box. I was alone. It seemed strange. There was a large bar. I peered inside. It was a drunks delight. I opened a Heineken and watched Aerosmith bring the crowd to its feet. They played for an hour and a half and the audience reluctantly let them leave the stage. I opened a Miller Lite. It was time to watch the waistline.

When the Stones came on stage it was with a burst of fireworks, a set of large screens that showcased each of the four members and a sound system that Hunter Thompson couldn't afford. The fifteen other musicians who actually played the music were in the background. During the Stones last tour, Hunter Thompson purchased their sound system and piped Irish music through it while he shot at doors. The Colorado countryside was never the same. Then he committed suicide. So my guess was that Hunter wouldn't buy this sound system. He was in heaven or hell. Or maybe somewhere else.

It was after the first hour that my suite opened up and suddenly there was a crowd. Chastain Johnson was the first to show up.

"Hello," she said.

"What no insults?" She looked nervous.

"Trevor, this is my boss Agent In Charge Bruce Jones." He looked like an insurance salesman. He also acted like one.

Why do FBI agents have generic names? I wondered but kept it to myself. "Hello Bruce, nice to meet you, some of my San Francisco friends are disguised as a Bruce." He didn't laugh, Chastain didn't laugh. I didn't laugh.

"Let me get you something to drink." Bruce had Perrier and Chastain, much to my surprise, had a Dos Equis. Nothing like Mexican beer before the Stones do their greatest hits. A selection of hits including "Satisfaction" blared as eight Samoans and Don Gino marched into the room.

"Ah, Agent Jones. Nice to see you."

"Gino Walker, it's been a long time." Agent Jones smiled. They began talking in subdued but serious tones. They were almost too close to each other. I had to control my dirty mind.

My suspicions were confirmed. The FBI used gangsters to solve its crimes. Then Agent Jones shook hands with each of the eight Samoans and called them by name. I still didn't know their names. I knew America was in good hands. The mafia still made its money the old-fashioned way-loan sharking, gambling and protection. Drugs and prostitution could get you killed in Don Gino's neighborhood. The FBI obviously liked the way that Don Gino kept things in order in the San Francisco area.

The Don and AIC Jones were discussing Napa Valley Merlots. Both were wine connoisseurs and they were extolling the virtues of the Jordan Cabernets and a wide variety of Merlots. Then they began talking about the Cakebread wines. It sounded like a foreign language. They hadn't seen "Sideways," so they didn't know that Merlot was no long a fashionable wine. So much for aficionados.

"Hello Trevor." I turned to see a smiling Detective Sanchez. He didn't have a Rolling Stones t-shirt. He was impeccable in an Armani suit. Zandra Filippi came in with a scotch and water and two napkins. One for his drink and the other with her various six phone numbers. He hadn't lost his touch.

"Detective, join the party." He looked around and headed for AIC Jones and Don Gino. Soon they were talking about San Luis Obispo wineries. Something about the earth not being quite right for the grapes. I think everyone had forgotten we were solving a series of brutal murders. Or we were at least attempting to end the murderous spree. They were also ignoring the Stones. The fun continued as Joyce Byers walked into the suite.

"What is this San Francisco north?" I looked lovingly at Joyce.

Joyce looked unhappy. "Well you are supposed to be my boyfriend. I never see you. Unless you are horny and can't get laid elsewhere."

The truth hurt. "Joyce, the world's greatest detective is at work." Sorry Elvis Cole.

"At work," she laughed. "You have more help than any detective in history."

I couldn't disagree. So I decided to share a nugget of information with her. "It's all on napkin 96."

She looked stunned. "What in the hell are you talking about?"

I explained the 96 napkins and my clues. She looked skeptical. Then I told her about napkin 97. Now she was interested. Then she thought about it. She knew that I had something in the way of a solution to the case.

"The answer is in the napkins, Joyce."

"Let's go back to your room and look them over." I agreed. I bade everyone farewell as Mick launched into "Start Me Up." Not a good sign. The Start Me Up band could lose another drummer.

We hailed a cab. A guy with a Turban stopped. He drove like a mad man and dropped us off at Joyce's hotel, the 6th Avenue Inn. It was only two blocks from the Warwick. As the driver dropped us off, he asked which way to the 5 freeway. He was obviously directionally challenged. That sounds better than calling him a raghead who couldn't drive. We got her files at the 6th Avenue Inn and walked over to my hotel. The room was a mess. The napkins were neatly piled. I laid out the 97 napkins and convinced Joyce that the next night I would have the killer's identity. I would wait until we got back to San Francisco to reveal it. She looked over the evidence and liked my four key suspects. Any one of them could be the killer. I didn't tell her my plan to lure the killer out in San Francisco. She agreed that basketball, female impersonators and the Rolling Stones were the key to solving the crime.

We rode the elevator downstairs and I hailed a cab to buy Joyce dinner at Canlis. We had a Russian cab driver. He drove even faster than the Indian. In ten minutes we were seated overlooking Lake Union. She ordered a medium rare steak, I had the chicken Florentine, we started with spinach salad and a bottle of Cakebread Merlot complimented the meal. I had no idea how much Cakebread cost. When I got the bill I was shocked $185. But things did get better. Peter Canlis, Jr., was an old friend, and he brought over a baked Alaska on the house. He also tore up the bill. He knew my cheap ways. I left $50 on the table for the waiter. Peter smiled. We had gone to Stanford together. He majored in American literature and hadn't worried about making a living. He knew that the family business would keep him in Russell Banks books.

Peter Canlis loved to tell me about Banks novel "The Sweet Hereafter" and how its description of a school bus accident from four different perspectives influenced his life. I was bored with his explanation but a free dinner helped me to listen. Peter walked us outside the restaurant. We hugged and he hailed a cab. We were picked up by a white cab drive, "Call Me Warren," he took off for downtown. I wondered were all white cab drivers named Warren.

As we rode back in the cab, Joyce told me she had to leave that night. She couldn't make the Start Me Up bands sold out Key Arena show. Just as well. It could be dangerous. She took the cab to the airport. I went to bed early. Alone. I wondered if Mick and Keith were now early to bed. Probably, with some young girl.

Chapter 28
THE START ME UP BAND AT THE KEY ARENA

The next evening was one that I anticipated. There were certain things that Don Gino, Detective Sanchez, the eight Samoans and the FBI had overlooked. I went to bed thinking about the next day. I was gleeful with anticipation. The Warwick Hotel Coffee Shop was filled the next morning. Not only had the Start Me Up band checked into the hotel but also there were more than 100 fans that followed the band. I spotted Guitar Jac in conversation with other members of the band. I wonder how Charlie Watts felt. An African American sitting in on the drums with a degree from Stanford was a strange sight. He was also a millionaire but so was Charlie. Touché. All of this made for speculation. Not even Mick could beat Guitar Jac's credentials.

I found a booth in the corner and noticed that the Seattle Post Intelligencer featured an article on McKenzie Dee's tribute to Ersel Hickey. They quoted his brother McArthur who talked about beating his brother over the head with a pail when they were four years old. Lunacy ran in that family. I scanned the reviews and the Stones were praised to heaven. Their review was no longer than McKenzie's. That was weird but who could figure out the press. McKenzie Dee was a Seattle star. Go figure.

I anticipated breakfast. My spinach and sausage omelet was placed in front of me with a fruit plate and tomatoes. Nothing like a low carb breakfast before solving a killing. No one talked to me. It was nice not to have a gang of journalists after me. As I left I noticed Don Gino coming in the front door with AIC Jones. They looked like they had been partying. I didn't want to know about last night.

After going back to room 808, I put on my sweat pants, t-shirt and gym shorts. I took a walk to the YMCA to shoot some hoops. I walked in and was stunned. Elliott Shonestein was shooting hook shots. I remembered that move from watching films of the 1960s. I had forgotten. He was a center for the University of California, Berkeley, It was a strange sight. He looked in shape. I thought he was kidnapped or dead. Or both. I wasn't happy to see him. It was too late.

"Trevor, good to see you."

"My thoughts exactly. Where have you been?"

"It is a little complicated. I didn't vanish, get kidnapped or anything else. I had to go through a 12 step program."

I looked stunned. "But you don't drink or smoke."

"I know, it is a little embarrassing."

Am I still your private detective?"

He looked stunned. "Of course."

"Then share the facts."

"I just went through a 12-step gambling program. It's a disease, an addiction."

"No shit." I was frustrated. Almost a hundred napkins and Shonestein was no longer one of my prime suspects.

There was a prolonged silence. I grabbed a nearby basketball and went into the Trevor Blake III dribbling act. When I was a kid I was known as lefty the dribbling whiz. Lefty was on the court. Elliott broke the ice.

"My addiction was gambling. I lost over two million dollars to the gangsters who are Don Gino's competitors."

"Does he know that Elliott?"

"Yes," Elliott looked nervous. He should. "I have the money to pay the gangsters, they have vanished. Don Gino says I should donate the money to a Catholic charity of his choice. Do I have an option? He doesn't know I'm in town."

"Not if you want to stay alive," I continued. "The Mission Dolores restoration project will thank you."

Don Gino didn't allow anyone else to control San Francisco gambling. Even Mayor Gavin Newsom thought that Don Gino's control of illegal gambling kept San Francisco safe from real criminals. Why does everyone talk about Don Gino as if he isn't a criminal? I confess I never understood the Mayor's reasoning. But to piss off the Mayor and Don Gino was not my cup of tea.

I had to take charge. "Elliott, I will let Don Gino know."

"Fine, Trevor." He smiled. He knew what Don Gino would do to the competition. The dog food plant would have new canning materials. We shot some hoops and Elliott beat me four times in horse. Then we played a half court game and he beat me at that. Then we shot fifty free throws. My game. I made 42, he put in 46. I conceded. We talked some more about the Start Me Up band. Then I realized that napkin 97 didn't include all the reasons that he was a suspect. I was about to solve the crime but had left him out of the equation. So I made napkin 98. Nothing like a back up plan.

I walked back to the hotel and got dressed for the night. But first dinner. I sauntered down to First Avenue turned right and got a table outside at the Axis. The Belltown area of Seattle is a strange place. They have the best California inspired menu. The California food with an Asian touch was excellent. The salmon in a crab sauce came with a vintage selection of fresh vegetables and a garlic mashed potato. I polished off a bottle of Jordan Cabernet Sauvignon and finished up with a cappuccino. The low carb diet wasn't on my mind. A cab pulled up as I left the Axis and I got into a car that smelled of curry. The cabbie took me directly to the Key Arena. He didn't talk. God was watching over me. He kept swatting at a fly on the dashboard. No curry for that bugger.

As I departed the cab, I was eager to solve a case. I didn't want to become one of those world-weary private dicks who lacked depth and subtlety. I also didn't want to be a boozing and smoking private eye. Just one who ate too much and got laid. I also wanted to be imaginative and allegorical. I also wanted to drink fine wine and gourmet dinners.

When I confided these thoughts to Guitar Jac, he reminded me that I had stayed too long at Stanford. At least I could drop the name. I could point out my two degrees. No one knew I had made my money in real estate. That is no one except McArthur Dee. He became napkin 99.

My backstage pass worked perfectly. Guitar Jac was in the corner looking like Guitar Jac. I didn't expect him to become Charlie Watts overnight. The rest of the band had people doing their hair, putting on make up and tuning guitars. Elliott Shonestein whirled around the room.

No one seemed to notice or care that Shonestein had been missing for some time. So much for the loyalty of the rock and roll crowd.

I walked over to the catering table. There were eight Samoans feeding a sample of each food item to three dogs. I didn't want to know what that was about. The Samoans were dressed in purple tuxedos. Not exactly a surprise. There was no sign of anyone else. No Don Gino. No AIC Jones. No Chastain Johnson. No Detective Sanchez. Maybe there was a God. I looked everything over. The room had no apparent problems. I walked on stage and there was nothing out of the ordinary. Something was wrong. I couldn't put my finger on it. I could feel it. The sixth sense of the private eye.

The Start Me Up band came on stage. The lead singer, Adrian Kirschbaum, had disguised his New York accent and with plastic surgery he looked just like Mick. "Give it up Seattle for Guitar Jac, our new drummer." There was thunderous applause and Guitar Jac strode on stage with a suit and hat that had the 1960s Charlie Watts look. There was another round of thunderous applause. No one seemed to notice that he was African American. Racial progress came in strange ways.

The concert started without a hitch. Then after six numbers Guitar Jac came out from behind the drums and Adrian Kirschbaum took over. He was about to adjust the microphone. Suddenly I realized what was wrong. I ran on stage shouting, grabbed a mike stand and hurled it at the drums. Kirschbaum fled to the right of the stage. It missed the Mick Jagger look alike and the mike fell to the floor as the drum kit exploded into small pieces. Kirschbaums's lips were singed and his eyebrows almost burnt off. He was alive. Suddenly, he looked like a Kirschbaum. Old. A New Yorker and Jewish. He stumbled backstage. The police rushed out on stage. The place was in pandemonium. They discovered that six of the dynamite sticks in the drums hadn't gone off. I was floored. I only saw an electrical wire designed to kill him. I had saved the day and didn't know it.

`Elliott Shonestein came out on stage and tried to quiet the crowd. Then a gunshot was heard. Someone fired a series of shots at the stage. The police grabbed a guy with a beer belly, a bad haircut and a Ronnie Dawson t-shirt. It was McArthur Dee. The police slapped handcuffs on him.

"He's not the killer." I screamed.

Who the hell are you," a twenty five year old cop with pink cheeks and a crew cut hollered

. "I'm Trevor Blake III, Private Eye."

The cop laughed. "A private eye, what next."

"He isn't the killer. He is simply drunk and an asshole. Not exactly against the law."

McArthur Dee burped and threw up on the floor. "Trevor you're going to get a real estate wedgie." McArthur passed out.

A policeman picked up McArthur's gun. It was his bee bee gun full of small b. b. s. On the stock the words "Hammond" were carved. It was a reference to a home he once lived in while his parents worked in Indiana. Weird! He couldn't kill anyone with this gun. He could make them uncomfortable. Just being around McArthur made anyone uncomfortable.

Suddenly everyone was there. Detective Sanchez deferred to the local police. Chastain Johnson lit a cigarette. AIC Jones looked pissed. The eight Samoans surrounded Don Gino. No one looked happy.

AIC Jones took charge. "We need to take over this investigation. It involves interstate drug smuggling, murder and multiple violations of international law. Suddenly the case was becoming complicated. Everyone turned and looked at McArthur. He woke up. He was trying to tell jokes and make people laugh. He was too stupid to realize the trouble he was in. He proceeded to bore everyone with a story about a hash pipe. They handcuffed him and took him to jail.

"You're going to get a real estate wedgie," he remarked to me as they took him out toward the stage door. "You have a bank account worth almost a million dollars," McArthur hollered. "You will still get a wedgie." McArthur had a one trick pony mind.

I looked stunned. The others didn't know that he had hacked into my bank account and every piece of information in my computer. So I had to take over.

"Well folks, meet McArthur Dee. He works for the killer. He has spent half his life in private diagnostic facilities. In other words, he is nuts."

"You're gonna get a wedgie, Trevor." He smiled. The rest of the room looked at him like he was nuts. He was. Finally, they got him out the back door. He was hollering something as he left. The word "wedgie" was once again in the air.

"There is no use trying to question him. He works for the killer but has never met him. They use a mailbox.

I sat down with Don Gino, Detective Sanchez, the FBI and the local police. It took some talking but I told them part one of the case. I explained how McArthur had been fooled into working for the Chef. It began as McArthur collected Rolling Stones records, books, memorabilia and autographs. The chef was the best-known Stones collector. The

Chef paid McArthur in memorabilia to help lay the groundwork for the killings.

Detective Sanchez couldn't believe what he had heard. He asked: "When McArthur does the killers bidding, does he have any idea that he is aiding and abetting a homicide?"

I tried to think of a nice answer. I couldn't. "He is too stupid, I continued, "he continues to tell us that he has committed no crimes. At least none in his mind. What is left of his mind."

Chastain Johnson got into the explanations. She pointed out that when the police explained to him that his role was to set them up, he looked befuddled.

"I think he should be locked up for 72 hours. " Chastain then lit a cigarette as the Seattle police led McArthur to a police car in handcuffs. No one still had any idea about the Chef. I did but he was now in San Francisco. He had caught the last Southwest Airlines flight to the Golden State. The Chef was cheap and this made it easy to find him.

I had enough of Seattle. It was time to fly home. The killer had made a big mistake. He had showed up at both Seattle concerts. Anonymous. But he was there. It was the dynamite that was the main clue. There were now four key suspects but only one had training with dynamite. The answer to who that was resided in San Francisco.

I looked at the room. "Sorry folks, I have to leave I have a plan to trap the killer."

"What a minute, Trevor," Don Gino remarked, "I have resources that can help you."

"No, thanks." I smiled at the Don.

AIC Jones remarked: "We have to put the FBI behind you." I smiled at Chastain. She glowered.

"No, this will work only my way."

Everyone wanted to help me. The answer was no, no, no. I looked at everyone in the backstage lounge. "The killer isn't in Seattle, he isn't in this room, and he isn't around. This dunce, McArthur, wired the microphone. He was told that he would get a naked picture of Keith Richards."

"That's so disgusting," Chastain Johnson remarked.

"I don't know," Don Gino smiled.

"Let's stay on top of this, no pun intended," AIC Jones giggled.

"I'll see you all in San Francisco," Detective Sanchez remarked as he left the room. The young girl who was serving drinks left with a slip of paper for Sanchez. I have to find out his secret. Maybe it's the Armani suits.

The Seattle Police Department had McArthur sitting in the backseat of a squad car. He was hollering that Brian Jones would kill all of us. He may have a point. The two Brian Jones that I met earlier were scary dudes. I took a cab back to the Warwick Hotel. I was shocked. The cabbie was a guy in his sixties. "Hi, I'm Warren, your token non-Indian cabbie." He laughed and talked baseball on the way to the hotel. He looked just like cabbies did before the towel heads took over. He was witty, getting his act together and he was a street corner philosopher. He was also erudite and funny. I needed this.

I made napkin 100 in the hotel and it had three lines, basketball, female impersonators and the Rolling Stones. The crime was solved. Now all I had to do was lure the perpetrator into a trap.

As I packed the door chimed. I looked out. It was Elliott Shonestein. He came into the room. He was also a prime suspect. He pulled a gun.

"Hand over the napkins, Trevor."

"Gladly, I think you misunderstand."

"Not at all. I am being set up to take the blame."

I paused. Elliott looked agitated. "You're not the killer." He looked perplexed. He picked up the napkin.

"Trevor, basketball, female impersonators and the Rolling Stones. I'm connected to all three."

I have to admit I didn't consider him the killer. Maybe I had solved the crime unwittingly. My reward was to be murdered. I guess I would be famous. But not like Elvis Cole, Shell Scott or Red Diamond. The door burst open and Chastain Johnson stood with a gun in her hand.

"Put your hands in the air, asshole." We both put our hands up. "Not you Trevor." I thought my other name was asshole.

"Oh, sorry," I replied with surprise. She cuffed Elliott and began reading him his rights. AIC Jones came into the room. He looked scared. This wasn't a good sign.

`"Put him in a cell with McArthur. Let McArthur know that he has a great deal of Rolling Stones memorabilia. Then have a guard there when McArthur tries to strangle him. He will talk." Obviously Agent Jones knew a thing or two about beating someone with a rubber hose. Even if it is a limp wristed one.

"We are flying both of them to San Francisco," AIC Jones remarked. "You can see them down there."

"Ok," I guess I was finally a player in this little drama. I picked up my 100 napkins and added a 101. I promised that this was my last napkin. I picked up my suitcase and waved down the first turban who showed up and his cab took me to the airport. H spent the whole time telling me about the Sikh Indian Independence movement. I listened politely. I gave him a ten-dollar donation to the independence movement. He didn't smile. I wandered into the Seattle Air Port and had a cup of Ivar's soup. It was time to put the final stages of my detection plan into operation.

I had my plan. It would take some luck. The strings were being pulled outside Elliott Shonestein's office. He wasn't the killer. He was set up to look like it. The key was still basketball, female impersonators and the Rolling Stones.

We landed in San Francisco in the early evening. My cab driver didn't have a turban. I thought that I might have a psychological reaction. I didn't. I returned home expecting to find young women and other surprises. The reception was indeed a surprise. Bennie and Bertie were standing in front of my apartment. The building that they owned was looking shabby. Maybe it needed a paint job. More likely they needed a life. Bennie's belly was heaving, Bertie had a scowl. They were mad. What about, I had no clue. I paid the cabbie and took my suitcase to the front door.

"Trevor, we need to talk."

"Ok, No problem, but what about?"

"You don't know."

"No." Now I looked confused.

"That naked picture of Janis Joplin on your wall can be seen from the street. We voted for George Bush for president to stop that sort of nonsense. Now our quasi-brother in law is a pervert."

"Quasi brother in law," I repeated in astonishment. "Have you forgotten I divorced your sister. I also have a naked picture of Janis in my apartment."

"Disgusting," Bertie screamed.

I brought them up to the apartment and gave them some brie and a glass of Jordan Merlot. It calmed them down. I took down Janis and threw here in the garbage. I put up a picture of the Partridge Family. They looked happy. They also told me that they were going to see Elvis.

"Didn't Elvis die taking a dump in 1977?"

"Trevor, you're so crude." Bertie burped. Obviously, she didn't think that was crude. She looked in my hall mirror admiring her grey hair and clothes from K-Mart. "We are going to see the top Elvis impersonator, Bennie opens the show at the Elks with his magic tricks. Do you know anything about Elvis?"

I said: "No, I just remember going to Graceland and found it boring." Suddenly it hit me. Boring. They would love the place. They polished off the rest of my brie and left.

I spent the rest of the night hatching my plan.

Chapter 29
THE KILLER COMES DOWN AN ALLEY

The next morning I got out of bed and read the San Francisco Chronicle. Joel Selvin was praising Bono for saving the world. Everyone was praising Bono. A prank by a Los Angeles disc jockey stating that Bono would head the World Bank turned into reality. He was considered for the position. There was too much Bono for me. Van Morrison was the only Irishman that fit into my listening needs. Van was a cranky dwarf who was a musical genius.. I needed to clear my head, so I walked down to Starbuck's on Chestnut Street and got a decaf mocha to go. Nothing like a mocha without caffeine.

One can never be too careful about their blood pressure. I looked over in the corner and I swear that there was a guy who looked like Pam Wong. He wasn't even a cute guy. I needed to get out of San Francisco. My sexuality was undergoing a serious challenge. Then again the pressure of the case was taking a toll. I needed to think. So it was off to my office. Today I catch the killer. I got in my car with what was left of the mocha and drove up Fillmore toward the Haight. I noticed the midget dressed as Mick Jagger on Fillmore Street walking up the hill to Broadway. He looked ready to expire from the steep hill. I smugly drove up the hill, slowly and gave the midget the finger.

Not only is driving in San Francisco a joy; it gives one time for reflection. I knew that the killer was close to the Start Me Up band. How I wasn't sure. Then it dawned on me. There was a level of frustration in the killer. I got it. He was a musician. One who had never made it in the business? Suddenly things were coming together.

I drove over to the Haight Ashbury. When I saw the street sign, I felt at home. The Haight Ashbury sign is a bit crooked because of people leaning on it. It is also faded and unpainted. So much for urban renewal. The two fat guys who sell ice cream, Ben and Jerry, offered to replace it. A big billboard with their picture dominates Haight Street. They gave the city officials a million-dollar donation and no one questioned the sign. So much for San Francisco's honest politics. A group of local hippies organized a campaign to ban the Ben and Jerry's sign. The city refused. Ben and Jerry repainted the sign and enlarged it. Now the fats guys are legends.

The locals were up in arms over corporate infiltration into the Haight. The post 1960s political types failed to notice that virtually everything was corporate in the Haight. Most everything was corporate in San Francisco. So much for the counterculture revolution.

I drained my coffee and threw it on the car's floor.

After finding a parking space, I wondered down to Emilio's. He had a new sign advertising real Italian Donuts. I was afraid to ask. Were there fake Italian donuts.. What in the hell was a real Italian Donut? Maybe we had been eating fake ones. There was a cartoon of a pizza maker in the window. Beside the cartoon an exhaustive explanation of the health benefits of Italian Donuts attracted the reader. Emilio was now selling Donuts as a health food. Only in San Francisco. I entered and Emilio gave me a big smile. Then again he gave everyone a big smile.

"Trevor, haveee Donut." The counter was full of people eating real Italian Donuts. His patrons smiled at him. He smiled at them. It was sickening. They were obviously liberals who loved his explanations of why George Bush had screwed up the Iraq war. He loved to talk politics in broken English.

Emilio smiled and walked over with a plate of two different Donuts. One was a French cruller and the other was his new Italian Donut. It was shaped like a pizza. Was nothing sacred? He was back in his immigrant rhetorical mode. "Letee goee in backee room." I blanched. He smiled at everyone and led me through a door into his office.

Once we entered his office, he dropped the accent and got serious. He asked what I knew about the killer. I talked at length with him about the case. He had been a high-ranking military officer in Vietnam and then a policeman. Emilio was a deductive thinker with a fine mind. He was also a criminal. He left Vietnam with a lot of money and he was under an investigative cloud. In America, Emilio had fulfilled his dreams. The Donut shop was for fun. It was also a way of laundering money. His latest IRS filing indicated that the Donut shop grossed over a million dollars a year. His good friend, former Mayor Gavin Newsom, didn't know about Emilio's sideline as a cat burglar. Emilio lived in the exclusive St. John's Wood area of San Francisco. He had completed his

M. A. in American literature and was writing a novel. He was definitely a complex man. He gave me some thoughts on trapping the killer. Against my better judgment I wrote out napkin 102. Emilio had some thoughts on the crime. He zeroed in on the musician type who committed the murders.

"It's one complicated man, Trevor. He may have an assistant."

"Are you sure?"

"Yes, he is not the man you think he is, the other person is a mystery." Emilio concluded.

"I don't need riddles, I need facts."

"The napkins tell it all, Trevor."

There was one clue he gave me that I had missed. Not a good sign. But I was ready to solve the crime. Deductive reasoning at work.

Emilio looked at the napkins. He helped solve the case. There was more than one killer. Emilio made that clear. While the Chef was the ringleader, he had a number of accomplices. Or maybe just one accomplice. Now it was time to figure who the accomplices were and how did everything fit together. I needed to walk awhile and think some more. Leaving Emilio's Donut shop I bought a San Francisco Chronicle. I looked at the entertainment section. Rereading Joel Selvin's column on 1960s musicians brought out the final clue. The lyrics to "Looking For The Woman" were in Selvin's article. I had it, the final clue.

I walked up to Haight and Ashbury and looked once again at the Ben and Jerry's sign. No ice cream for me this week. I had overdone it in Seattle. I walked up the stairs. My office was untouched. No one broke in to clean it. There was more mail than I realized. I went through the sixty odd pieces and wrote ten checks. A private eye has to pay his bills. I wonder if Sam Spade worried about his credit rating. As I mulled over my napkins, Guitar Jac bound into the door. He was dressed in his blues-performing outfit. This was a pair of Jordache jeans. I didn't realize that Jordache even made jeans. Then I found out that Jac had them custom tailored. There was a blues work shirt that was not only custom fitted but made with a faded denim and the whole outfit was completed with sandals made by Dave Page Cobbler in Seattle. Ralph Lauren socks were visible beneath the sandals. Not exactly the outfit of a poor man. Jac smiled. He obviously had something important to discuss. Jac was a meticulous thinker and I knew that he would have a plan.

"Well, Jac, what do you have to offer?"

"Nothing." He smiled. "Nothing except I know the killer's identity."

Good old Jac. Nothing like understatement. "You mean that my trusty assistant has solved the crime."

"No, not exactly, you have to do it on your own. I have it down to four people and the Chef is the ringleader. But he has accomplices."

"You haven't been talking to Emilio, have you Jac?" I went to our refrigerator. I paused to open a can of diet coke.

"That stuff is bad for you Trevor."

Always the health nut, Jac was often not fun. "Let me put it this way my good guitar friend. You have identified everyone surrounding the case. That is hardly a solution to my problem."

He laughed. "No the answer is pretty simple and Emilio must have a handle on it." Guitar Jac paused. "Trevor, the Chef likes to eat at Bill's Place. "

"What!" I couldn't believe it. I had missed the most important clue.

"I found a Bill's menu at the scene of some of the killings." Guitar Jac blushed. He had looked into the crimes without sharing with me. It was his habit. He was a perfectionist who never explained anything until he had all the facts.

"What does the menu show?" I paused and took a swig of coke. "So he ate a hamburger."

"You don't get it Trevor, he planned the murders at Bill's and you simply lure the killer there with a series of cryptic telegrams. He planned the murders using Bill's napkins. Like you he has a stash of napkins with carefully planning on them." Jac pulled out a napkin. "I found this one on the floor at Bill's when I dropped a guitar pic."

"Let me get this straight, Jac, I am going to send a telegram to everyone asking for the murder suspect to come to Bill's for a burger. Then have them write on a napkin and compare the handwriting."

"No, you are going to send a clue in the telegram."

"To whom am I sending the telegram." The P. I. always has to appear logical.

"Simple, Trevor, to RCA Records, they have signed the Start Me Up band and simply request that the telegram be forwarded to the songwriter, specify a time and meeting place. The telegram should read: "the jig is up, I have got you, Trevor." I looked at Guitar Jac in astonishment.

"The jig is up, how embarrassing is that phrase. Not to mention it is politically incorrect." I looked with curiosity at Jac. His reasoning left a lot to be desired.

"I will supply the last clue when the killer responds." Guitar Jac looked smug. Maybe he had solved the crime. He wasn't sharing the solution with me.

"Good, Jac, but just what is this clue. I might need to know it."

"You got it. The clue is that you have discovered who wrote "Look For The Woman." Remember the Chef and his use of poison." Jac continued. "Send the secret clue."

"Jac, you are a genius." I had forgotten about the poison. Only the killer knew about it. The police had never mentioned the poison. The newspapers had never written about the poison. I had never talked about the poison. I looked for napkin 42, it had the details of the poison on it.

Jac proceeded to give me some ASCAP information. This was the New York company that copyrighted songs. The clue led to four people. Welcome to the party. I had the same four suspects. There was another clue. One only the killer knew. I was ready to send the telegram. Now I realized I had to send four telegrams. The P. I. business is complicated but I am on the case.

I looked at Jac. I was surprised. He was on to something. He was ready to leave town. "Your suitcase on your desk looks packed."

"It is. I have just signed a recording contract with Warner Bros. I fly to Hollywood tonight. Dan Bourgoise of Bug Music will copyright my songs. The Rolling Stones have agreed to cut three of them for their new album."

"Congratulations." I was stunned. I knew that Guitar Jac was talented but this was unexpected. I also knew that I had to solve the case on my own.

"They were going to pay me a bit more than you do." He laughed. "But, hey man, I owe it all to you. I will be back at work for our next case. That is unless I become James Brown."

"Don't worry, Jac, James Brown isn't James Brown anymore."

Guitar Jac laughed. "Keep my desk and name plate, I will return."

"Ok!" What else could I say. He left. I sat in my chair stunned. The picture of Van Morrison over my doorway had a grumpy look. But Van Morrison always had a grumpy look, so I didn't take umbrage. I put on the Morrison CD "Magic Time" and listened to the title track talk about a better life. I needed that lift. Then "Celtic New Year" began playing and my plan came to fruition. Maybe Van Morrison could join my firm and sing to criminals so that they would confess.

I called the San Francisco Chronicle. I asked for Hiram Johnson. He was the apprentice rock critic. He came on the phone.

"Trevor, how's it hanging?"

"Loose." I smiled. He was silent.

"You want something?"

"Of course, why else would I call."

"Let me have it."

"What I need Hiram is a short story on a benefit to be held in two nights at Slim's."

"Impossible." He laughed. "There is a Boz Scaggs show that night."

"Well then let's make the benefit at Bill's Place."

"Need I remind you, Trevor, that Bill's Place sells hamburgers, it isn't a music venue, it has never had a music facility. Not now. Not in the past. Never. Not even in the future. Is that clear." I could almost hear him exhale. I loved rock music critics. They were so damned precise it was embarrassing.

"Calm down, Hiram, I'm solving a case.

"Need I remind you Trevor, that you have yet to solve a case or for that matter get a date."

"Touchy, touchy, Hiram." I always had to endure Hiram talking to me like I was an idiot. It was part of our relationship. He always did me the favors. "Just put in the Chronicle that the benefit will be in the garden eating area."

"Trevor, the garden seats twenty people."

"It's a small benefit, Hiram."

"Ok, I owe you but I will need a favor. When this crime is solved. I want to be the first to know the musical connection. It could be a hell of a story. Murder by the Rolling Stones. I could get a Pulitzer. I would be the first rock journalist to do a serious story involving murder. I might even get on Court TV. Nancy Grace would call me to appear on her show. She is one ugly bitch. I would make an exception for her.

"Any thoughts on my story," Hiram exhaled.

"Say the benefit concert is by invitation only. Telegrams will go out to the invitees."

"Telegrams," Hiram asked quizzically.

"Just write the story." I fumed.

"Ok," he hung up.

I drove out Clement Street and rented Bill's Place for a private party. It took a thousand dollars but they agreed. I called Don Gino and told him my plan. He agreed to have the eight Samoans there. They would serve the food. I drove down to the Irvington Brothers Third Street Warehouse and printed up invitations. It wasn't a long guest list. But the killer was in the mix. As I left, the receptionist sneered at me. No invitation for her. No expense was spared for the P. I. about to solve his first case. Each invitation was complete with a copy of the Rolling Stones new CD. It was a classy touch for an embryo detective. It was also an expensive touch. Maybe Don Gino could get into the CD pirating business. I was about to emerge from detective limbo. I could almost see the headlines.

After walking down to Western Union, I was ready to send four special telegrams. I sent out another sixteen and walked down to Fed EEX and sent the invitations. Only the four suspects would get two invites. The four main suspects were instructed to meet me in the alley to learn about a special substance. I walked over the tenderloin and bought a stun gun in a pawnshop. One could never have too much protection. Sam Spade would never be caught dead with a stun gun. Shell Scott would smile with his glistening teeth, snarl and the bad guys would confess. I didn't have their look or their style. Shell Scott also used his fists. Times had changed. I abhorred violence. Stunning someone, not killing them, was my motto. Maybe that's why I am not yet a household name as a private eye.

I walked back to Embarcadero One. It is a strange name for a place more than a mile from the Embarcadero. It was time for a brew. I headed over to the Holding Company. For twenty years this had been my bar of choice. It was located on the second floor between the Embarcadero One and Two complexes. It seemed to straddle them. Free food was the draw. The hors d'ouvres were the best in San Francisco. I ordered an Anchor Steam beer grabbed a plate of chicken wings, some ribs, a large chunk of veggies and a Chinese noodle salad. The last item was new. A paean to cultural diversity. I sat down and looked up at Sports Center on the television. I watched as Charles Barkley told the viewers that the Phoenix Suns couldn't play defense. A group of people distracted me. Suddenly four people sat down. I didn't know any of them. They had on dark suits, they looked unfriendly and they ordered Perrier. My guess was the FBI. I was in for a shock.

"Hello, Trevor," a guy with perfect teeth and muscles that seemed to scream I'm tough looked at me. The others fidgeted nervously in their suits.

"Hi guys."

"I'm Malcolm Dodd, President of RCA Victor." He had a suit on that screamed mafia. He spent more money styling his hair than I spent on my car.

He looked like a hoodlum. So it fit. A record executive. "Hello!" I was lost for words. So much for the FBI. They were criminals but ones in the music business. I was relieved I knew that they were criminals, but they were friendly ones. They looked Italian. I guess extortion and racketeering didn't pay as well as the record business. Maybe my instincts were right. They were simply looking for a new act.

"Hello guys, what can I do for you?"

"We want you to come to work for us. You need to find Elvis." I looked at them in amazement. I was in the middle of solving a case and RCA wanted me to find Elvis. I hoped that they knew he died some years ago. I looked speechless. Fortunately, I recovered and blurted out a rather silly line.

"Elvis died in 1977." I wondered if Bennie and Bertie had sent them. You know hire a joke to harass the serious private eye. This turned out not to be the case. They were in fact legitimate record moguls. They not only showed me their ids but also pointed to the six bodyguards standing in the corner. Where were the eight Samoans when I really needed them?

"We know that you are busy. What we have to offer is a case that is very complicated. Your current investigation is winding down. We have a check for $25,000." Suddenly I was all ears. The big, in shape guy put his card on the table, it read Malcolm Dodd, President, RCA. So he was legitimate. He laid an envelope on the table. "There is a $25,000 check in this envelope and a contract. If you're interested, this is your second case." They had obviously done their research. I thanked them and opened the envelope. I read it quickly. All I could think about was the $25,000. Famous private eye gets recognition before he deserves it. He also gets the money. I signed the contract and told them I would be off to Memphis to solve this little caper. That is after I found the Chef and had him arrested. Things were going well. I had money. I had the case solved. I could afford to take a taxi. But I had to think.

I decided to walk home. I needed the exercise. The Holding Company had so much free food I could hardly move. The chicken wings were heavy on my stomach. My car was safe in the Irvington Bros. parking lot. That is unless the secretary slashed the tires. It was a real possibility. I walked over to Van Ness Avenue and wandered into Harris' Steak House for a glass of wine. It was a twelve-dollar glass of Jordan Merlot. I should have taken an eight-dollar cab ride home and saved four dollars. A blonde who looked like Chastain Johnson sat at the end of the bar. I went to the bathroom and she was gone when I returned. I finished the exquisite Jordan Merlot and felt energized. Or maybe a little tipsy. So I decided to walked down to Lou's Pier 47 and see some blues. Pier 47 is a local blues club that has three acts every day. Bobby Webb was playing and he was in a saxophone groove. The closing act Jimmy McCracklin and the Blues Blasters played all of the legends hits. That is one song "The Walk." It was why I came to see McCracklin. He sneered at the audience as he left the stage. What an asshole. He flipped me the finger. I had a long history with Jimmy; I was once his manager. I paid myself a few times. He never forgave me.

Lou's Pier 47 allowed me four hours of drinking and blues. There was nothing like a celebration for catching the killer. Even if that celebration was a day before I closed in on the unsuspecting unsub. When I got home there were no messages on my answering machine, no young girls at my door and no hoodlums. Bennie and Bertie were in Memphis and I was alone with my thoughts. I didn't feel well.

I took a Tylenol and went to bed. The next morning I woke up and turned on the radio. The Rolling Stones new album was all over the stations. Mick and Keith had written all the songs. I don't think they needed the money. Then to my surprise Guitar Jac's voice came over the air. His first release had been recorded months earlier and Warner Bros put it out with a heavy promotional push. The song, "Murder By The Rolling Stones," told the story of a young girl who killed for Rolling Stone memorabilia. I wondered if McArthur Dee was the co-author. It was getting weird.

The day of the party arrived. I took a cab downtown and retrieved my car. No slashed tires. Maybe the receptionist loved me after all. I drove out to Bill's Place and checked the back alley. That was to be my trap. I walked in and let the cook know that it was carte blanche on the meals. My guests could have what they wanted. Even though it was all hamburgers, they were the best in San Francisco. I was ready to find the killer. I went downtown and rented a tuxedo. They wanted to know if I desired a purple one. I told them no.

With my tuxedo on, it was show time. I took my car home. I grabbed a Gucci brief case that I kept for special occasions. It was a knock off.

One I got in Hong Kong for ten dollars. It looked original. Who could tell the difference? I grabbed a cab. The driver wasn't wearing a turban. Progress. I had the cab let me off two blocks from Bill's Place. I wondered up the alley. I looked into the garden. All the usual suspects were there. But I knew that the killer would show up later in the alley. The telegram made it a convenient meeting place. It was obscured from Bill's Place and it was hard to see the darkened alleyway. The perfect place to kill a private eye. I looked out onto the street. Hiding in a corner of the darkened alleyway I watched as the killer came into my trap. Down the alley the killer sauntered. He looked gorgeous. He was dressed in a formal gown.

"Hello Pam." I smiled.

"Ah Trevor, you did figure it out. I am probably Cambodia's foremost female impersonator. Do you know how many men have had sex with me." I was afraid to ask. There were some things that I didn't need to know. I had escaped that fate. Then down the alley came Elliott Shonestein.

"Trevor, so good to see you."

"We still have one more accomplice." I knew the whole story.

"Yes, we do," Elliott remarked. "But we have a surprise for you. Look into Bill's Place. What do you see?"

"People." Oh shit, I thought. I don't know any of the people.

"We intercepted all the invitations and hired professional party crashers." He smiled. I was nervous. "Now Trevor, let me introduce the third criminal." Down the alley came Sheldon Foreskin. It all came together. He wrote the songs for the Start Me Up band, the publicity over the dead members was meant to sell a subsequent album. Who was the fourth culprit. I wondered. I guess there were only three criminals. I looked and down the alley came three more people. It was getting crowded. They were hoodlums with machine guns. I Don't think they were coming to help me. Pam Wong barked orders at them.

"They were once a part of the Cambodian army, Trevor, their expertise is disposing of people without a trace. That is your fate." She smiled and lit a cigarette. I was nervous. I looked down the alley and two people were walking slowly toward us. I was shocked. It was Don Gino and Emilio. They were walking down the alley unarmed. Emilio did have a sword in his hand. He also had some kind of funny bandana tied around his head. I wanted to tell him that it was not exactly the weapon to combat a machine gun. Don Gino wasn't smiling and neither was

Emilio. They also didn't appear scared. I was ready to go to the bathroom in my pants from fright.

"There is some old queer and a little Chinaman coming down the alley," one of the machine gun hoodlums hollered. I shuttered. Pissing off the Don was not good for one's health. Calling Emilio a Chinaman was not going to buy his friendship.

Pam Wong looked up the alley: "Run up and check them for weapons." One of the machine guns went up and saw no weapons. Just an old sword. Emilio smiled as his fingers ran over the blade.

Don Gino smiled. "Allow me to introduce Emilio." That is General Emilio late of the North Vietnamese Army. With his machete and the bandana around his head, Emilio looked like he was auditioning for a part in the Karate Kid. He also looked fierce. He also looked pissed off. Don Gino now had a frown. Not a good sign.

Don Gino walked up to Elliott. Don Gino looked agitated. "You were my partner and betrayed me. What do you have to say for yourself?"

Elliott laughed. "We are holding machine guns on you. You have an old Chinaman with a machete and you're lecturing me. Have you lost your mind?" I couldn't wait for the answer.

"Well gentlemen, if you will look at your chest area, tell me what you see." I saw a red dot on everyone's chest except mine. "My associates have laser equipped rifles pointed at you. One move and you die." Don Gino walked over and slapped Elliott in the face. "The nerve of you to call me an old queer." He walked over to Pam Wong. He ripped off her wig and dress. He punched him/her in the mouth. She was an ugly man. Then the Don walked over and took the three machine guns from the frightened Cambodians. Without anyone noticing eight Samoans materialized with eight machine guns and six body bags. Sheldon Foreskin passed out. I didn't think that things could get weirder. They did. Detective Sanchez, AIC Jones and Chastain Johnson came down the alley. A stenographer followed them. It was now crowded in the alley. They talked for a time. Then Detective Sanchez took out a tape recorder, a table was set up and everyone confessed.

Then the fun began. I asked the questions. Everyone knew that I had the answers. It was a strange setting for a police interrogation. The story came out in bits and pieces. I relayed the facts while everyone listened. Sheldon Foreskin had been an All Big Ten basketball player at the University of Michigan. He had also majored in chemistry. He hurt his knee and failed his tryout with the Chicago Bulls. His 1970s glam rock band, Foreskin Loves You, had one album on Capitol and they vanished from sight. He wrote songs under the name E. Baylor. When I checked his full name E. Baylor was a pseudonym. Since Foreskin was a fan of former Los Angeles Lakers basketball great Elgin Baylor, it all made sense. He had written five songs that made small sums of money. His plan was to get the Rolling Stones to record his music. He met Pam Wong at Aunt Charlie's Lounge. This San Francisco transvestite bar was home to Foreskin who was a cross dresser. He had won ten amateur hour singing contests at Aunt Charlie's. He was banned from performing in anymore, as he was deemed a professional. He brought McArthur Dee in as a computer specialist. McArthur stole all the Stones' memorabilia and tipped off Chastain Johnson to Foreskin's activity. She led Trevor to the solution.

Pam Wong was to make the connection to the Stones management to sell the songs and Elliott Shonestein would make money out of the controversy. I wasn't sure who killed the drummers. Then it dawned on me, Sheldon Foreskin left behind a clue. He was the killer. The clue was an expensive Bumble Bee pomade. He left gobs of it behind. He was six feet seven inches and the pomade stuck on the top of the door jam. The crime was solved but there were still loose ends.Once I looked into his culinary background, I knew that Foreskin was the culprit. He was also known in Aunt Charlie's as the Chef.

I pointed out that there was still the question of Oblivion. That was an easy one to solve. When Elliott Shonestein vanished, he had dressed up as Oblivion. He was not only a cross dresser but a female impersonator. He had been a drummer in a series of rock bands. They all had substantial connections in the music business. Pam Wong was really a Cambodian man. Thank god I didn't sleep with her. At least I think I didn't. Who knows! With everyone cuffed and the case solved I felt good.

There was relief when I was told that I could leave. I did. When I got home Joyce Byers had let herself into my apartment. She was naked and in bed. I tried to tell her the story. She hopelessly distracted me. But she knew all the details. My mind was also on other things. Police do communicate with each other. Joyce left and I went to bed. That is to sleep. I was exhausted. My first case was solved and I felt good. I didn't realize that the loose ends would go one forever.

I looked over at my clock radio. It was past two in the morning. I was bothered by the unanswered questions. There was time to reflect on the future. Maybe I would get another real case. Then again maybe I had reached my professional nadir.

Chapter 30

THE AFTERMATH OF MURDER BY THE ROLLING STONES

I awoke the next morning feeling refreshed. Why not I had just solved my first major crime. It was all over. I could finally relax. I dressed and walked down Chestnut Street to Starbucks. I had my usual venti decaf coffee and a bagel with low fat cream cheese. I had to watch the waistline, if I was going to be famous. I congratulated myself on a job well done. No one else seemed to notice my first class detective skills.

"Hello dickhead," I turned to see Chastain Johnson. She looked gorgeous in a colorful Custo top. She had on a pair of D & G Jeans. I remembered their ad it said "With Booty." Chastain sure had booty.

"Trying to hang out with a famous detective." She laughed, not a good sign.

Chastain said: "Buy a newspaper and try to catch up on the loose ends." She lit a cigarette, blew smoke at me and took off out the door.

After finding four quarters, I picked up the San Francisco Chronicle. The headline stunned me. "Trevor Blake III Solves Mystery and Loses The Bodies." I wasn't sure what that meant. I read the story. Detective Richard Sanchez announced that I had secured a taped confession. Sanchez then said that I called the police and had the primary suspect handcuffed to a car. I also left a tape recorder and a series of more than 100 napkins that contained all the clues to solving the crime. There were some loose ends, the Chronicle reported, that didn't make sense. When the police arrived, they found some of the criminals missing. Later that evening a respected citizen, Gino Landry, turned up at the police station. The three suspects escaped in his car before the police arrived on the scene and his purple Cadillac crashed and burned. The bodies were burnt beyond recognition. Mr. Landry, the Chronicle reported, found the charred remains of the passengers. He was able to extract identification from papers blown out the car window. Mayor Gavin Newsom praised Mr. Landry for his civic-minded duty. Civic minded, my ass. They had all pissed off the Don by using the q or the h word. One even called him a faggot. Not a smart thing to do. Pissing off the Don was not good for ones health.

Jesus, I thought. Don Gino incinerated them. The story went on to conclude that the car fire was so fierce that identification was possible only through DNA testing to identify the remains. As I suspected Don Gino had a small part of the remains. The DNA identified the suspects. Now deceased.

I needed to see Don Gino. I dressed in my Van Morrison tour t-shirt, a pair of twill pants from L. L. Bean and my Air Jordan tennis shoes. I was Mr. Yuppie. I needed to look respectable as I was going to ask Don Gino some hard questions. It was a strange time. I had solved the crime but as the San Francisco Chronicle reminded the readers I had lost the bodies. Not exactly the work of a seasoned private eye.

I drove down to Don Gino's office in the Mission District. He wasn't there. He wasn't in his Castro office either. I was directed to his dog food plant. I found Don Gino on the canning line smiling at his product.

"Don Gino, what happened?"

"Trevor, relax, evil has a way of being taken care of."

"Ok, what really happened?"

Don Gino smiled and looked at the finished dog food cans. My God. He ground them up and put the three bodies in the dog food. "They're a good source of protein, Trevor."

I thought that I might be sick. "What about Chastain Johnson, AIC Jones and Detective Sanchez? They were all on the crime scene."

"They were called away Trevor. Justice was best served with me in charge." He smiled and lit a small cigar. He looked troubled. There was no doubt that Don Gino's Catholic conscience was giving him trouble.

"What's wrong Don Gino?"

"I do have a conscience." He looked sad.

I didn't know what I could say. "Is there anything I can do for you Don Gino?"

"Yes, there is." He pulled out his cell phone and made a call. "Come with me."

I wasn't sure what was up. But there was no reason to piss off the Don. We got into his purple limo and headed for the Mission Dolores. It was San Francisco's initial Franciscan Mission built in 1776 and it still had an operational parish church. The purple limo pulled up next to the church and we got out. I wasn't sure what was going on.

"Come with me, Trevor. You will see the kind of man I am."

I was confused. I thought he was a cold-blooded killer. Remember me not to share my thoughts with the don. I walked inside. Don Gino took me to a confessional. I stood outside. He began his confession and I could hear everything. He told the priest that he had ground the bodies into a meal for his dog food. Then he had canned the bodies. The priest forgave him and told him to perform twenty-five Hail Mary's. No need to upset the Don. Then as Don Gino prepared to leave this private and confidential confession, the priest told him that he would see the Don at bingo next Wednesday. Nothing like a Don with morals.

Don Gino walked out front. He looked at the front of the church. It was aging. The paint was gray. There were bird stains on the roof. The grass was in need of attention. The shrubs and flowers looked as though they were in need of repair. If not outright replacement. Don Gino pulled out his cell phone. He called Mayor Gavin Newsom. They agreed that the city would come out and renovate the grounds. Then he called Sunset Landscaping and they agreed to plant new shrubs and flowers. Then Don Gino told Sunset Landscaping that they would get a city contract to beautify the Mission District. Don Gino thanked the Mayor and they worked out the Sunset Landscaping deal. Then Don Gino reached into his pocket. I shuttered. He pulled out a checkbook. He wrote a check for $500,000. No sense waiting for renovations. They would start immediately. He sent one of the Samoans into the Mission Delores to deposit the check in the collection box. He smiled at me.

"Well, Trevor, you did pretty good."

"Thanks." I hoped that was the right answer.

"I've got a present for you."

Now I was nervous. "Fine." I hoped it wasn't Elliott Shonestein's head.

He handed me ten rare Rolling Stones CDs. "These are bootleg copies, I believe they are illegal, but they contain the essence of every Stones performance so far on the tour. They were headed for McArthur Dee, but he has been committed to the Sedro Wooley Mental Hospital north of Seattle. He is in the ward for record collectors with mental impairment. I don't think they allow CD players. Not good for ones mental health." Don Gino laughed at his joke. So did I. No sense pissing off the Don. I went back to my office.

I stopped and looked at the Haight Ashbury sign. I never got tired of it. I glanced over at Ben and Jerry's. It was time to celebrate. I walked across the street. I had two scoops of Cherry Garcia on a waffle cone. I returned to my office and bound up the twenty stairs. I walked in and looked at my Janis Joplin picture. It was next to the Van Morrison. She always excited me. Van never did. I turned and was shocked.

There stood Mick and Keith. Were they the real Mick and Keith? Or were they part of the Start Me Up band? They were all in town. Trying to be a cool P. I. I remarked: "Hey guys, great show in Seattle."

"Yeh, except for that fucking Aerosmith. We topped 'em but it wasn't easy."

Now I was in shock, it was the real Mick and Keith. I could think of only one thing to do. I had them sign the ten bootleg CDs. They thanked me for my help and reminded me to find Elvis. I think it was the drugs. I had no case involving Elvis. But they knew more than I did. It turned out that was my next case. I guess that's why Mick and Keith are still on top of their game. I had forgotten about finding Elvis.

I needed to spend some time in my office. It was time to clean up the bills. The case had provided more than $50,000 in fees and the expenses were only about $20,000. Blake Investigations was solvent for the first time. I was finally in the big time. There was a knock on the door. Mick and Keith left. They explained it was probably fans.

I hollered: "Come in."

"Hello Trevor," Zandra Filippi remarked. "I have been fired by the Stones. Do you need some help?" She licked her lips. I found that erotic. I was tempted. I didn't tell her that Mick and Keith had just left via the back door.

"No, Zandra, but let me talk to Guitar Jac." I called Jac and he hooked Zandra up with Jack Sudden at Elvis Presley Enterprises. The next day she was on the plane for Memphis. She was appointed the new Executive Director of Publicity for Elvis Presley Enterprises. I bet Elvis Cole never accomplished so much. Then again he never met Zandra.

I drove home and there on the front door stood Bennie and Bertie. "Trevor, we are so proud of you." They hugged me. Bertie gave me a sweater she had knitted with a reindeer on it and they had bought me a Mervyn's shirt for my birthday. I would soon be a fashion disaster. Nothing like a fashion plate dressed in a Mervyn's shirt. They left by praising my detection skill. They seldom praised me, so I accepted it in a gloating way.

"By the way Trevor," Bennie said, "we have doubled your rent." So much for the famous detective having money.

"Fine." I said. "The famous private eye has to pay for his fame."

"We are on our way to Memphis to see where Elvis is buried." They walked out onto Chestnut Street. Bennie was working on magic tricks and Bertie was reading a self-help book. I loved them. Why, I don't know.

I watched them drive away. They were to be gone for a month. I had the feeling I was in for a vacation.

I soon found out that Memphis was in my future. It would be my second case.

I went over to Paradise Bakery, Nilda made me an omelet and I got ready for fame and fortune. I also took out my first napkin and began writing notes on how I would find Elvis. Ron interrupted me and suggested that I go into another line of work. I ignored him.

The End

ABOUT THE AUTHOR

Howard A. DeWitt is Professor Emeritus of History at Ohlone College, Fremont, California. He received his B. A. from Western Washington State University, the M. A. from the University of Oregon and a PhD. from the University of Arizona. He also studied at the University of Paris, Sorbonne and the City University in Rome. Professor DeWitt is the author of twenty books and has published over 175 articles and more than 200 reviews in a wide variety of popular and scholarly magazines. He writes in the fields of U. S. and California history, the history of rock and roll and he was also a political scientist. His books on foreign policy, as well as his doctoral dissertation, are ones widely used in major universities.

For more than thirty years he has taught two college level courses in the History of Rock n Roll music. He continues to teach the History of Rock and Roll music on the Internet. In a distinguished academic career, he has also taught at the University of California, Davis, the University of Arizona, Cochise College and Chabot College. He was a research assistant at the University of Oregon. In addition to these teaching and research assignments, Professor DeWitt is a regular speaker at the Popular Culture Association annual convention and at the National Social Science Association meetings.

He wrote the first book on Chuck Berry, which was published by Pierian Press under the title **Chuck Berry: Rock N Roll Music** in 1985. DeWitt's earlier brief biography, **Van Morrison: The Mystic's Music**, published in 1983, received universally excellent reviews. On the English side of the music business DeWitt's, **The Beatles: Untold Tales**, originally published in 1985, was picked up by the Kendall Hunt Publishing Company in the 1990s and is used regularly in a wide variety of college courses on the history of rock music. Kendall Hunt also published **Stranger in Town: The Musical Life of Del Shannon** with co-author Dennis M. DeWitt in 2001. In 1993's **Paul McCartney: From Liverpool**

To Let It Be concentrated on the Beatle years. He also co-authored **Jailhouse Rock: The Bootleg Records of Elvis Presley** with Lee Cotten in 1983.

Professor DeWitt's many awards in the field of history include founding the Cochise County Historical Society and recognition by a number of state and local government organizations. DeWitt's book, **Sun Elvis: Presley In The 1950s**, published by Popular Culture Ink. was a finalist for the Deems-ASCAP Award for the best academic rock and roll book.

Professor DeWitt is a renaissance scholar who publishes in a wide variety of outlets that are both academic and popular. He is one of the few college professors who bridge this gap between scholarly and popular publications. His articles and reviews regularly appear in **Blue Suede News**, **DISCoveries**, **Rock 'N' Blues News**, the **Journal of Popular Culture**, the **Journal of American History**, **California History**, the **Southern California Quarterly**, the **Pacific Historian**, **Amerasia**, the **Western Pennsylvania Historical Magazine**, the **Annals of Iowa**, **Journal of the West**, **Arizona and the West,** the **North Beach Review**, **Ohio History**, the **Oregon Historical Quarterly**, **Montana: The Magazine of the West**, **Record Profile Magazine**, **Audio Trader** and **Juke Box Digest** among others. For forty plus years DeWitt has combined popular and academic writing.

During his high school and college years, DeWitt promoted dances in and around Seattle, Washington. Such groups as Little Bill and the Bluenotes, Ron Holden and the Playboys, the Frantics, the Wailers and George Palmerton and the Night People among others played at such Seattle venues as the Eagle's Auditorium and Dick Parker's Ballroom.

Howard has two grown children. A daughter, Melanie Stoa, is a teacher in the Los Angeles area and a son; Darin completed graduate work in public policy at the London School of Economics and is presently completing a PhD in Political Science at the University of California, Los Angeles. His wife of forty plus years, Carolyn, is a teacher and artist. She is presently retired and vacationing around the world. The DeWitt's divide their time between homes in Scottsdale, Arizona and Los Angeles, California.

Criticism and praise can be sent to Horizon Books, P. O. Box 4342, Scottsdale, Arizona 85261. DeWitt can be reached via e-mail at Howard217@aol.com Also See the Horizon-Books.com website.

www.ingramcontent.com/pod-product-compliance
Lightning Source LLC
Chambersburg PA
CBHW031951040426
42448CB00006B/309